THE STORY OF
archaeology

THE STORY OF
archaeology
IN 50 GREAT DISCOVERIES

Justin Pollard

Quercus

CONTENTS

Mayan terracotta figure

Great Pyramid at Giza, Egypt, with sphinx in the foreground

Ancient fortress, Novgorod, Russia

P-38 Lightning on a Greenland glacier

5

INTRODUCTION

The word 'archaeology' was coined less than 400 years ago and the subject, in its modern sense, has existed for just half that time, but it fulfils a need that people have felt for much longer. One of the sons of Ramses II, living some 4000 years ago, wondered about his ancient ancestors and set about collecting their artefacts and ordering the restoration of their tombs. Since the Renaissance, a Western world reawakened to its classical predecessors has sought out the ancient statues, coins and artefacts considered most beautiful and placed them in public galleries and private salons for admiration and learned contemplation. It was only in the 19th century, however, with the realization that the history of mankind must stretch back far further than biblical chronologies allowed, that the subject of archaeology as we understand it today really came into being.

Those first archaeologists were faced with an awesome task. Suddenly thousands of years of human activity opened up, but they were for the large part dark years

3.75 mya	2 mya	1 mya	50,000 ya	10,000 ya	5000 BC	4000 BC

3.75 mya (million years ago) Hominid bipedal footsteps from this date at Laetoli, Tanzania

*c.*1.8 mya–250,000 ya *Pithecanthropus erectus* (reclassified as *Homo erectus*), Java, Indonesia

*c.*40,000 ya **(years ago)** Mungo Man, Australia

*c.*13,000 ya Cave paintings at Altamira, Spain

*c.*4000 BC Hypogeum, Hal-Saflieni, Malta

*c.*40,000–25,000 ya Mungo Lady, Australia

*c.*7000 BC Kennewick Man, North America

c.3.2 mya Lucy (*Australopithecus afarensis*) lives at Hadar, Ethiopia

*c.*32,000 ya Cave paintings at Chauvet-Pont-d'Arc, France

*c.*9400–8000 ya Çatalhöyük, Turkey

120,000–40,000 ya
Middle Palaeolithic (Old Stone Age)

4300–3000 BC Mesopotamia, Uruk-based cultures

3500–500 BC Bronze Age

9000–3000 BC Neolithic (New Stone Age)

2.3 mya–120,000 ya
Lower Palaeolithic (Old Stone Age)

40,000–10,000 ya
Upper Palaeolithic (Old Stone Age)

10,000–3000 BC
Mesolithic (Middle Stone Age)

without written records to tell us what people were thinking and doing. Prehistory was an impossible mass of objects and sites which might be hundreds, thousands or tens of thousand of years old, but which seemed to lack order or meaning. The job of archaeology ever since has been to uncover, arrange and understand these silent remnants of earlier times and to try to make sense of these fragments from the shipwreck of time.

Since its inception, archaeology has benefited from the interest and support of people from far beyond the narrow confines of academia. Books written by archaeologists about their great discoveries have been best-sellers, and new discoveries attract media attention in a way that many other subjects can only dream of. And yet professional archaeology has not always been grateful for this public enthusiasm. It is still, in part, a subject that agonizes over being misunderstood as a form of treasure hunting, that feels dogged by an 'Indiana

3500 BC	3000 BC	2500 BC	2000 BC	1500 BC	1000 BC

c.3600 BC Neolithic temples, Ggantija, Gozo

c.2900 BC 'Great Death Pit of Ur', Mesopotamia

c..2560 BC Great Pyramid, Giza, Egypt

c.1600 BC Knossos is rebuilt as the main palace on Crete

c.3400 BC City-states emerge in Sumeria (southern Mesopotamia)

c..2560 BC Khufu's boat, Egypt

c..1500 BC Final stage of construction of Stonehenge monument, England

c.2300 BC Amesbury Archer, England

c.1450 BC Mycenaean Linear B script is developed, Greece

c.3300 BC Ice Man (Ötzi), Italy

2800–1450 BC Minoan civilization

c.1346 BC Akhetaten founded in Egypt

c.3100 BC Skara Brae, Orkney Islands

c.1324 BC Tomb of Tutankhamun, Egypt

1450–1150 BC Mycenaean kingdom

c.3000 BC Troy founded in northwestern Turkey

c.1279 BC Tomb of Seti I, Egypt

c.2600–1700 BC Indus Valley civilization flourishes

c.1200 BC Basket Maker culture, North America

c.2800–1100 BC Aegean Bronze Age

c.3100–30 BC Egyptian dynasties (1st–Ptolemaic)

Jones' image which it believes has led those outside the profession to view it as a swashbuckling, gold-seeking adventure. This does the large numbers of people who follow archaeology a disservice. The tales of those long-dead fortune hunters, many of which are included here, do have their place in the story of archaeology, but that place is firmly in the past. They are important not simply because of the astonishing discoveries they made, but because their roguish methods have taught later generations what not to do. Frankly, these stories also still inspire us with wonder, for there is something of the treasure hunter in every archaeologist. The difference is that the treasure we now seek is not of the gold or silver variety, but simply the desire to uncover clues to the lives of people who have lived here before us. If it is Indiana Jones who first inspires someone's interest in archaeology, then I for one am all in favour of it. It is for archaeologists then to explain that the subject is wider, more complex and more wonderful than anything that can be encompassed in a mere two hours of a Hollywood movie.

1000 BC	900 BC	800 BC	700 BC	600 BC	500 BC	400 BC

c.1000 BC Flag Fen causeway

c.950 BC Solomon builds the Temple of Jerusalem

c.880 BC Nimrud rises to prominence as the capital of Assyria

776 BC Earliest known Olympic Games, Olympia, Greece

c.700 BC Nineveh is established as Assyria's capital

c.400–300 BC Lady of Elx, Spain

c.400 BC Ice Maiden, Siberia

c.400–15 BC La Tène culture, Europe

c.3100–30 BC Egyptian dynasties (1st to Ptolemaic)

c.800–400 BC Hallstatt Iron Age, Europe

c.750–c.31 BC Roman republic

In that respect, archaeology has a unique advantage. Whilst most written history, at least until very recently, has been mainly concerned with powerful people and landmark events, every human and every minor event can leave a mark in the archaeological record. That is the true pulling power of archaeology – it is the testimony of us all – and it is that which attracts us to it. As such, a broken pot or a test tube of ancient pollen can be just as much 'treasure' as the mask of Tutankhamun, for they all tell a part of the story that helps us to understand who we are and how we got here.

This book attempts to trace the history of modern archaeology from its beginnings to the present day through 50 iconic excavations. Some of these discoveries are of the swashbuckling type – lost tombs filled with precious artefacts – but others are of bricks and letters and pieces of flint and pottery which have, in the story they tell, proved to be yet rarer and more valuable. The choice of sites is of course a personal one, made from many thousands of

300 BC	200 BC	100 BC	AD 1	AD 100	AD 200	AD 300

c.300 BC Ptolemy I founds the Serapeum at Saqqara, Egypt

c.150–100 BC Antikythera mechanism

AD 9 Battle of the Teutoburg Forest, Germany

79 Vesuvius erupts and buries Herculaneum and Pompeii

Second Century BC Petra flourishes as the centre of the Nabataean culture

c.21 BC–AD 61 Dead Sea Scrolls, Qumran, Israel

210 BC Terracotta army, China

9 BC Ara Pacis, Rome

c.100 Lindow Man and Lindow Woman, England

196 BC Rosetta Stone, Egypt

105 Vindolanda tablets, England

Third to Ninth Centuries Maya rise to prominence, Central and South America

221–210 BC China, Qin dynasty

c.300 BC–AD 800 Nazca culture, Peru

c.31 BC–c. AD 476 Roman empire

excavations across the world, all of which could rightfully claim to have their place in the story of the development of the subject – indeed every excavation has a place in that story.

I have also had to decide what constitutes a 'discovery'. In some cases, sites have remained hidden from all human sight for thousands of years, and knowledge of them has been completely forgotten. But in the case of places such as Easter Island and Angkor Wat, local people have in fact never lost them at all – the story here is of how the outside world has rediscovered them and in the process learned that every culture and country the world over has its own unique and precious past.

The choice of sites has been made using a number of criteria. Firstly, I have looked for excavations which in their day were considered ground-breaking either in the techniques employed or because of the previously unknown part of history or prehistory that they uncovered. Secondly, I have chosen sites

Kennewick
Little Bighorn

Mesa Verde

Tenochtitlán
Palenque
Port Royal

Nazca
Machu Picchu

Easter Island

| 400 | 600 | 800 | 1000 | 1200 | 1400 | 1600 | 1800 | 2000 |

6th–7th Centuries
Sutton Hoo burials, England

9th–14th Centuries
Novgorod, Russia

1797 John Frere questions accepted theory of earth's antiquity

c.615 Palenque, Mexico

1000 Easter Island *moai* statues

1460 Machu Picchu, Peru

1876 Battle of Little Bighorn, North America

*c.***306–1453** Byzantine empire

c.1130–1300 Cave Dweller Pueblo civilization, North America

1545 *Mary Rose* sinks off the coast of southern England

1250–1581 Aztec civilization, Mexico

c.1200 Great Zimbabwe, Africa

1692 Port Royal, Jamaica, submerged

c.1150 Angkor Wat, Cambodia

1942 'Glacier Girl', Greenland

12th–15th Centuries
Inca civilization, South America

*c.***300 BC–AD 900** Classical Mayan civilization, Central America

1325 Templo Mayor, Tenochtitlán, Mexico

450–1300 Mesa Verde, North America

*c.***400–600** First settlers arrive on Easter Island

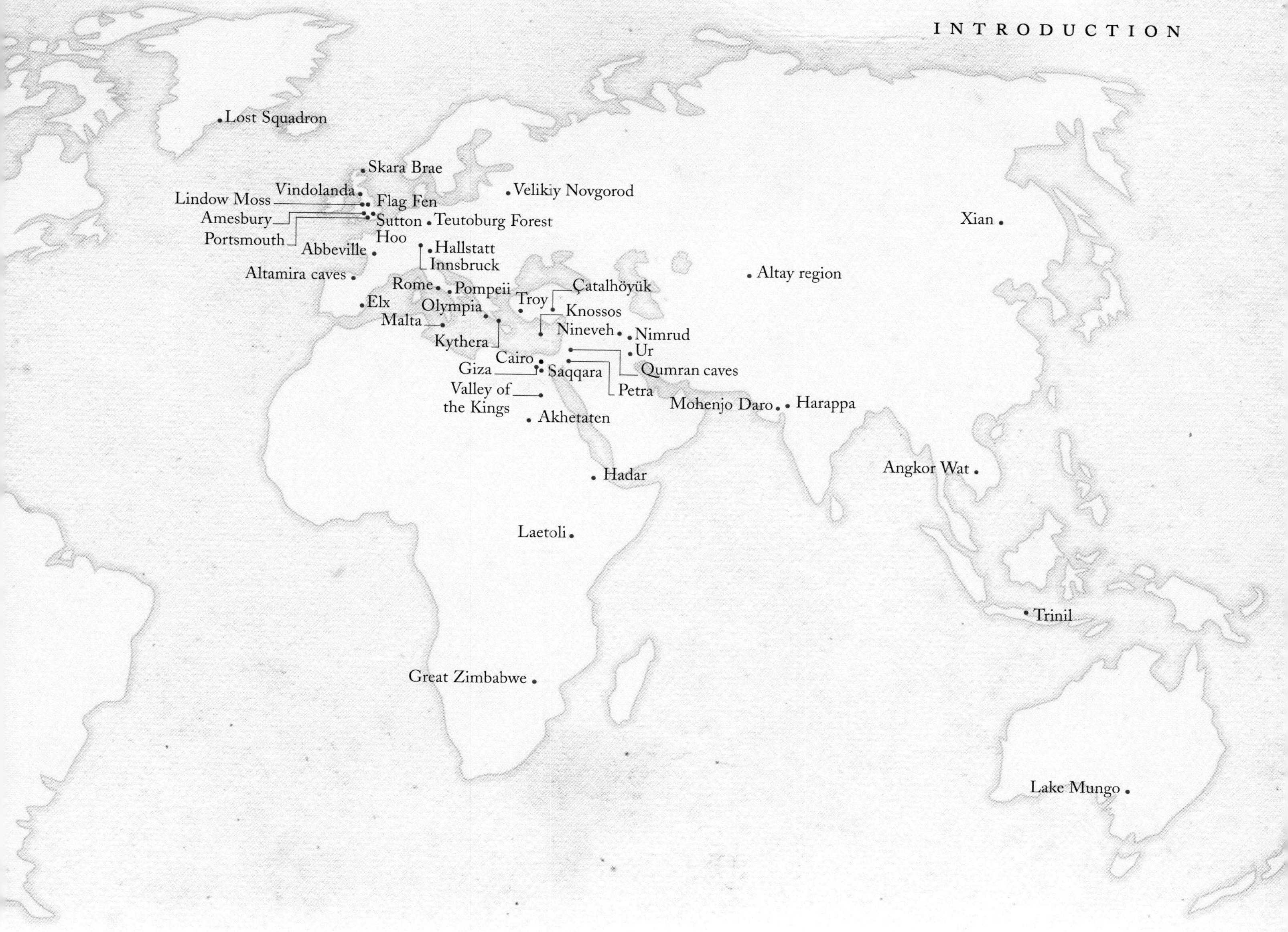

Lost Squadron

Skara Brae

Vindolanda
Lindow Moss
Flag Fen
Velikiy Novgorod
Xian
Amesbury
Sutton
Teutoburg Forest
Portsmouth
Hoo
Abbeville
Hallstatt
Innsbruck
Altamira caves
Altay region
Rome
Pompeii
Troy
Çatalhöyük
Elx
Olympia
Knossos
Malta
Nineveh
Nimrud
Kythera
Ur
Cairo
Giza
Saqqara
Qumran caves
Valley of
the Kings
Petra
Mohenjo Daro
Harappa
Akhetaten
Angkor Wat

Hadar

Laetoli

Trinil

Great Zimbabwe

Lake Mungo

whose 'treasures' may be well known but where the stories of their discovery and
their discoverers are rarely told. In all these cases I have added text boxes which
will, I hope, explain something of the archaeological techniques used then and
now, the cultures that have been discovered and the personal stories of the
people who discovered them.

Finally, I have simply chosen those sites and those stories which inspired
me when I was a child – the tales of explorers finding lost cities, of the
decipherment of ancient languages, of walking into a room where no-one
had stepped for 3000 years. These are the stories of wonder and excitement
that first led me and many other archaeologists into the field and which kindled
and continues to fuel the wider public interest in our subject, without which
modern archaeology would not exist.

Justin Pollard
NORFOLK 2007

GIGANTIC WORKS

Antonio da Magdalena at Angkor Wat, 1586–9

'*At Ongcor, there are ... ruins of such grandeur ... that, at the first view, one is filled with profound admiration, and cannot but ask what has become of this powerful race, so civilized, so enlightened, the authors of these gigantic works?*'

HENRI MOUHOT *Travels in the Central Parts of Indo-China, Cambodia and Laos during the Years 1858, 1859 and 1860*

Antonio da Magdalena, a Capuchin monk from Portugal, travelled to the Far East with a mission. It was 1586 and the Portuguese empire was rapidly expanding into new overseas territories. For the merchant of the Portuguese fleet this meant access to new wealth, to luxuries that would certainly fetch a high price in Europe. But for Antonio da Magdalena it meant access to new souls.

Converting what most Europeans considered to be the barbaric and heathen natives of their colonial empires went hand in hand with their subjugation. Little attention was paid to the indigenous culture, which it was usually more convenient to brand as 'primitive' and hence suitable for conquest. But when Antonio da Magdalena returned from his journey to the interior of Cambodia, he had a very different story to recount to the official historian of the Portuguese Indies, Diogo do Couto. He told him that on trekking into the jungle interior they had come across a ruined city:

'*... surrounded by a moat, crossed by five bridges. These have on each side a cordon held by giants. Their ears are all pierced and are very long. The stone blocks of the bridges are of astonishing size. The stones of the walls are of an extraordinary size and so jointed together that they look as if they are made of just one stone.*'

It seemed to him to be a city of goliaths, filled with elaborately decorated palaces and watercourses, now all slowly disappearing back into the enveloping jungle. But just under 2 miles (3 km) beyond it lay something yet more wonderful: a temple, which his local guides told him was called 'Angar'.

'*It is of such extraordinary construction that it is not possible to describe it with a pen ... it is like no other building in the world. It has towers and decoration and all the refinements which the human genius can conceive of. There are many smaller towers of similar style ... which are gilded. The temple is surrounded by a moat, and access is by a single bridge, protected by two stone tigers so grand and fearsome as to strike terror into the visitor.*'

Opposite: The largest religious structure in the world, the temple of Angkor Wat is thought to symbolize the Hindu cosmos: the surrounding moat represents the oceans and the five central towers resemble the five-peaked Mount Meru, home of the Hindu gods.

The place da Magdalena had stumbled on was the ruins of the Khmer temple of Angkor Wat, a vast structure surrounded by 2.2 miles (3.6 km) of wall and moat, crowned with five huge towers. In the minds of Westerners this was an almost impossible find and it seemed beyond belief that it was the work of any native civilization. Hypotheses were put forward concerning its origins, including that it was a lost Roman city built by the emperor Trajan or perhaps a Greek outpost. Marcello de Ribadeneyra, another Portuguese missionary who visited the site at the end of the 16th century, heard tell that Alexander the Great had built it and marvelled, '… *no-one lives there now, it is inhabited by ferocious animals, and the local people say it was built by foreigners'*.

In fact, the city these Portuguese missionaries 'discovered' had been abandoned for only about a century when da Magdalena visited, and parts of the temple were still in use. And it had not been built by foreigners but by an indigenous civilization which had flourished in the region from the ninth to the 15th centuries.

High peaks and bas-reliefs

It has taken many years of excavation and restoration to uncover the story of Angkor and even in the 19th century it was widely believed in the West to be Roman work. By restoring and studying the miles of bas-relief that decorate the main temple of Angkor Wat we now know that it was built early in the 12th century by Suryavarman II (r.1113–50), king of the Khmer empire, who dedicated the temple to the Hindu god Vishnu. It stood as the centrepiece of his great city of Angkor, a representation in sandstone of Mount Meru, the home of the gods. Built in three rising rectangular galleries, the temple was topped by five towers representing the five peaks of that mythical mountain. The beautifully carved bas-reliefs that line the walls depict stories from the

TIMELINE

802 Jayavarman II establishes Kambuja as an independent kingdom, marking the start of the Khmer empire

*c.*900 First city built at Angkor

*c.*1150 Temple at Angkor Wat completed

LATE 12TH CENTURY The golden age of the Khmer empire under Jayavarman VII sees a new capital built at Angkor Thom

1431 Khmer empire is attacked by Thai forces and Angkor falls; a year later the capital is moved to Phnom Penh

1586 Antonio da Magdalena discovers the ruins of Angkor Wat

Temples at Angkor Thom also contain walls decorated with bas-reliefs, including this section from the Bayon Temple, depicting Khmer warriors fighting the Cham army. The Bayon was built by King Jayavarman VII, a practising Buddhist, as his state temple.

ancient Sanskrit epics the *Ramayana* and the *Mahabharata*, along with a processional scene showing Suryavarman II and episodes from the life of Krishna (an incarnation of the god Vishnu). Pilgrims visiting the temple would walk past these familiar tales, sometimes leaving inscriptions telling of their own good deeds, before climbing steep stairs (which represent the difficulty in climbing to the kingdom of the gods) to the next level of terraces, cloisters and galleries. Those who were allowed to climb to the top saw the five towers standing before them, the central tower raised above the rest, its shrine containing a statue of Vishnu who stared out over one of the greatest cities on earth.

Impressions of a Chinese visitor

Thanks to the records of visiting Chinese diplomats, we even have first-hand accounts of the living city. Zhou Daguan (1266–1346) arrived in Angkor in August 1296 and after a year at the Khmer king's court he returned home to write a description of what he had seen. All business, he tells us, was carried out by women who would sell goods from mats spread in the great marketplace, on pitches they hired from the state. He described how both men and women went bare-chested and barefoot, lived in houses without tables or chairs and ate their meals from tiny bowls made of leaves. But for all their apparent simplicity, this was not a poor or unsophisticated place. The temple towers and palaces he describes as encased in gold and bronze and in one account he describes how the king, Srindravarman II (r.1295–1308), went in state from his palace.

> *'When the king goes out, troops are at the head of the escort; then come flags, banners and music. Palace women, numbering from three to five hundred, wearing flowered cloth, with flowers in their hair, hold candles in their hands, and form a troupe. Even in broad daylight, the candles are lighted. Then come other palace women, carrying lances and shields, the king's private guards, and carts drawn by goats and horses, all in gold, come next. Ministers and princes are mounted on elephants, and in front of them one can see, from afar, their innumerable red umbrellas. After them come the wives and concubines of the king, in palanquins, carriages, on horseback and on elephants. They have more than one hundred parasols, flecked with gold. Behind them comes the sovereign, standing on an elephant, holding his sacred sword in his hand. The elephant's tusks are encased in gold.'*

By the time the Portuguese arrived at Angkor, the city was deserted apart from a few devotees at the great temple which had since been converted to Buddhist use. All signs of the Khmer empire, at least to Western eyes, had gone save for the silent stones. The job of archaeology would be to retell their story, but in the 16th century archaeology was as unknown as the wonders it would one day uncover.

THE KHMER EMPIRE

No written records survive from the Khmer empire except inscriptions carved on temples and palaces, so its history has been pieced together from reliefs at places like Angkor Wat, records of Chinese visitors to the region and archaeological investigations.

The Khmer kingdom of Angkor could be said to have begun in 802 when King Jayavarman II (r.802–50) ostentatiously declared himself 'king of the world'. He had grown up in the sophisticated Javanese court, possibly a hostage from one of Java's Cambodian vassal kingdoms. On returning to Cambodia, he had set about rapidly increasing his influence by conquering neighbouring kingdoms, forming in the process a land he called Kambuja which, through his 802 declaration, he announced independent from Javanese rule. Although he was casting off the overlordship of Java, his years in the court there had not been wasted and his memories of its refined civilization were the seeds from which Khmer art would grow.

Under Jayavarman II's immediate successors Kambuja's central location meant that conquest could give way to trade, providing the wealth with which the first city of Angkor was built sometime around 900. As well as spending on building projects, the Khmer invested heavily in agriculture and irrigation, building a series of huge reservoirs, providing a further impetus to trade and allowing the population to expand.

In the early 12th century the Khmer empire began looking beyond its borders and an era of aggressive expansionism began. Under Suryavarman II kingdoms were conquered in Burma, the Malay Peninsula and Thailand, extending to the borders of Laos. It was during this period that the city of Angkor reached its height and the great temple of Angkor Wat was built, taking 37 years to complete.

Expansionism brought its own problems and, following Suryavarman's death – probably during an attempted invasion of Vietnam – the Khmer empire was briefly conquered. It rose again under the Buddhist King Jayavarman VII (r.1182–c.1206), who built a new capital at Angkor Thom ('the Great City'). Under his enlightened rule much of the infra-structure of the empire was laid down, including the construction of over 100 hospitals and an extensive road system linking the old and new cities, complete with inns for merchants and government officials.

The empire came under increasing pressure after Jayavarman VII's death and began to contract in the face of Thai expansion and threats from Mongol China. By the time the Chinese diplomat Zhou Daguan arrived in Angkor the golden age of Khmer rule was already over, so his dazzling descriptions of the court of King Srindravarman can only hint at the wealth and power his predecessors must have enjoyed.

After Srindravarman's death in 1308, records become scarce. There is evidence that later kings' belief in a more personal form of Buddhism may have eroded their authority, and archaeology shows that around this time much of the extensive water management system that supported the empire began to fall into disrepair. The empire never regained its former power and finally, in 1431, it was conquered by the Thai Ayutthaya kingdom. There is evidence that Angkor was not entirely abandoned at this time but, as the rump of the Khmer state moved south to the area around Phnom Penh, slowly the economic value of the site dwindled. By the time Antonio da Magdalena arrived in 1586 the surrounding jungle had grown back enough to convince him that this 'lost city' was not simply abandoned but had been empty for centuries.

Under Suryavarman II the Khmer empire controlled all of modern Cambodia and most of Thailand and Laos but its area of influence was eroded by the 15th century.

'THE CITY DISINTERRED'

The Discovery of Herculaneum and Pompeii, 1594–1763

*I stood within the City disinterred;
And heard the autumnal leaves like
light footfalls
Of spirits passing through the streets.*

PERCY BYSSHE SHELLEY *Ode to Naples* (1816)

In 1594 the Neapolitan architect Domenico Fontana (1543–1607) was commissioned to dig a tunnel from the River Sarno to supply water to an estate on the southern flanks of the volcano Vesuvius, on the outskirts of Naples in southern Italy. At one point the projected tunnel was required to pass under a low hill known by the locals as La Cività. It was an odd name for an area of farmland (La Cività means 'the town'), and when Fontana's men began tunnelling he discovered why. What his miners found under the metres of pumice and volcanic dust were ancient ruins – marble panels, fragments of frescoes and two inscriptions. Noting these, Fontana moved on and the new waterway was completed.

Just why Fontana did not explore the strange ruins remains uncertain. Later excavators on the site believed they were digging areas that had previously been explored, which implies that Fontana's men did more than just remove those pieces of masonry in their way. It has even been suggested that they stumbled upon some erotic Roman frescoes and, god-fearing men that they were, hurriedly reburied them and went on their way.

The well of statues

Whatever the reason, the hill of La Cività kept its secrets, and more than 100 years passed before the ancient world intruded for a second time on the lives of Neapolitans. Water would again be the reason for this intrusion. In 1709 a workman was digging a new well for a monastery in the town of Resina (modern Ercolano) but instead of striking water he hit a slab of rare marble, which proved to be a seat from a previously unknown and deeply buried Roman theatre. News of the find soon reached the Austrian occupiers of Italy and one of their cavalry officers, Maurice de Lorraine, Prince d'Elbeuf (1677–1763), decided to investigate. He built a villa near the monastery and ordered that the well excavations be expanded. Soon other antiquities began to appear, including parts of classical statues and an inscription bearing the name Appius Pulcher, a man known from historical sources as a friend of the Roman orator Cicero. The statuary was just the sort of decoration a civilized cavalry officer needed for his villa, and de Lorraine ordered the site to be stripped clean. In this way perhaps the best preserved theatre in the ancient world was robbed, the finds and their locations going largely unrecorded.

It would be wrong to lay too much blame on de Lorraine. Archaeology as we know it did not exist in his day. The classical past had come to the attention of Europeans in the Renaissance and it was fashionable to collect ancient works, but anything other than art was considered merely the rubbish of a bygone age. Discoveries predating the classical, such as Angkor Wat (see pages 12–15), received even less attention – they were simply travellers' tales. Maurice de Lorraine was not aware that his villa stood on the site of a forgotten Roman city; all he knew was that he owned a well which produced statues.

News from Resina soon percolated through the European courts. So, in 1735, when Charles of Bourbon, later Charles III of Spain (r.1759–88), made himself king of the Two Sicilies (a kingdom consisting of Sicily and southern Italy, including Naples), he ordered the work to be expanded to provide relics fit for a royal collection. Charles employed his own royal antiquary, Marcello Venuti, and one of his first jobs on arriving in the city was to be lowered down the 'statue well'. In the gloom of the excavations Venuti made one of the first genuine archaeological discoveries. Until that point it had been assumed from an inscription found earlier that these treasures came from an

Ruins of the Forum at Pompeii. At the heart of Roman cities, these public meeting places were where most of the town's business was carried out. The main roadway was paved, with wide walkways on either side.

17

isolated temple of Hercules. Venuti, a classical scholar, read the inscription with different eyes and saw that the word 'Herculanenses' referred not to a temple but to a city. It was a city whose name he already knew from ancient sources, a city that had been destroyed in a terrible catastrophe in AD 79 – the city of Herculaneum.

But Venuti's discovery did not mark the start of archaeological excavation as we know it. His master wanted art, not history, and the site was attacked by military sappers with pickaxes and explosives. Their task was to find beautiful objects, which they did: jewellery, pieces of bronze horses, statues (including one of the emperor Augustus), capitals, columns and inscriptions were unearthed and removed. No records were kept and any items not considered 'art' were simply shovelled away. As soon as a tunnel was considered worked out, it was quickly backfilled with rubble to prevent subsidence on the surface.

Artefacts preserved among the ruins at Pompeii, such as hair pins, jewellery and cooking utensils, provide evidence of the everyday objects used by Romans in the first century AD.

Early excavations at Herculaneum and Pompeii were careless and seem to have been little more than hunting parties for beautiful objects. It was not until Karl Weber oversaw the work at Pompeii that items removed were properly recorded.

Charles was delighted but suspicious that others would exploit his treasure hoard. He ordered the finds locked away in his palace where he alone would see them. Reports on the site were banned and even sketches of the finds forbidden. By 1745 the site was believed to be worked out and Charles needed a new source of ancient works. His attention returned to the small hill that Fontana had dug through.

The reawakening of Pompeii

In 1748 excavations were ordered to be carried out at La Città by Turkish slave labourers. Work proceeded quickly as the soft soils and volcanic ash of the region proved much easier to excavate than the hardened subterranean mud of Herculaneum. The work also took a different course. The Spanish military engineer Rocco de Alcubierre, who had hacked his way through Herculaneum, was joined by Karl Weber (1712–64), a Swiss architect whose insistence that every room be excavated individually and recorded exasperated Alcubierre. It also marked Weber out as possibly the first true archaeological excavator, the first person to try to discover more in ancient ruins than just treasure. In 1763 the reward for this patient approach finally came when an inscription from the site was recovered which proved that this was the lost city of Pompeii, a place whose terrible fate on 24 August AD 79 was recorded by some of ancient Rome's greatest writers. Pliny the Younger (63–c.113) had described how on that day Vesuvius erupted:

> '… night came upon us, not such as we have when the sky is cloudy, or when there is no moon, but that of a room when it is shut up, and all the lights put out. You might hear the shrieks of women, the screams of children, and the shouts of men; some calling for their children, others for their parents, others for their husbands, and seeking to recognize each other by the voices that replied; one lamenting his own fate, another that of his family; some wishing to die, from the very fear of dying; some lifting their hands to the gods; but the greater part convinced that there were now no gods at all, and that the final endless night of which we have heard had come upon the world.'
>
> PLINY *Letter LXVI, to Tacitus*

The open-air excavations at Pompeii proved harder to hide than the subterranean caverns of Herculaneum and news of the discovery quickly spread. Pompeii became the world's first archaeological visitor attraction and the intense scrutiny it attracted resulted in changes to working practices, including the abolition of slave labour in 1765. The buildings as well as the finds began to influence the visual arts of the era.

TIMELINE

79 (24 August) Vesuvius erupts, burying the nearby cities of Herculaneum and Pompeii and killing thousands of inhabitants

1594 Domenico Fontana discovers ancient ruins beneath La Città while tunnelling but does not realize their significance

1709 A workman at a monastery at Resina unearths a marble slab, which proves to be part of a buried Roman theatre; shortly afterwards, Austrian cavalry office Maurice de Lorraine appropriates the site and strips it of its statuary

1735 Charles of Bourbon orders excavations to be stepped up; Marcello Venuti identifies the site as the lost city of Herculaneum

1748 Excavations begin at La Città; Karl Weber demonstrates painstaking technique in excavating and recording finds

1763 Inscription reveals La Città to be Pompeii

1860 Giuseppe Fiorelli leads the excavations at Pompeii and introduces the technique of filling voids with plaster to create casts of people and animals who perished in the disaster

THE DESTRUCTION OF POMPEII AND HERCULANEUM

By the first century AD many Roman settlements clustered around the base of Mount Vesuvius in the Bay of Naples, growing rich from the fertile volcanic soils on its slopes. The volcano around which they crowded was not dead however, just sleeping, and the region was well known for the type of minor earthquakes which we know today often precede an eruption, but which the Romans did not recognize.

In AD 64 the historian Suetonius recorded an earthquake in the region, although he was more interested in the fact that it might be a message from the gods (Emperor Nero was making his first public singing performance there at the time) than a warning from the mountain. Other small earthquakes followed; in the spring of AD 79 local people began reporting that wells were unexpectedly drying up. By August there were frequent earth tremors that increased in violence up to the afternoon of 24 August. Then, suddenly, Vesuvius erupted.

A depiction of Pliny and his mother at his uncle's villa at Misenum in AD 79 as Vesuvius pours forth its poisonous ash, by the 18th-century Swiss artist Angelika Kauffmann.

During the initial eruption the writer Pliny the Younger, who was staying nearby, marvelled at the huge column of ash and smoke rising into the upper atmosphere, but had little idea what it meant for the inhabitants of the towns nearer to the volcano. Pliny noted, *'Soon afterwards, the cloud began to descend, and cover the sea'*.

What he was describing was a pyroclastic flow – a cloud of super-heated ash and gas, which emerged from the volcano at more than 800 degrees Celsius and travelled down its sides at incredible speed. Ash and pumice were now raining down even where Pliny was, some 22 miles (35 km) from the eruption, and violent earthquakes were making buildings there unsafe. As the cloud blotted out the sun and darkness descended, he noted that the sea had been sucked away – leaving marine creatures stranded on the beach – before surging back in what we know today as a tsunami.

Closer to the volcano two towns had taken the brunt of the eruption. At Pompeii thick, choking ash was covering streets whilst earthquakes brought down buildings, crushing people inside. Those who escaped into the street faced a hail of rocks falling from the sky and the savage blast and heat from the pyroclastic flows.

Herculaneum was even closer than Pompeii to the eruption but, thanks to the direction of the wind, was spared much of the thick ash rain. It was only a temporary respite, however, and the pyroclastic flows, hurtling down the volcano's sides, would scorch the town, setting fire to the roof timbers before burying everything beneath about 20 metres (66 ft) of hot mud, ash and rock.

By the time the eruption finally stopped there was almost nothing left of Pompeii and Herculaneum. Indeed the whole area around the Bay of Naples had been changed. The violent earthquake had raised the beach level and altered the course of the River Sarno, while the volcano's flanks were a wilderness of sulphurous, lifeless ash and pumice.

We do not know how many people perished in the eruption as large parts of both towns remain buried. In any case, we have only a rough idea of how many people lived in them. To date, the remains of some 1500 people have been found, and many more certainly lie buried in the ruins. We do know that those who survived chose never to return, and two Roman towns slipped out of history for 17 centuries.

The excavator Giuseppe Fiorelli poured liquid plaster into the holes left by bodies enclosed in ash at Pompeii. These people were probably overcome by fumes and would have suffocated to death. The casts sometimes show details of clothing and footwear.

In Britain the Neoclassical style became popular in public and private building works – porches were replaced with porticoes and cooking hearths with Adam fireplaces – while in France Pompeii's influence could be seen everywhere, from the architecture of Versailles to the paintings of Jacques-Louis David.

The past speaks

Attitudes to the people who had once called Pompeii home were also changing. More methodical excavation brought discoveries of a personal nature. The eruption of Vesuvius had preserved a moment in time and excavators began unearthing everyday items that spoke of the lives of the citizens – the remains of meals, workmen's tools, children's toys and even graffiti. The appointment of Giuseppe Fiorelli (1823–96) to lead the excavations in 1860 brought another remarkable discovery: the remains of the Pompeians themselves. During his excavations he noticed strange-shaped voids in the pumice and ash that filled the streets and buildings. Unsure of what had caused them, he injected plaster of Paris into them before excavating the surrounding debris. What emerged were casts of the bodies of those who had failed to escape the eruption 1800 years before. There were adults and children holding hands and a man still grasping an axe with which he had tried to break out of the room that would become his tomb.

These discoveries helped to bring about a realization in Europe that Pompeii and Herculaneum, and by extrapolation any archaeological site, might hold more than just artworks. The buildings, the everyday objects and the remains of the people themselves could hold clues to ancient lives and, even without historical records but by means of careful excavation techniques, they might be persuaded to speak.

THE NAVEL OF THE WORLD
The Mystery of Easter Island, 1722

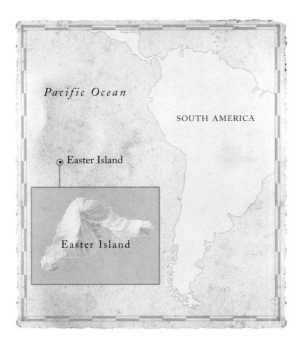

Pacific Ocean

SOUTH AMERICA

Easter Island

Easter Island

On 5 April 1722 the Dutch navigator Jakob Roggeveen (1659–1729) saw an island 9 miles (14 km) distant and ordered his flotilla to set course for it. He was in the South Pacific looking for '*terra australis*' – a great continent first suggested by Aristotle, which many believed lay on the other side of the world from Europe and which even appeared on some of the more optimistic maps and charts of the day. *Terra australis* would prove to be a myth, but the island Roggeveen was heading for was as real as it was unexpected.

Covering an area of only 63 square miles (163 sq km), this small scrap of land in the Pacific lay 2200 miles (3600 km) off the South American coast and 1290 miles (2075 km) east of Pitcairn Island. It was so remote that no European had visited it, although some claimed to have caught sight of it. In accordance with Dutch customs of the day, Roggeveen summoned the captains of his ships – the *Arend*, the *African Galley* and the *Thienhoven* – to pass a resolution claiming discovery of the land. They also needed a name for it. Since the date was Easter Sunday, the commanders agreed that it should be marked on the chart as 'Easter Island'. What he could not know was that the island already had a name that spoke of its great isolation – *Te pito o te henua* (the Navel of the World). Because of the exceptionally calm weather another day passed before Roggeveen could anchor off the coast and, as he did so, he encountered a surprising sight. With their backs to the sea were the remains of numerous huge stone figures. And standing by those statues were people. Easter Island was inhabited.

An enigmatic culture

After landing on the island Roggeveen claims to have found a land devoid of trees but with rich soil producing enough bananas, sweet potatoes and sugar cane to support a large population. There were many thousands of inhabitants, and his men opened fire on some of them within minutes of landing. But Easter Island was and remains the most isolated inhabited island on earth, so where had these people come from and why were they living in a land of fallen statues? These questions, together with the mystery of what became of the culture that built the immense stone statues, or *moai*, were among the greatest puzzles in the history of archaeology.

It was the late 19th century before archaeologists came to Easter Island and began their investigations, and over a century more before most of the answers came to light. In

1955 the Norwegian explorer Thor Heyerdahl (1914–2002) arrived with an American anthropologist and archaeologist, Dr William Mulloy (1917–78), who studied the origins of the island's population. Mulloy was the first archaeologist to take pollen samples – he removed soil segments from different stratigraphic levels and identified plant pollens (which survive very well in archaeological contexts) remaining in them. From these he built up a picture of an island that was very different from the one Roggeveen had described. In the mid-first millennium AD the first settlers of Easter Island had arrived to find a lush broad-leafed rainforest. The settlers brought with them new crops – sweet potato, banana, paper mulberry and taro – and domesticated animals, including chickens as well as the less welcome rats.

Levels of burning in Mulloy's excavations show that the settlers wasted little time in beginning to clear the forest to make room for fields. From that moment, the ecology of Easter Island began to change. Human predation and egg-taking by rats forced the wild

Almost 900 colossal maoi *statues, carved from hardened volcanic ash, punctuate the barren landscape of Easter Island. Although their original purpose is unknown, it is thought that the figures may be representations of powerful chiefs from the island's past.*

23

Rock paintings at Ana Kai Tangata cave near Orongo depict the 'birdman' (Tangata Manu). Orongo was the site of an annual competition to determine the leadership of the island.

bird populations onto the small islets surrounding the main island, but the clearance of the forest revealed a rich and productive soil which allowed the human population to grow and flourish.

The golden age

From around AD 1000 Easter Island entered its greatest era, during which the *moai* statues were constructed. These massive stone heads on truncated torsos were mainly carved from single pieces of compressed volcanic ash. The largest *moai* ever erected, known as *paro*, was nearly 10 metres (33 ft) tall and weighed 76 tonnes (84 tons). One unfinished example is 21 metres (69 ft) tall and would have weighed 274 tonnes (302 tons). The finished statues were erected at ceremonial sites, often on beautifully worked stone platforms (*ahu*), and excavations of examples which fell face down have shown that the characteristic deep eye sockets of the heads originally held large coral eyes.

Exactly what was the purpose of the 887 known *moai* is uncertain, although the most widely accepted theory is that they represented the spirits of dead ancestors and may have embodied the power of living chiefs descended from them. Their construction certainly required huge resources and during this period the island's population swelled to between 10,000 and 20,000.

Conflict and destruction

By the 18th century Easter Island was almost devoid of trees and the destruction of the forest to provide wood for building and boats (and perhaps rollers for moving the *moai*) and to clear areas for agriculture led to a progressive impoverishment and erosion of the soil. These factors, together with the pressures caused by a growing population, meant that Easter Island society began to change rapidly. At the main *moai* quarry over 400 figures still lie abandoned in various states of preparation. Archaeological sites of this era also contain something new – large numbers of obsidian spearheads and daggers, suggesting increasing conflict in the society. Finally, the *moai* themselves were toppled.

When Roggeveen arrived on the island no *moai* remained standing. Nearly all the trees had gone and legends told of a terrible period of starvation and cannibalism causing the population levels to fall dramatically to 2000 or 3000. Archaeology shows that the diet changed around this time: the remains of fish and seafood disappear from rubbish pits, perhaps because of a lack of wood for making fishing boats. Birds, driven offshore by predation, also disappeared from the menu.

But the culture Roggeveen found was managing to adapt. At the ceremonial village of Orongo, stone carvings show the emergence of a new 'birdman' cult in which tribes vied to be the first to bring back an egg from the offshore nesting grounds of the sooty tern. Each year boys would climb down the cliff, swim half a mile (1 km)

TIMELINE

*c.*400–600 Original settlers arrive on Easter Island; they name the island *Te pito o te henua* (the Navel of the World)

*c.*1000–1600 'Golden age', in which most of the *moai* statues were constructed and erected

1722 Jakob Roggeveen's flotilla first sights Easter Island on 15 April

1862 Peruvian slave traders abduct one-third of the island's population

1877 Population drops to 111

1888 The island is annexed by Chile

1947 Thor Heyerdahl sets out on his *Kon Tiki* raft to prove Easter Island's original inhabitants sailed from South America

1955 William Mulloy arrives with Heyerdahl and takes soil samples which provide the first ecological explanations for the island's decline

out to the rocky islet and wait for the migratory terns to arrive. The first to take an egg, then swim back and climb the cliff won for his tribe the right to manage food distribution for that year. Perhaps the Easter Islanders had succeeded in replacing warfare with a competition.

The re-erected *moai* whose eyeless heads now stare across the treeless landscape that their culture transformed bear witness to one of the most famous man-made ecological disasters ever uncovered by archaeology. But it is the outside world which must bear responsibility for Easter Island's final decline. The culture Roggeveen found may only have been a shadow of what had gone before, but it was adapting. When news of Roggeveen's 'discovery' of Easter Island reached Europe, however, it brought more than archaeologists to the island. In 1862 slave traders landed from Peru and abducted one-third of the remaining population. Fifteen abducted islanders who eventually returned brought with them a disease which had never before threatened their remote island home – smallpox. By 1877 only 111 Easter Islanders survived.

EXPERIMENTAL ARCHAEOLOGY

Experimental archaeology enables us to understand how archaeological events or processes might have occurred by reconstructing and re-enacting them, using the technology that was available at the time. By trying to re-create pottery or build structures using only the tools that the original craftspeople had, archaeologists hope to gain greater insight into the methods used in the past, and perhaps solve long-standing mysteries.

The enigma of Easter Island has been a test bed for such theories, including major experiments to try to understand how people first came to the islands and what destroyed the culture that created the *moai*. The experiments have shown both the strengths and the limitations of this approach.

Easter Island had come to the attention of Norwegian explorer Thor Heyerdahl before the Second World War. It provided crucial evidence for his theory that the islands of the Pacific were originally colonized by an ancient, fair-skinned people from Peru. He had noted in Roggeveen's account of the islands the presence of 'surprisingly' fair-skinned inhabitants, and in the structure of the *ahu* platforms on which the *moai* figures stood he thought he saw a technology identical to that used in South America.

In an attempt to give credence to his theory, Heyerdahl organized an experiment. Using only the materials and techniques that were available in pre-Columbian South America he constructed a balsawood raft and, with five other crew, set off across the Pacific with no modern equipment except a radio. After 101 days the raft was wrecked on a reef off the Tuamotu Islands on 7 August 1947, 4300 miles (7000 km) across the Pacific from where it set sail.

The story of the voyage of the *Kon Tiki* (the name Heyerdahl gave the raft) became an instant best-seller but has also caused controversy among archaeologists. Proving that something was possible using ancient technology is not the same thing as proving that it happened – indeed, there is no substantiating archaeological evidence that any such voyage ever took place. Furthermore, however much Heyerdahl and his crew tried, they could not put themselves into the mind-set of pre-Columbian Peruvians, nor could they escape from the fact that they had all received a 20th-century education – knowledge that was useful in preparing for and surviving the voyage.

More recent DNA studies on human skeletons on the island have found them to be of Polynesian origin. This suggests strongly that Easter Island and many other Pacific islands were in fact colonized by peoples coming not from South America, which lies to the east, but from the other side of the Pacific Ocean in East Polynesia.

OLYMPIA REBORN

Locating the Site of the Ancient Olympics, 1766

Not all archaeological excavations are simply about recovering information about the past. A few inspire excavators and visitors to such an extent that they gain a new life in the present. Of these there is one that began as a small classical dig but became a worldwide cultural phenomenon and in the process made the name of an ancient site in Greece known across the world – Olympia.

Some ancient towns survived the collapse of the classical world and were never abandoned nor forgotten, but this was not the fate of Olympia. By the time the antiquarian Richard Chandler (1738–1810) visited Greece in 1763, Olympia had been relegated to the history books as an unidentified place where the Greeks had once held games. Chandler was in Greece with a painter and an architect at the request of the Dilettanti Society, which had been founded by a group of wealthy landowners who had been on the fashionable Grand Tour of Europe. Inspired by having seen the wonders of the classical world at first hand, they had formed a dining club in 1734 with the intention of sponsoring the study of the ancient world and commissioning new artworks in the classical style. Part of this involved funding expeditions to find and record ancient sites.

So it was that in 1766, as his expedition drew to a close, Chandler found himself in a vineyard in the northwest Peloponnese. It was a typical rural Greek scene, apparently ageless and natural except that between the vines he could see the stubs of ancient walls. As he explored further he noticed more and more of them and began to see the drums of slender columns in the Doric style overgrown with vines and weeds. It was clearly a major site and the style of the columns dated it to the classical Greek period. In this far-off corner of the Peloponnese that could mean only one thing and, making no attempt to uncover any more of the ruins, he marked the place on his map 'Olympia'.

Early visits and excavations

The later history of Olympia had been unhappy. After the banning of the Olympic Games in AD 393 by the Christian emperor Theodosius, who considered them 'pagan', the town had lost much of its importance. Yet it had remained inhabited and a Byzantine settlement had grown up over the ruins, which were progressively robbed to provide stone for the walls intended to keep out an ever-increasing number of invaders. Eventually those defences had failed and the site had been sacked. With the fields untended and the river untamed, winter floods slowly covered the site with thick mud and the town of Olympia slipped from view.

Chandler's publication of the location of Olympia in his 1776 book *Travels in Greece* brought the site to public attention once more and visitors soon began returning to the ruins. In May 1829 the French Expédition Scientifique de Morée began the first excavations on the site. It recovered parts of one of the most famous buildings, the temple of Zeus, which had once housed the chryselephantine (gold and ivory) statue of Zeus, carved by the great Phidias and recorded by Antipater of Sidon as one of the Seven Wonders of the World. The finest pieces of sculpture were shipped back to the excavators' own country and they can still be seen in the Louvre in Paris. Hearing of these unauthorized exports, the Greek government immediately banned further excavations.

The idea that the treasures of ancient Olympia might still lie in the ground did not die however. The Prussian art historian Johann Joachim Winckelmann (1717–68), who was familiar with the description of the site by the ancient writer Pausanias, had enthused that a rediscovered Olympia would yield *'statues of young and manly figures … wonderworks of art by the thousand'*.

The ancient Greeks celebrated the victories of their greatest athletes by erecting bronze or marble statues of them at the site and Pausanias, who visited Olympia in the second century AD, had written of a veritable forest of such figures there. Winckelmann in turn inspired his fellow countryman Ernst Curtius (1814–96), who applied to excavate the site in 1853. Thanks to the elaborate diplomatic manoeuvres necessary to persuade the Greek authorities that this would not be another 'smash-and-grab' raid on their antiquities, excavations began only in 1875. These excavations would provide the first proper archaeological investigation of a classical site.

Surviving columns from the Palaestra at Olympia, a building used for wrestling and boxing events.

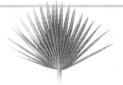

TIMELINE

776 BC The first Games are held at Olympia

C.AD 170 Pausanias visits Olympia and describes its glories

393 The Byzantine emperor Theodosius bans the 'pagan' Games

1763 Richard Chandler visits Greece to record ancient sites

1766 Chandler discovers Olympia

1776 *Travels in Greece* published

1829 French excavations reveal many important buildings and statues, but unauthorized exportation of sculpture leads to a ban on further investigations

1875 Following a lengthy application by Ernst Curtius, detailed archaeological excavations begin

1894 Pierre de Coubertin presents his idea for a revived Olympic Games

1896 Athens hosts the Games of the First Olympiad

The ancient Olympic Games were held to honour the Greek god Zeus. In this representation of the temple of Zeus at Olympia, the enthroned god dominates one end of a colonnaded hall. Pausanias described the statue in detail: 'In his right hand a figure of Victory made from ivory and gold. In his left hand, his sceptre inlaid with all metals, and an eagle perched on the sceptre. The sandals of the god are made of gold, as is his robe'.

Olympia was dug stratigraphically, the team removing each layer of silt and rubble one at a time to reveal the long history of the place. The sculptural friezes from the temple of Zeus were found where they had fallen during some long-forgotten earthquake, and the layout of the buildings around it proved to be much as Pausanias had described. Here was the Prytaneion where the officials who ran the ancient Olympic Games were housed, the Phillipeion that once contained a memorial statue to Alexander the Great's father, Philip of Macedon, the Bouleuterion where the games were administered and even the workshop of the sculptor Phidias.

As for the bronze statues, Winckelmann would have been disappointed, for it seems that the valuable metal had been removed and melted down long ago. Only fragments of their inlay survived as a scattering of lips, irises and eyelashes around the bases for the statues. More than 5000 of these bases have been recovered, bearing the names of the greatest victors in the ancient Olympic Games.

But the Prussian excavations at Olympia did more than recover artefacts. At the time the work was one of the best examples of modern archaeological techniques and practice, with the people of Greece retaining all the finds from the site in return for the right of the excavators to publish their work. Furthermore, the site was landscaped after excavation and a purpose-built museum was constructed (the first site museum in the world) to encourage visitors. Publication of the work was prompt and meticulous, and the reports of the wealth of finds coming from the site inspired one man in particular.

Revival of the Olympics

Baron Pierre de Coubertin (1863–1937) had been seeking an explanation for the French defeat in the Franco-Prussian war of 1870–1 and had come to believe that the main reason was the lack of physical education and sporting spirit amongst French youth. He was aware that in Britain a much greater emphasis was placed on sports in schools – the British had been inventing new sports and codifying old village games since the Industrial Revolution. He had even visited Much Wenlock in central England in 1890 to learn about their Olympian Society Annual Games, which had been revived for much the same reason. Ironically, it was the flood of reports coming from France's old enemy, the Prussians, at Olympia that provided the real impetus. At a congress in Paris in 1894 he presented his ideas for a revived Olympic Games in which the world's youth could test their mettle on the sports field rather than on the battlefield. In 1896 Athens hosted the Games of the First Olympiad, and the new Olympic movement was born.

Today the ancient site of Olympia still provides the vital first spark in the celebration that its excavation revived. On the original running track, uncovered by a German team during the Nazi occupation of Greece, a parabolic mirror is used to light the flame that is then carried across the world to the location of the games and which remains burning for their duration. It is a unique link between the ancient past, an archaeological excavation and the greatest sporting event the world has ever known.

THE HERMES OF PRAXITELES

Although there was some disappointment during the 19th-century excavations at Olympia that so little of the bronze statuary that once filled the site was recovered, it was hardly a surprise. The finest bronzes had often been stolen or taken as war booty in the distant past. Some had then been lost and others melted down. Indeed many of the most famous Greek sculptors known from historical sources had no surviving works that could be attributed to them. Some Roman copies of statues were known but almost all the originals seemed to have succumbed to the ravages of 2500 years of history.

But if the Prussians were disappointed by the lack of bronze, Olympia's earth was holding another great secret for them. Marble is more difficult to remove and harder to reuse than bronze and, in 1877, the site of the ancient Olympic Games offered up one of the finest examples of marble statuary ever discovered.

Hermes Bearing the Infant Dionysus, *from the temple of Hera at Olympia. Praxiteles's statue, excavated in 1877, dates from c.330 BC.*

masterpiece by the Greek sculptor Praxiteles (fl. fourth century BC).

Praxiteles was already known to classicists from descriptions of his sculptures in the writings of ancient authors, and many museums already possessed later copies of his works. The Vatican owned two copies, including one of Aphrodite, the original of which had been made for the people of Cnidus (in present-day Turkey). They valued it so highly that they would not sell it to King Nicomedes even when he offered to cancel the huge debt the city owed him.

The discovery of an original work caused a sensation. Carved in white marble from the island of Paros, then the finest source of marble known, it shows Hermes resting on his journey to hold up something to amuse the infant Dionysus (the arm holding whatever it was is missing). The style is characteristic of other known copies of works by Praxiteles: the main

Hermes Bearing the Infant Dionysus was discovered on its original base in the ruins of the temple of Hera, just where Pausanias had seen it some 1700 years before. It shows Hermes, the messenger of the gods, taking the baby Dionysus to be reared by the nymphs following the death of his mother Semele. She had been consumed in flames when she saw the child's father, Zeus, in all his terrible glory. Unlike so many ancient statues, this not a copy but the original

figure lounges against some drapery and his head is tilted and turned slightly. As might be expected, experts have argued about whether it is really an original work by Praxiteles, but the mastery of the carving, the fact that it was found exactly where Pausanias saw it and the lack of any definitive evidence to the contrary makes this probably the only original Greek masterpiece to have come down to the modern world.

'A VERY REMOTE PERIOD INDEED'

John Frere and the Antiquity of Man, 1797

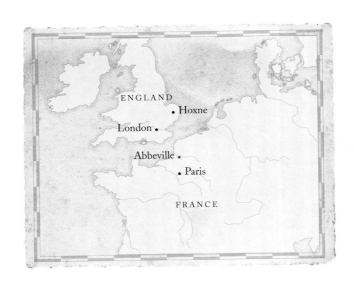

On 22 June 1797 the secretary of the Royal Society of Antiquaries in London stood up and read a letter to the distinguished gentlemen who had gathered in their meeting rooms:

'Sir, I take the liberty to request you to lay before the society some flints found in the parish of Hoxne, in the county of Suffolk, which, if not particularly objects of curiosity in themselves, must, I think, be considered in that light from the situation in which they were found.'

This was the opening paragraph of the letter and with it began the story of prehistoric archaeology. The letter was from John Frere (1740–1807), a member of that society, who made a modest income from land he had inherited in Norfolk in eastern England and from a London grain mill in which he had, with great foresight, installed the revolutionary new steam engine sold by Messrs Watt and Boulton. This income gave Frere time to indulge in his hobby, antiquarianism.

Focus on the classical past

Since the Renaissance there had been a growing interest in objects recovered from the past, and European collectors vied with each other to secure the ancient artefacts they considered the most beautiful and valuable. Much of this antiquarianism centred on the classical world where excavations or, more accurately, treasure-seeking expeditions occasionally turned up Roman and Greek sculpture, inscriptions and pottery.

These investigations made no attempt to distinguish layers of remains or to recover anything other than items that were considered 'art'; nor was any serious effort made to use the finds to reconstruct the history of the sites. These were, after all, Roman towns and Rome was known from written history. Artefacts themselves, unless they contained inscriptions, were deemed to be silent witnesses to that history, jumbled in the earth in a meaningless lucky dip, waiting for a fortunate prospector to find them.

What had taken place before the age of literate civilizations was rarely considered a worthwhile question for antiquarians to ask. By Frere's day educated men and women were perfectly well aware that strange objects such as flint arrowheads and axes which were sometimes brought up by the plough were the product of primitive peoples who did not have the use of metals. But who those people were and when they lived was thought to be irrelevant and generally impossible to know. When John Conyers (*c.*1633–94) had uncovered a flint handaxe associated with what he described as 'elephant' bones (probably mammoth bones) in Gray's Inn Lane, London in about 1690, the logical conclusion seemed to be that the axe belonged to an ancient Briton who had used it to kill one of the elephants that history told him had been brought to England by the emperor Claudius. How else had an elephant got there?

A biblical explanation

The problem with understanding anything that happened before recorded history was not simply that it was 'unknowable'. Most people believed there really wasn't much to know. That was because the early history of life on earth could easily be reconstructed through the one book which definitively explained events of the past – the Bible. Most Europeans in the late 18th and early 19th centuries took the Bible as the literal truth: the world had been created in six days. The planet, its plants and animals were made first and humans were then fashioned as their custodians.

The discovery of Palaeolithic tools like these (found in the Czech Republic) prompted John Frere to question the popular belief that earth was created in 4004 BC.

The Old Testament contained elaborate genealogies going back to the first humans, Adam and Eve, so it was even possible to establish a date for when all this had happened. The most precise calculation had been made in 1650 by the archbishop of Armagh, James Ussher (1581–1656), in *Annales veteris testamenti, a prima mundi originae deducti* ('Annals of the Old Testament, deduced from the first origins of the world'). He concluded that creation had begun just before dusk on 23 October 4004 BC.

TIMELINE

1650 Archbishop James Ussher calculates the date of earth's creation to be 23 October 4004 BC

1669 Danish scholar Niels Stensen reasons that the youngest layers in earth's strata must be those at the top, and the oldest must be at the bottom

1690 Discovery of so-called elephant bones and handaxe in Gray's Inn Lane by John Conyers

1797 John Frere writes to the Royal Society of Antiquaries describing flint implements found in a layer of earth beneath layers containing shells and animal remains

1830–3 Charles Lyell publishes *Principles of Geology*, followed in 1838 by *Elements of Geology*, in which he demonstrates that the processes which changed the earth in the past are continuing

1847 Boucher de Perthes sets out his ideas on the existence of prehistoric humans and the evidence for climate change in the past

1858 Hugh Falconer, Joseph Prestwich and John Evans visit Abbeville to study de Perthes's collection; they confirm his theories about the antiquity of man

1859 Prestwich reports his findings in the Proceedings of the Royal Society. Charles Darwin publishes *On the Origin of Species by Means of Natural Selection*

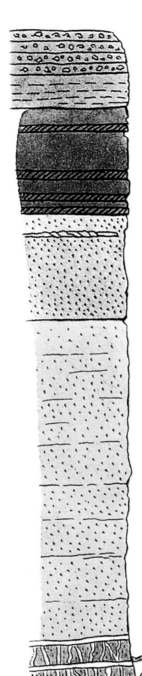

Many of Frere's friends in the Royal Society of Antiquaries took this as a definitive date. The earth had its origins just over 4000 years before the Romans arrived in Britain, and all pre-Roman material must therefore fall within this period. There were some who had reservations about this, who realized that the huge layers of sediment that could be seen in rock faces and the presence of strange fossil bones of animals that no longer existed suggested that the earth had undergone many changes in its past. They understood that these transformations must have occurred over long periods of time and that the planet could not have been created in its 'perfect' modern form. They concluded, however, that whilst the earth might be older than Ussher's date, these previous worlds had settled down into their present form around 4000 BC and that humans had appeared only after that time.

John Frere begged to differ. In his letter to the Royal Society of Antiquaries, he went on to describe the flint implements found in a brick clay pit in Suffolk as:

> '... weapons of war, fabricated and used by a people who had not the use of metals.'

No doubt this would have seemed perfectly reasonable to the members of the society, but what bothered Frere was exactly where he had found them. He stated that they came from beneath 4 metres (12 ft) of undisturbed soil and gravel, below a layer of sand and shells (suggesting that the site had once been underwater) and below the fossilized bones of animals that were now extinct. As Frere and many others knew, this was problematic. The Danish scholar Niels Stensen, often known as Nicolas Steno (1638–86), had established in 1669 that the lowest layers of a geological profile must be older than the higher ones, so Frere's stone tools had to be older than the extinct animals and the bed of an ancient sea. This brought Frere to a dramatic conclusion:

> 'The situation in which these weapons were found may tempt us to refer them to a very remote period indeed; even beyond that of the present world.'

Planting the seeds of modern archaeology

With this statement Frere planted the seeds of modern prehistoric archaeology. He had taken silent artefacts from prehistory and, using a combination of geology, paleontology and straightforward logic, made them speak of their origins in a time long before the modern world – before 4004 BC.

Frere's brilliant deduction did not start an immediate revolution, however. His letter was duly read to the society and published in its journal, but it excited little interest among scientists or the general public. The enormity of his

Early 19th-century geologists studied earth strata and found that each layer contained different fossil remains. Charles Lyell used this evidence to demonstrate that the earth had developed very slowly over a long period of time.

BOUCHER DE PERTHES

John Frere's ideas were only finally proved in the 1850s by a French archaeologist, Jacques Boucher de Crèvecœur de Perthes (1788–1868), who was director of the customs service at Abbeville in France. His prestigious, well-paid but relatively undemanding job allowed him time to pursue an interest in archaeology and it was this that brought him to the Somme valley. While excavating the gravel terraces here, he came across pieces of flint which he believed showed evidence of having been shaped into primitive tools. What was surprising, this being northern France, was that the tools came from layers in the gravel in which he was also finding elephant and rhinoceros bones.

De Perthes made a crucial contribution to proving the existence of prehistoric humans.

In a Europe where many people still took the Old Testament as a literal narrative of earth's early history, this was a potentially explosive discovery. For 17 years de Perthes continued quietly collecting evidence and refining his ideas before setting them out, beginning in 1847, in his three-volume *Antiquités celtiques et antédiluviennes* ('Celtic and Antediluvian Antiquities'). He made two important deductions. Firstly, from his finds he saw that people had lived alongside animals which were now extinct. The geology and the fossil finds also suggested that the climate must have changed significantly in the past – as well as temperate times, the region had experienced periods of tropical warmth in which hippopotamuses roamed the region and cold periods

in which ice sheets extended from the poles down across the Somme.

Like those of Frere 50 years before, de Perthes's findings did not gain immediate approval. This was partly because some of the ancient stone tools he had discovered were so primitive as to cast doubt on whether they were man-made at all (not helped by the poor illustrations in his book) and in part because of the perceived slight against the church that his findings implied.

In 1858 the Scottish geologist Hugh Falconer (1808–65) visited the Somme and happened to see de Perthes's collection at Abbeville. He was certain that the finds were man-made and persuaded his colleague Joseph Prestwich (1812–96) and the archaeologist John Evans (1823–1908) to visit the site. Aided by the geological heavyweight of the age, Charles Lyell, they quickly agreed that the flints were indeed tools and that they came from the same deposits as the extinct animals he had found.

The new science of geology could also now prove they were extremely old; indeed we now know that de Perthes's tools are at least 500,000 years old. It was the ammunition they had been looking for, and Prestwich quickly published his report in the *Proceedings of the Royal Society*. The following year Charles Darwin published *On the Origin of Species by Means of Natural Selection*. The spell of biblical chronology had been broken, and the age of archaeology could begin.

suggestion – that earth had existed for a far greater time than the Bible allowed for – and his innovative use of logic to determine the relative ages of objects by their position in the ground went almost completely unrecognized.

Over the next 50 years, however, Charles Lyell (1797–1875) would prove that the earth's surface was in a process of constant, slow change (and was not a static, finished entity) and Charles Darwin (1809–82) would develop his theory of natural selection, finally demonstrating that the history of earth and of mankind was immeasurably longer than Archbishop Ussher could have imagined.

'A ROSE-RED CITY HALF AS OLD AS TIME'
Burckhardt at Petra, 1812

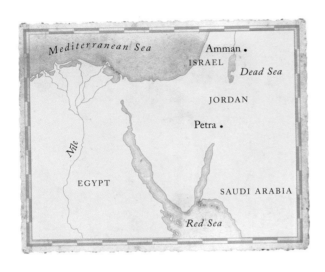

J. L. Burckhardt was known by many names, which he changed to suit his environment. On the European continent he was officially Johann Ludwig Burckhardt, his family in Switzerland called him Jean Louis and when he set sail for England in 1806 he changed his name to John Lewis. It was as John that he left England, from the port of Cowes on the Isle of Wight in March 1809, but by the time he arrived at his first port of call, Malta, he was known as Sheikh Ibrahim Ibn 'Abd Allah.

Burckhardt (1784–1817) was not an archaeologist but an explorer. At the time he was in the pay of the London-based Association for Promoting the Discovery of the Interior Parts of Africa. As he travelled he carried in his pocket an eight-year contract to find the source of the River Niger in Africa. The Association had sent many before him, including Mungo Park (1771–1806), and none had returned, so Burckhardt had proposed a new plan. He would travel undercover dressed as an Arab, first to Malta where he would perfect his Arabic, and then to Aleppo in Syria. From there he would travel to Cairo, where he would wait for an Arab caravan travelling to Timbuktu. He would then proceed to the source of the Niger – wherever that might be.

It was a plan full of dangers but with many advantages. Travelling as an Arab he could move among the people of the Middle East and North Africa without arousing suspicion. He could visit places where Westerners were unwelcome and, in theory, he stood less chance of being robbed and murdered. By living among the Arab people and learning their survival skills he was also less likely to succumb to the harsh desert itself. If his identity was ever discovered, however, his life would swiftly be cut short.

The route south
From Malta Burckhardt travelled to Aleppo in Syria, now confident in his ability to speak the language and to blend in. From Aleppo he began taking short journeys into the desert to see whether he would pass unnoticed among the tribesmen. Confident that he could, he started for Damascus. In Damascus he had a choice – he could travel down the coast through Jerusalem and Gaza and across Sinai or he could take a longer route, following the trail of the Muslim *hadj* (pilgrimage to Mecca). It was a dangerous route; indeed the *hadj* had not taken place for the previous six years for fear of attacks from

Emerging from the narrow mile-long ravine, known as the siq, *which leads to the ancient city of Petra, Burckhardt was rewarded by the magnificent sight of the 'Treasury'* (al-Khazneh). *It is thought to have been a tomb or temple and, when Burckhardt stumbled across it in 1812, a stream ran in front of the building.*

THE NABATAEANS

Ancient references to the city Burckhardt found in the desert were rare and all that was known about the people who built it and lived there was their name – the Nabataeans. Exactly who they were remains a mystery even some 200 years later. We know that they were a literate people because a great deal of graffiti has been found at Nabataean sites. However, none of their literature (if they produced any) has survived and their temples carry no inscriptions to provide information about their builders or their purpose.

The strength of Nabataean culture seems to have been trade. From their location in central Arabia the Nabataeans controlled a number of important trade routes from the Arabian peninsula and the Red Sea ports as well as caravan routes to Asia and west into Egypt. This loose confederation of communities was ruled from Petra, a city which had much to offer. It was well defended by natural cliffs on all sides, secluded enough to avoid unwanted attention, at the centre of many valuable caravan routes and, most important of all, a source of water in the desert. The Nabataeans were great hydraulic engineers and the flash floods which beset the region were controlled in Petra by a series of aqueducts, canals, dams and cisterns which collected the excessive rains of the flood season and eked them out through the scorching summer droughts.

The exact date when Petra was founded is not known, but it appears that people were living there before the Nabataeans, possibly in the fifth or fourth centuries BC. The tombs they cut for themselves in the cliff walls show Greek, Egyptian and Syrian influences, but in the second century BC, when both the Egyptian and Persian dynasties were weak, Petra really came to the fore as the heart of a thriving kingdom.

The city continued to flourish under Roman rule until, early in the third century AD, building work and production of coins and pottery suddenly came to an end. Just what happened to Petra remains a mystery. It has been surmised that a Persian invasion brought about its fall, that an earthquake destroyed the intricate water system or simply that the rise of the city of Palmyra and changes to trade routes drew business away from the city.

There is evidence that the city survived in some form, perhaps as a religious centre, into the early fifth century but nothing is heard of it after that. In the Middle Ages Petra was a local curiosity, visited by tribesmen and traders in search of buried treasure, but outside the region the city's location was completely forgotten – until a Swiss adventurer disguised as an Arab merchant stumbled upon the ruins in his search for the source of an African river.

local tribes. But the route promised Burckhardt something he was unable to refuse: a chance to travel into unknown areas to the east of the Dead Sea, to places no European had ever seen. His mind was made up.

He left Damascus on the evening of 12 June 1812, riding past piles of rocks by the roadside that marked the graves of murdered travellers. He was heading into a land of extremes, where the temperature was blisteringly hot by day and bitingly cold at night, where the desert people might rob you of everything but your underclothes as you travelled but would always offer you hospitality at night after a long ride.

From Damascus he travelled south, past the ruins of the Roman city of Jerash to Amman, today the capital of Jordan but then nothing more than another Roman ruin. By now his guides, when he could find any who were willing to make the journey, were becoming suspicious. Why would an Arab trader be so interested in these old ruins and why would anyone waste time in such exposed locations where robbers might see them?

The journey continued, however, down to Kerek to the great Saracen castle of Shobak which still bore the name of Saladin, the first Ayyubid sultan of Egypt, carved on its walls. It was among the castle ruins that Burckhardt took the decision that would change his life and make his name. Instead of pressing on towards Cairo, he decided

Above: At the time of Burckhardt's visit to the Middle East, Jaffa (modern Tel Aviv-Yafo in Israel) was an important sea port. This watercolour of Jaffa was made by the Scottish painter David Roberts in 1839.

Below: Leaving Kerek, Burckhardt deviated from his plan of travelling straight to Cairo. Instead of heading west he was tempted south by tales of some interesting ruins - his curiosity was rewarded when he discovered Petra.

to take a small detour to Wadi Mousa – the Valley of Moses – where he had heard from locals that ancient wonders were to be seen.

His guides were less enthusiastic and he was forced to invent a story about wishing to sacrifice a goat to the prophet Aaron whose tomb lay at the head of the valley. Following his guides, Buckhardt travelled as far as the mouth of the valley where a local man was persuaded, in return for two horseshoes, to take him to the tomb. He was heading into a land unseen by Europeans for over 1000 years.

First glimpse of the ancient city

Passing ancient tombs along the route, the pair plunged into a narrow ravine, its sides so high that they could not see the sky. After nearly half an hour winding through this dark passage, the path opened up. In front of them:

> *'A mausoleum came into view, the situation and beauty of which are calculated to make an extraordinary impression upon the traveller ... It is one of the most elegant remains of antiquity existing in Syria; its state of preservation resembles that of a building recently finished.'*

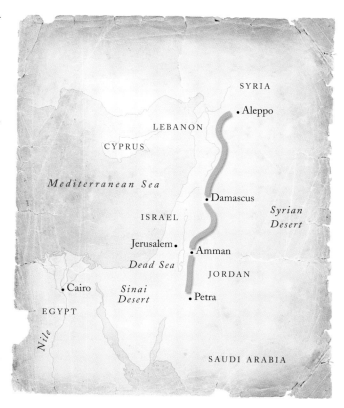

TIMELINE

SECOND CENTURY BC
Petra enjoys its heyday as a thriving city and the centre of the Nabataean culture

AD 105 The Roman emperor Trajan annexes the Nabataean kingdom, which becomes the Roman province of *Arabia Petraea*

EARLY THIRD CENTURY
Building work and production of pottery and coins stop in Petra

511 A severe earthquake (one of many) occurs in the region

1784 (24 November) Jean Louis Burckhardt is born in Switzerland

1806 Burckhardt travels to England

1809 After making extensive preparations for his journey, Burckhardt sets out to discover the source of the River Niger

1812 En route from Damascus to Cairo Burckhardt makes a detour and discovers the lost city of Petra

1817 Burckhardt dies, aged 32

1819–29 Burckhardt's accounts of his travels in the Middle East are published posthumously

This was the building now known as the 'Treasury', actually a vast tomb, over 40 metres (130 ft) high, cut into the cliff face. On a pretext Burckhardt went inside, passing through elaborate doorways into three huge rooms, but nowhere was there a sign of any writing or painting that might suggest who had built this awe-inspiring structure.

Nor did this building stand alone. Further on more tombs, each one slightly different, stood out from the pink sandstone of the cliff face. On one side stood a semi-circular theatre, also cut into the rock, that had once seated over 3000 patrons, and on the plain beyond, hemmed in on all sides by the precipitous mountains, stood *'heaps of hewn stones, foundations of buildings, fragments of columns and vestiges of paved streets; all clearly indicating that a large city once stood here'.*

Burckhardt had an idea where he was. The Greek geographer Strabo (64/63 BC–after AD 23) had referred to a desert city protected by high cliffs on all sides and home to a people called the Nabataeans. He also had a name for the place, from the Greek for 'rock' – Petra.

By now the guide was becoming nervous and suspicious. When Burckhardt began heading up the cliff face towards a spectacular Corinthian tomb which the locals called 'The Palace of Pharaoh's Daughter', his guide shouted out:

> *'I see now clearly that you are an infidel, who have some particular business amongst the ruins of the city of your forefathers; but depend upon it that we shall not suffer you to take out a single part of all the treasures hidden therein.'*

It was a common belief among local people that this ancient city must house hoards of lost treasure. If word got out that Burckhardt had found some, however unlikely that was, he would never leave the place alive. Realizing it was time to leave the city, he returned to the path and continued on to a clearing below the tomb of Aaron. Here he sacrificed the goat his guide had carried there and prepared to leave. It was time to set out again for Cairo and for new discoveries. What he could never know was that he had already made the greatest discovery of his life. He was indeed riding through the remains of Petra, the city that John Burgon (1813–88) would later immortalize in his sonnet, *Petra* (1845):

It seems no work of Man's creative hand,
by labour wrought as wavering fancy planned;
But from the rock as by magic grown,
eternal, silent, beautiful, alone!
Not virgin-white like that old Doric shrine,
where erst Athena held her rites divine;
Not saintly-grey, like many a minster fane,
that crowns the hill and consecrates the plain;
But rose-red as if the blush of dawn,
that first beheld them were not yet withdrawn;
The hues of youth upon a brow of woe,
which Man deemed old two thousand years ago,
match me such marvel save in Eastern clime,
a rose-red city half as old as time.

JEAN LOUIS BURCKHARDT

Jean Louis Burckhardt was born in 1784 in Lausanne, Switzerland. As a young child he became fascinated with stories of lost civilizations, particularly of the Roman empire. But another empire was at this time in its death throes, and the French Revolution would bring an end to his happy childhood. Although Switzerland was neutral, Jean's father's business interests had made him enemies in France and he found himself marked as an 'enemy' of the new French state. Fearing reprisals, the council in his family's home town of Basle convicted his father of treason and imprisoned him. Two years later, in 1798, France invaded Switzerland, which became subject to French rule.

Burckhardt dressed as an Arab merchant. In order to travel safely in the Middle East, he assimilated the Arabic language and customs.

The 14-year-old Burckhardt was left without family or money and was forced to provide for himself. From school in Neuchâtel he moved on to university in Germany but, unwilling to live in poverty, he ran up huge debts. To escape these, he sailed for England in 1806. Burckhardt arrived in London with no money and few prospects, but his intellect and love of history soon brought him to the attention of some powerful figures, including the future consul in Cairo and the librarian of the British Museum.

He also met Sir Joseph Banks (1743–1820), a wealthy naturalist and a prominent member of the Association for Promoting the Discovery of the Interior Parts of Africa (also known as the African Association). The Association had been founded to fund expeditions into Africa, a continent still largely unknown at the time in the West. The purpose of the expeditions was to discover and map new lands with a view to their future exploitation by the rapidly expanding British empire.

In recent years the Association had found it difficult to recruit men to undertake its perilous journeys into Africa. For all its wealth and erudition, the Association underestimated the difficulties of such expeditions and had a long and growing list of field agents posted as missing or dead. It needed men of learning and skill, who could combine academic prowess with extreme physical resilience, practical

knowledge and a fearless desire for adventure. In March 1808 Burckhardt applied and was accepted.

Considerable efforts were made to ensure that Burckhardt would be ready for his assigned mission – to locate the source of the River Niger. He studied astronomy (for navigation), mineralogy (to identify Africa's mineral resources) and medicine (to ensure his own survival). He also took the opportunity to begin learning Arabic so he might travel through North Africa as an Arab merchant, and he designed for himself a rigorous exercise regime to help him deal with the heat. Early in 1809 his preparations were considered complete and the African Association handed him his orders. He was to sail for Malta and from there head to the Middle East, journeying down to Cairo, where he would await a caravan to take him into the uncharted regions of Africa.

But if Burckhardt hoped to be remembered as an African explorer his dream was not to be realized. After his detour to Petra, he arrived in Cairo to find that no caravan destined for Fezzan – his initial goal – was expected, and no-one knew when the next one would leave. To pass the time he decided to prepare himself further physically and mentally by travelling up the Nile into Sudan disguised as a Syrian merchant. Next he cut across the desert to the Red Sea coast and then followed the *hadj* to Mecca. In one respect the journey served its purpose. He was now toughened to desert life, used to sleeping on the ground and to surviving on vegetables and water and he passed among Arabs without comment. But the gruelling journey had damaged his health and by the time he returned to Cairo he was sickening.

As he waited once more in Cairo, news came that the Fezzan caravan was finally ready to leave. But it was too late for Burckhardt. He had developed dysentery and he died on 15 October 1817, aged 32. He would never reach his goal; in fact he had barely started, but during his excursions in the Middle East he had discovered something greater – Petra, the lost city that would be his legacy.

IN THE LAND OF OZYMANDIAS
Belzoni in Egypt, 1817

Giovanni Belzoni (1778–1823) had been in Egypt for two years when, in 1817, he came to the valley of Beban el Malook with a permit to dig. Having arrived in Egypt at the start of the antiquities rush, he had twice travelled up the Nile in search of the finest objects for museums and collectors hungry for Egyptian art. He had encountered a world of frontier law, where bribery and threats were the currency of daily life and his competitors spent as much time plotting against each other as they did ransacking ancient sites.

Despite the best efforts of his main rival Bernardino Drovetti (1776–1852), collecting on behalf of the French, Belzoni had had some stunning successes. He had located and shipped back to Cairo the colossal statue of the 'Young Memnon' (which we now know to be of Ramses II), said to be the inspiration for Shelley's *Ozymandias of Egypt* (1818):

> *'My name is Ozymandias, king of kings:*
> *Look on my works, ye mighty, and despair!'*

On the island of Philae in the River Nile Belzoni had identified what he believed to be the most perfect hieroglyphics and added them to his collection. Journeying south he had located the temple of Abu Simbel, one of the most impressive monuments on earth. But he had had his share of reverses. Returning to Philae, he found that Drovetti's men had smashed his hieroglyphics. In Luxor he found the temple of Karnak already in French hands and his name a cause of suspicion and unrest among local Arab rulers. Being unwelcome and unable to dig in Thebes, the one-time capital of ancient Egypt, he was forced to move across the river to the Land of the Dead, to a place called Beban el Malook – now known as the Valley of the Kings. Belzoni began digging, initially in search of inscribed papyri and small objects to sell. His methods were primitive: he cut small holes into tombs and squeezed through to rifle their contents. In one mummy pit:

> *'When my weight bore down on the body of an Egyptian it crushed it like a band-box …*
> *I sunk altogether among the broken mummies, with a crash of bones, rags and wooden*
> *cases … and every step I took I crushed a mummy in some part or other.'*

Such destruction may seem shocking but Belzoni was a man of his time, providing what the market required. He was also, to his credit, still learning. As he crashed through tombs he began to understand how they were constructed, what common elements they contained and how they differed from the ancient descriptions made by the Greeks, which until his time were the only references available to academics.

Tomb beneath a torrent

Belzoni soon gained a reputation as a tomb-finder. The graves on the west bank at Thebes were unlike the pyramids of earlier pharaohs. They were not meant to be displayed, indeed they were hidden to prevent looting. But Belzoni had a knack of finding them. Scouring the craggy valley walls, he searched out rock falls which might have obscured an entrance and sorted through the outwash from seasonal rivers which might have brought down artefacts from higher tombs. This was the way he was working on 16 October 1817 when:

'I caused the earth to be opened at the foot of a steep hill, and under a torrent, which when it rains, pours a great quantity of water over the very spot I have caused to be dug.'

The colossal head of Ramses II, the 'Young Memnon', was found by Belzoni in 1816 and is now in the British Museum.

His workmen thought he was mad. Who would build a tomb under a river course? The following day, Belzoni's hunch was proved right and, after removing tons of silt and rubble, *'… in the evening we perceived the part of the rock that was cut, and formed the entrance'*.

The next day the workmen continued to excavate around the opening, revealing a large tomb choked with rocks. Chipping away at one area, they cut a passage just big enough for Belzoni to crawl into. *'I perceived immediately by the painting on the ceiling, and by the hieroglyphics in basso-relievo … that this was the entrance into a large and magnificent tomb.'* What he could not have known, since the hieroglyphics on the wall remained an impenetrable mystery, was that this was the tomb of Pharaoh Seti I, father of Ramses II.

Belzoni crawled past the earth-strewn mouth of the tomb until he could stand. At the end of the first, rubble-strewn corridor he came to a flight of steps which led down into the mountainside. He followed them until he came to another corridor. Certain that he was now in a royal tomb, he rushed on and only just pulled back from the edge of a pit 9 metres (30 ft) deep. Beyond lay a small opening in the wall only half a metre square (5 sq ft).

TIMELINE

1778 (5 November) Giovanni Belzoni is born in Padua, Italy

1803 Moves to England and begins touring theatres with his 'strong man' act

1815 Belzoni and his wife settle in Cairo where Belzoni works on hydraulic machines for use in irrigation; at about this time he meets Jean Louis Burckhardt

1816 At Thebes Belzoni locates a colossal statue of Ramses II, known as the 'Young Memnon'. He transports it to Cairo and it later becomes one of the first major Egyptian antiquities in the British Museum collection

1817 Belzoni discovers the temple of Abu Simbel. Later that year (16 October) he locates the entrance to the tomb of Seti I and over the course of the next few days he explores the entire tomb complex

1820 On his return to England he mounts a successful exhibition and enjoys celebrity status but receives no remuneration from the British Museum for the sarcophagus from the tomb of Seti

1823 He returns to Egypt intent on finding the legendary city of Timbuktu in West Africa but contracts dysentery and dies at Gwato in Nigeria on 3 December

1825 In London Sir John Soane buys Seti's sarcophagus and hosts parties in honour of 'The Great Belzoni' and his impoverished widow

THE GREAT BELZONI

During his lifetime the Italian strong man and explorer Giovanni Belzoni was known by many epithets – the Italian Hercules, the Patagonian Sampson and Jack the Giant Killer – but the name which has stuck and which he called himself is 'The Great Belzoni'.

Belzoni was born in Padua on 5 November 1778 but moved to Rome when still young. He was preparing to take monastic vows when the sudden appearance in the city of the conquering French interrupted his plans. He moved to England, where he took up a rather different profession, touring theatres with his 'strong man' act. Since he was tall, prodigiously strong and a great showman, this undoubtedly suited Belzoni better than a monastery.

His show proved to be a great success. It also allowed him to indulge a passion for hydraulics, which he claims to have studied in Rome and which he certainly put to use in his show, adding elaborate fountains and waterfalls to his act. This unusual hobby led him in 1814 into the pay of the new governor of Ottoman Egypt, who was keen to update the country's antiquated irrigation system.

Belzoni and his English wife Sarah arrived in Alexandria on 9 June 1815 and made their way to Cairo. They took a dilapidated house and settled down to life in the volatile city. Work proceeded painfully slowly on the water wheel he had promised the governor. Belzoni's local workforce were suspicious of the flamboyant Westerner and resentful of his Turkish master and, in the end, the project failed. But to Belzoni this no longer mattered – a greater adventure beckoned.

Almost as soon as he had arrived in Cairo Belzoni had become fascinated by the pyramid fields of the Giza plateau, which lay on the outskirts of the city. By chance he had also met the adventurer Jean Louis Burckhardt (1784–1817), who discovered the lost city of Petra (see pages 35–9). Burckhardt was in

'The Great Belzoni' was an impressive figure. During his stay in Egypt he wore local dress and grew a substantial beard.

Cairo waiting for a caravan to take him into central Africa and he persuaded Belzoni that his future lay in searching out the treasures of Egypt.

In March 1820 Giovanni and Sarah returned to London and by then Belzoni was famous. *The Times* claimed he had *'distinguished himself above all European travellers in modern times'.* His exhibition in the Egyptian Hall in Piccadilly, which included facsimiles of Seti's tomb, was a huge success. Belzoni became the talk of London but the Western collectors for whom he had undertaken his expeditions proved less effusive in their praise. The alabaster sarcophagus of Seti I he had uncovered in the Valley of the Kings was impounded by the British Museum but the museum refused to buy it, preventing Belzoni from realizing his share of the profits.

Depressed, he sold up his exhibition and his thoughts began to return to the meeting with Burckhardt that had started his career. Burckhardt had died in 1817, before his caravan could set off, but Belzoni now decided to undertake a similar journey to seek the legendary city of Timbuktu in West Africa. Neither friends nor family could dissuade him and he set out in 1823.

Having been refused permission to travel through Morocco, he headed down the Guinea coast but fell ill shortly after reaching Benin and died in the village of Gwato. Official sources said he died of dysentery but the contemporary explorer Richard Burton (1821–90) maintained he was robbed and murdered.

In London, the British Museum finally released Seti's sarcophagus but still blanched at the £2000 price tag. Belzoni's prize was instead snapped up by the architect Sir John Soane (1753–1837). On three successive nights in 1825 he held parties for London's high society to come and marvel at the object and perhaps make a donation towards the welfare of the now destitute Sarah Belzoni. Each night the toast was to 'The Great Belzoni'.

In front of it was a rope, now over 3000 years old, by which the last person to go in or out of the tomb had gained access. He reached across but the rope turned to dust at his touch.

The treasure within

The following day he returned with wooden planks to bridge the gap and hauled himself through the opening to emerge in a decorated hall. Having christened this the 'Drawing Room' he moved on into a small chamber alive with scenes of gods and goddesses, which he named the 'Room of Beauties'. Beyond lay another hall supported on two rows of three pillars with two small rooms off to each side, and past this Belzoni came to a larger space:

> 'The saloon is 31 feet 10 inches by 27 feet. On the right of the saloon is a small chamber without anything in it, roughly cut, as if unfinished, and without painting: on the left we entered a chamber with two square pillars, 25 feet 8 inches by 22 feet 10 inches. This I called the Sideboard Room, as it has a projection of 3 feet in the form of a sideboard all round, which was perhaps intended to contain the articles necessary for the funeral ceremony.'

When Belzoni first set foot inside the tomb of Seti I in 1817 it was the most magnificent ever seen in the Valley of the Kings. The unusual wall paintings – in raised relief – were in perfect condition and Belzoni had the foresight to take impressions of them. The illustration above is a detail showing Egyptian gods in an astrological scene.

One final chamber lay past the saloon. In the glimmer of lamplight it seemed at first a disappointment. Unlike the halls and chambers before it, it was not brightly painted but covered with a simple white plaster, although the dark blue ceiling glimmered with zodiacal signs. The floor was strewn with small wooden figures, among which was the embalmed carcass of a bull:

> 'But the description of what we found in the centre of the saloon … merits the most particular attention, not having its equal in the world … It is a sarcophagus of the finest oriental alabaster; 9 feet 5 inches long, and 3 feet 7 inches wide. Its thickness is only 2 inches; and it is transparent when a light is placed in the inside of it. It is minutely sculptured within and without with several hundred figures, which do not exceed 2 inches in height, and represent, as I suppose, the whole of the funeral procession and ceremonies relating to the deceased, united with several emblems. I cannot give an adequate idea of this beautiful and invaluable piece of antiquity, and can only say that nothing has been brought into Europe from Egypt that can be compared with it.'

Although as he walked through the tomb Belzoni was considering what the sarcophagus might bring financially, other ideas began to form in his mind. As well as ordering that the sarcophagus be shipped to Cairo, he arranged for wax impressions to be taken of the wonderful reliefs he had seen on the walls, instead of hacking off the originals. Belzoni was beginning to wonder about the people who made this place, about how they lived and what they believed. And so, in a way, the modern idea of archaeology was taking root. When a local military commander demanded that Belzoni show him the 'treasure' (which he had been told consisted of 'a large golden cock, filled with diamonds and pearls'), Belzoni simply laughed and asked him what he thought of the paintings on the wall. The commander was not impressed but Belzoni was beginning to realize that this was the treasure he had been seeking all along.

THE KEY TO EGYPT
The Secret of the Rosetta Stone, 1824

In 1798 Napoleon Bonaparte (1769–1821), then at the height of his powers, invaded Egypt, seizing power from the Ottoman rulers. But his was an unusual army of occupation. Along with the troops, who immediately began fortifying the coast against the British attack they knew was imminent, came scholars and draughtsmen by the thousand. They had been sent to explore and record the wonders of this ancient country.

They had their work cut out, for Egypt was full of ancient artefacts and monuments and the new building work on the coast was unearthing more treasures every day. So it was that a large black stone arrived in the offices of the Institut d'Égypte in Cairo in August 1799. It had come from near the Egyptian port of Rosetta (modern Rashid), where it had been discovered during the excavation of the foundations for the French coastal battery at Fort Julien. The stone had first been noticed by Captain Pierre-François Bouchard (1772–1832) who had alerted his general, Jacques-François de Boussay, baron de Menou (1750–1810), and so the object arrived in Cairo accompanied by a note from the two men.

Three scripts, a single text
The stone, made of a dark grey-pink granodiorite, stood 1.14 metres (3.7 ft) high and was inscribed on its largest face with an ancient Egyptian text. This was hardly unusual – as the members of the Institut were finding, the ancient Egyptians had seemed to delight in writing their script on anything and everything. What no-one in Cairo or elsewhere for that matter could yet do was translate these strange texts. And that was where Bouchard's powers of observation came in. He had noticed that the stone contained not one but three scripts, in two languages – classical Egyptian hieroglyphics, demotic (a cursive Egyptian script used for official documents and literature) and ancient Greek. If, as it appeared might be the case, the three scripts were translations of the same text, then this might prove to be the key to understanding hieroglyphics.

Getting the stone out of Egypt for scholars to study was not going to be easy, however. As expected, Britain had responded to France's invasion of Egypt by sending its navy under the command of Horatio Nelson (1758–1805) to engage the French fleet in Aboukir Bay. Following the defeat of the French at the Battle of the Nile, Napoleon had returned to France, leaving his soldiers and the gentlemen of the Institut to fend off British and Ottoman advances as best they could.

Napoleon in Egypt, *an oil painting by Jean-Léon Gérôme, 1863. Napoleon's Egyptian campaign was a military failure, but the 1000 or so civilians who accompanied the French forces – among them artists, botanists and surveyors – would bring back a lasting legacy in the form of priceless artefacts and hitherto unknown information about the ancient Egyptian civilization.*

The French held the British at bay until March 1801. In June of that year Cairo capitulated, and on 30 August the garrison at Alexandria where de Menou's force (and the Rosetta Stone) had been sent also surrendered. De Menou, however, refused to hand over the archaeological finds collected by the Institut and a standoff ensued: the British claimed everything as spoils of war, while the French threatened to destroy the entire collection.

Somehow during this dispute the Rosetta Stone came into British hands. One version of events claims that it was quietly handed over; another claims it was snatched from de Menou and borne away in triumph on a gun carriage. Whichever is true, in February 1802 the stone was loaded on a captured French frigate and despatched to London, leaving the French to return home with mere rubbings and plaster casts of the artefact.

Unlocking the puzzle

In March 1802 the Rosetta Stone was presented to the London Society of Antiquaries. Later that year it was finally put on display in the British Museum – where it remains to this day – and the painstaking work of translating it could finally begin.

It is perhaps the greatest of ironies that the majority of the translation work would eventually be carried out by a man who was denied direct access to the stone, the Frenchman Jean-François Champollion (1790–1832). His translation of the hieroglyphic text on the stone would not only reveal the world of its maker, the Greek ruler Ptolemy V, king of Egypt 205–180 BC, but would also provide the key to reading all ancient Egyptian texts from the days of the pyramid builders to the Roman occupation. This undertaking would open a window onto more than 3000 years of history.

The Rosetta Stone has been displayed in the British Museum in London since 1802. Despite its ordinary appearance, this stone provided the key that would unlock the secrets of the hieroglyphic script used in Egypt from about 3300 BC until the end of the fourth century AD.

CHAMPOLLION AND THE ROSETTA STONE

From childhood Jean-François Champollion displayed an extraordinary aptitude for languages. By his late teens he was fluent in well over a dozen languages, ancient and modern, including Latin, Greek, Amharic, Arabic, Syriac, Persian, Chaldean, Chinese and Coptic – the tongue spoken by the Christian minority in Egypt between the second and 17th centuries AD. So it is not surprising that Champollion's interest should have turned to Egypt – encouraged by the European craze for all things Egyptian which had begun with the French discoveries in that country – and in 1822 he began work on deciphering hieroglyphics.

Champollion was by no means the first nor was he the only researcher working on the problem. Several attempts had been made previously to translate the ancient Egyptian language, dating back to 1643 when Athanasius Kircher (1602–80) wrote *Lingua Aegyptiaca Restituta* ('The Egyptian Language Restored'), in which he correctly guessed that the language of the Egyptian Copts was descended from ancient Egyptian.

The Swedish diplomat Johan Åkerblad (1763–1819) had also produced a working alphabet for the demotic section of the text by taking the proper names in the Greek sections and finding their equivalents in the demotic version, hence assigning sounds to the demotic letters. The English scholar Thomas Young (1773–1829) had taken the work further with his realization that the demotic text was not simply alphabetic – with each glyph representing a sound – but also included symbolic glyphs which affected their meaning. He had also noticed that demotic was not an entirely different language from hieroglyphics but might be related to it. But Young could not go any further. Although he realized that the oval cartouches in the Egyptian text contained phonetic spellings of names, he had come to believe that hieroglyphics were largely symbolic with only a few phonetic elements and would therefore be impossible to translate fully. At this point Champollion stepped in.

Champollion continued Young's work in comparing the signs in cartouches with the royal names in the Greek text, thus assigning sounds to each of the glyphs. In this way he slowly began to construct a phonetic alphabet for the glyphs, based on their equivalent Greek sounds. Now he needed independent proof of his name translations and this came from a monument then resting at Kingston Lacy in Dorset, in southwest England – an obelisk taken from the temple of Philae near Aswan, which also contained a bilingual inscription in Greek and hieroglyphics. Champollion proved that the glyphs in the cartouches on this monument were the same as the ones on the Rosetta Stone – they represented the names Ptolemy and Cleopatra.

Champollion was just one step away from a working decipherment, and the final clue came from a language he had learnt as a boy – Coptic. Champollion guessed that, as an ancient Egyptian language, it might be related to hieroglyphics. He put this to the test when he received a drawing of a cartouche from the temple discovered by Giovanni Belzoni (1778–1823) at Abu Simbel in Nubia (see pages 40–3). Some of the glyphs in it matched glyphs on the Rosetta Stone to which he had allocated sounds, but some were different.

The first glyph was a circle with a dot in the middle followed by an unknown letter, then an 's' and another 's'. He guessed that the circle represented the sun, which in Coptic was pronounced 're', giving him 're – ? – s – s'. A name immediately sprang to mind. The name of a very famous pharaoh – Ramses – was already known from Greek texts so if the missing letter was an 'm' then Champollion had the name of the person who built the temple. It was a brilliant breakthrough and, after more painstaking work during which he identified one mystery glyph after another from reams of inscriptions, he finally published *Précis du Système Hiéroglyphique* in 1824. The language of the ancient Egyptians was back from the dead.

The result would be to transform Egyptology. No ancient civilization went to greater lengths to record its history, religion and private lives. Egypt's buildings were covered in hieroglyphics, including religious stories, itineraries, magic spells, lists of pharaohs and battle narratives. The dry desert conditions had also preserved all types of Egyptian correspondence from contracts written on papyrus to jokes and insults scrawled on walls and pottery fragments (known as ostraca). The Egyptians could speak for themselves once more, as they had always intended to, and the combination of their now translatable words and the archaeological evidence of their lives made them the most famous ancient civilization in the modern world.

'CARELESS OF COMFORT'
Layard Excavates Nineveh and Nimrud, 1839

'In the year 1820 Mr Rich, having been induced to visit Kurdistan for the benefit of his health, returned to Baghdad by way of Mosul. Remaining some days in this city, his curiosity was naturally excited by the great mounds on the opposite bank of the river, and he entered upon an examination of them ...'

A.H. LAYARD Introduction to *Nineveh and Its Remains* (1849)

In the autumn of 1839 Austen Henry Layard (1817–94) and his friend Edward Mitford set out across Mesopotamia, ostensibly on their way overland to Ceylon (Sri Lanka) to join the civil service. But from the opening description of this journey in Layard's own book it is clear that he had secretly already found his destination, here in the open deserts and ancient towns of what is present-day Iraq:

> *'We were both equally careless of comfort and unmindful of danger. We rode alone; our arms were our only protection; a valise behind our saddles was our wardrobe ...'*

It was during this dangerous journey that the pair camped in a village one night and looked down from the summit of a hill over the landscape that would make Layard's name:

> *'A line of lofty mounds bounded to the east and one of a pyramidical form rose high above the rest ... Its position rendered its identification easy. This was the pyramid which Xenophon had described, and near which the ten thousand had encamped: the ruins around it were those which the Greek general saw 22 centuries before, and which were even then the remains of an ancient city.'*

Secret excavations

This forgotten ruin was Nimrud and what Layard saw stayed in his memory. Two years later, having never reached Ceylon and by then in the pay of the British ambassador in Constantinople, he returned to begin his excavations in secret.

A view of the ruins at Nimrud. The city rose to prominence when the Assyrian king Ashurnasirpal II chose it as his capital in about 880 BC. Layard's excavations revealed some remarkable discoveries, including the spectacular palace of Ashurnasirpal with its acres of carved alabaster panels depicting the king's victories.

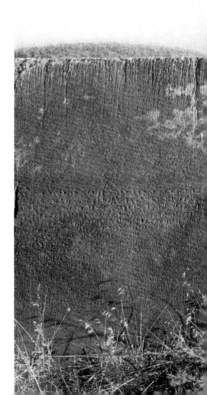

'On 8 November, having secretly procured a few tools, I engaged a mason at the moment of my departure, and carrying with me a variety of guns, spears and other formidable weapons, declared that I was going to hunt wild boars in a neighbouring village, and floated down the Tigris on a small raft constructed for my journey.'

Layard arrived at Nimrud at sunset and stumbled upon the hut of Awad, a man who had taken refuge in the ruins from the depredations of the local governor. After a sleepless night in the hut, the party set off for the main mound, which they found strewn with ancient pottery and fragments of cuneiform inscriptions. As Layard collected up the fragments, Awad pointed out a piece of alabaster sticking out from the soil:

'We could not remove it, and on digging downward it proved to be the upper part of a large slab. I ordered the men to work around it, and they shortly uncovered a second slab. Continuing in the same line we came upon a third; and, in the course of the morning, discovered ten more.'

Further excavations revealed huge bas-reliefs of warriors on chariots, besieged cities and grief-stricken women, tearing at their hair. On the burnt floors of the rooms, Layard found the remains of gilded ivory objects, including the image of a king carrying the Egyptian symbol of life, the *ankh*, and decorated flower borders that must once have adorned the walls. Layard was now convinced he had found what he had been searching for – the ancient city of Nineveh. In fact, he had stumbled upon the ruins of the biblical Calah (Nimrud) and was even now standing in the ruins of the palace of the Assyrian king Ashurnasirpal II (r. 883–859 BC). Ashurnasirpal had made the city the capital of his empire around 880 BC at a banquet attended by 50,000 guests.

TIMELINE

1820 Claudius Rich examines mounds at Kouyunjik near Mosul, believing them to conceal the ancient city of Nineveh

1839 Austen Henry Layard and Edward Mitford begin their journey across Mesopotamia

1840 Layard first sees the ruins of Nimrud

1842 Layard begins excavations at Nimrud. During a visit to nearby Mosul, he observes Paul-Émile Botta's dig at Kouyunjik and formulates the idea that the site is Nineveh

1845–51 Three royal palaces unearthed at Nimrud

1849 Layard orders a workforce to excavate Kouyunjik; over the next two years Sennacherib's palace and Ashurbanipal's library are revealed

1894 Layard dies in London

1988 Iraqi archaeologists unearth the 'Nimrud treasure', which is put on display in the national museum; it is lost during the Gulf War of 1990–1 and rediscovered in 2003

AUSTEN HENRY LAYARD

Austen Henry Layard was in many ways the quintessential Victorian Romantic. Born in Paris, he travelled widely as a boy before being sent to live in England with his uncle and aunt. Layard trained as a lawyer but, eager for adventure, he decided to take a post in the Ceylon (Sri Lanka) civil service. He and his travelling companion Edward Mitford refused the usual passage by ship and took a commission from the Royal Geographical Society to travel overland through the Middle East and Persia, recording the terrain as they went. Only Mitford would ever reach their destination.

Layard at one of his excavations. His work and writings whetted the appetite of the European public for information about the biblical civilizations of ancient Mesopotamia.

In the Middle East Layard found the adventure he was looking for. After contracting malaria in Constantinople (modern Istanbul) he undertook a series of reckless journeys into the Middle Eastern interior, visiting Petra alone and being robbed and nearly killed by tribesmen. It was during one such trip that he first saw the strange earth mounds opposite the city of Mosul (in modern Iraq), then being tentatively explored by the French consul Paul-Émile Botta (1802–70), and the idea struck him that this whole, vast area might be the ancient city of Nineveh.

By now Layard's money had run out and he returned to Constantinople, where he made the acquaintance of Sir Stratford Canning (1786–1880), the British ambassador to the Ottoman Turkish court. Canning was impressed by the young man and thought his knowledge of the local tribes, their languages and the remote border regions of Persia might prove useful. Layard must have told Canning about the mounds of Mesopotamia, and in October 1842 he paid for Layard to travel to the region and begin excavations. Work proceeded apace and soon the biblical city of Nimrud began to appear – although at the time Layard was convinced that this was Nineveh. Canning was delighted with the results and arranged for the best pieces to be sent to the British Museum in London.

With museum funding secured, Layard moved on to the mound at Kouyunjik, opposite Mosul, and at last he discovered what he had been searching for, the palace of the Old Testament tyrant Sennacherib in the long-forgotten city of Nineveh.

In 1847, exhausted and suffering once more from malaria, Layard was forced to return to England where he found he was a celebrity. His books on the discovery of Nineveh proved to be the first archaeological best-sellers, and were reprinted three times in one year. Scholars had recently managed to decipher Assyrian cuneiform script, and so the heavily inscribed objects and thousands of cuneiform clay tablets Layard had uncovered were telling the public stories they were eager to hear. Here were not simply events and names from some distant foreign past, but the characters of the Old Testament brought to life. The homes of the prophets and the palaces of their rulers were suddenly made real, no longer merely allegorical tales, but authenticated people and places from history. One tablet even contained an ancient version of the Flood story. In an age when some people were beginning openly to doubt the historical value of the Bible, here, it seemed, was the new science of archaeology coming triumphantly to its defence.

In 1849 Layard was well enough to return to Mesopotamia and continued excavations at Nineveh and Babylon, discovering in the process the huge library of Ashurbanipal, probably the earliest library ever created and the foundation for our knowledge of the Assyrian world. Just two years later, however, Layard turned his back on archaeology for good and decided to use his fame to begin a career in politics.

Layard died of cancer in 1894. He left a collection of paintings to the nation, and the treasures he brought back from Nineveh still stand in the British Museum's Assyrian galleries.

Layard continued his excavations between 1845 and 1851, uncovering the palaces of Ashurnasirpal, Shalmaneser III (r.859–824 BC) and Esarhaddon (r.680–669 BC) and shipping many of the greatest finds back to London, where they still form the centrepiece of the British Museum's Assyrian collection. Included among them is the famous Black Obelisk of Shalmaneser III, a 2-metre-high (6.6-ft) monument from the ninth century BC which contains the earliest reference to the Israelites in the form of King Jehu paying tribute to the Assyrian king. Also shipped back were the colossal human-headed winged bulls which flanked the doorway into the throne room of Ashurnasirpal which, thanks to the peculiarities of the British civil service, travelled to London via Bombay (modern Mumbai), where impromptu lectures were given about them on the quay.

The search continues

As excavations proceeded, however, Layard was becoming increasingly aware that this site, spectacular though it was, was probably not the romantic city of Nineveh he had been searching for. So in 1849 he began excavations on the mound opposite Mosul known as Kouyunjik, which the British resident in Baghdad, Claudius Rich, had investigated in 1820 in the belief that it was Nineveh. Layard believed that all the mounds in this area were parts of Nineveh and as he left Nimrud he mused on the sights that would have greeted travellers in ancient times:

This relief sculpture in limestone is from a throne base found at the palace of Shalmaneser III at Nimrud. It depicts Shalmaneser meeting the Babylonian king Marduk-zakir. Shalmaneser had helped defeat a revolt against Marduk-zakir in 851 BC and the two kings regarded each other with respect.

'The whole space over which the eye ranges from this spot was probably once covered with the buildings and gardens of the Assyrian capital – that great city of three days' journey. At an earlier period, that distant pyramid directed the traveller from afar to Nineveh … To me the long dark mounds in the distance were objects of deep interest. I reined up my horse to look upon them for the last time … and then galloped on towards Mosul.'

In reality Layard had overestimated the size of the Assyrian capital: Nimrud and the other mounds on the plain turned out to be many different biblical cities. But, unknown to him, the one he was now heading towards was his goal.

Arriving in Mosul, Layard quickly set his workforce to excavating Kouyunjik and after several days he was summoned to the site with news:

'I rode immediately to the ruins; and, on entering the trenches, found that the workmen had reached a wall, and the remains of an entrance. The only slab as yet uncovered had been almost completely destroyed by fire. It stood on the edge of a deep ravine which ran far into the southern side of the mound.'

A 'palace without rival'

Down that 'deep ravine' lay the palace of Sennacherib (r.705–681 BC) – a 'palace without rival' in the city described by Jonah as 'exceeding great'. Layard was standing at the gates to Nineveh. Over the following two years a palace of some 80 rooms was uncovered, richly decorated with alabaster wall reliefs and winged bull statues guarding the doorways. Here also were more cuneiform inscriptions, whole libraries gathered by

Sennacherib and Ashurbanipal (r.668–627 BC). At the time cuneiform was still in the process of being deciphered, so Layard could only guess at what stories the many thousands of clay tablets would eventually tell.

Subsequent excavations have shown that the city covered over 2.7 square miles (7 sq km) and was ringed by a great wall that contained 15 gates. Water was brought to the 100,000 inhabitants of the city by 18 canals and aqueducts which stretched up to the distant hills over 25 miles (40 km) away. At its height the city was twice the size of Babylon.

One hundred and fifty years after Layard's first tentative and secretive explorations at Nimrud the biblical cities of Iraq have still not given up all their secrets. Layard, like many of his era, has been accused of cultural imperialism, of searching only for valuable trophies to export to Europe (something he openly admitted). But he also brought to the world's attention a civilization previously remembered only through obscure references in the Bible and, by doing so, opened up new horizons in archaeology. Nor, it seems, did the people of Mesopotamia who had aided him in his discoveries think badly of him. On the last night of excavations before he left Iraq forever, a delegation of his workmen came to him asking for a note to certify that they had been in his service. This, they said, would provide them some protection on their journey home. They would also:

> '… *show my writing to their children, and would tell them of the days they had passed at Nimrud.*'

The Scottish artist James Fergusson painted this impression of Sennacherib's sumptuous palace at Nineveh as the frontispiece to Layard's second book, Discoveries of the Ruins of Nineveh and Babylon *(1853).*

THE NIMRUD TREASURE

'We may wander through these galleries for an hour or two, examining the marvellous sculptures … Here we meet long rows of kings, attended by their eunuchs and priests – there lines of winged figures, carrying fir cones and religious emblems … Some, who may hereafter tread on the spot when grass again grows over the ruins of the Assyrian palaces, may indeed suspect that I have been relating a vision.'

A.H. LAYARD *Nineveh and Its Remains* (1849)

The Nimrud treasure (ninth century BC), which includes this gold crown, was rediscovered undamaged in a Baghdad bank vault in 2003.

did excavations by Sir Max Mallowan (1904–78), the husband of Agatha Christie, begin to uncover a tale every bit as exotic and dangerous as those penned by his wife – the story of Ashurnasirpal II, the greatest of Assyrian kings, whose capital this once was.

Agatha Christie never missed a clue, but her husband did, and it was another 38 years before the Iraqi archaeologist Muzahim Mahmud, walking in the ruins in 1988, noticed an unusual patch of relaid tiles on the floor of the harem. Removing them, he uncovered a series of untouched royal tombs and a treasure unparalleled since the discovery of the tomb of Tutankhamun in the 1920s.

The 640 gold, silver and crystal objects which make up the Nimrud treasure once belonged to the queens of Assyria and were buried with them beneath the floor of the royal harem. But just 200 years after the last body was sealed in this vault, the Assyrian empire fell. Since then the tomb and its riches had lain sleeping, covered by the dust and sand of the Iraqi desert from which it had first been raised.

Only in the 19th century did Layard's excavations of the man-made hills on the banks of the Tigris show that one of them was the site of Nimrud, home of the Assyrian kings. Aided by the recovery of thousands of clay writing tablets from the royal libraries he unearthed at Nimrud, Nineveh and Babylon, a picture emerged of a society with its roots in the fifth millennium BC; a society that had pioneered writing, city dwelling, irrigation and farming. It soon became clear that this was also the great empire mentioned in the Old Testament, the home of the Tower of Babel and the story of the Flood. Here such biblical villains as Sennacherib, Nebuchadnezzar and Sargon the Great were not just names in the Book of Kings but were archaeological and historical flesh.

But Layard's work could only scratch the surface of the vast palace complex at Nimrud, and full excavations had to wait until the 1950s. Only then

But the country to which he was returning the treasure was a troubled one – the Iraq of Saddam Hussein (1937–2006) – and just two years after their discovery the country descended into war with Kuwait and then the West. As Saddam's regime tottered and its repression grew, the treasure mysteriously disappeared from sight.

Nothing was heard of this incredible find outside Iraq until after Saddam fell from power but then the news was more terrible than anyone had imagined. The national museum had been looted, many of its treasures were missing and it was feared that the Nimrud treasure had been stolen.

In the summer of 2003 a group of investigators looking for Iraq's missing antiquities was invited to a vault at the National Bank. For weeks engineers had been pumping gallons of sewage out of the room and they were finally ready to open the door. Inside lay three museum boxes with their seals intact, just as they had been left at the outbreak of war. In those boxes lay the Nimrud treasure. Iraq had its crown jewels back, and they could at last begin to tell their tale.

'SHATTERED BARQUES'
The Hidden Cities of the Maya, 1839

'*Cities like shattered barques in a green ocean, their masts gone, their names lost, their crews perished and none to tell from whence they came.*'

JOHN LLOYD STEPHENS *Incidents of Travel in Central America, Chiapas and Yucatán* (1841)

Frederick Catherwood (1799–1854) first met John Lloyd Stephens (1805–82) in London in 1836. Catherwood was an English draughtsman and architect and Stephens was an American diplomat and writer, but they shared a love of exploration. Both had travelled extensively in Europe and Egypt and had found that a good living could be made from telling an adventure-loving public of their exploits. But with Egypt already crawling with antiquities dealers and fortune-hunters, new revelations were needed to satisfy the growing appetite for ancient discoveries.

The two men were inspired by the work of Juan Galindo (1802–39), a Central American army officer who had recently published accounts of lost cities in the jungles of the New World. His writing sparked memories of the rumours of El Dorado – the city of gold – told to the first European visitors to the Americas, and Catherwood and Stephens decided to investigate. It was 1839 when the two men realized their goal. Stephens had been appointed Special Ambassador to Central America by the US government. He had formed an expedition to explore the Yucatán peninsula which separates the Caribbean Sea from the Gulf of Mexico, and he asked Catherwood to join him. During weeks of cutting through dense jungle, aided by local guides, they had found and recorded the Mayan city of Copán mentioned by Galindo. Now they were heading for another, more mysterious site – Palenque – and late in June they glimpsed a pyramid poking through the thick undergrowth. Arriving at the building known as the 'palace' they found evidence of earlier visitors, their names written in candle soot on the ceiling.

Surrounded by jungle, the ruins of the ancient city of Palenque look out across a low coastal plain to the Gulf of Mexico. The 'Temple of the Inscriptions' is to the left, and the palace and astronomical observatory tower are to the right.

The ruins in which they set up camp were surrounded by almost impenetrable rain forest whose rain-soaked creepers crawled over the pyramids, pulling apart the stonework. It seemed an impossible place for any civilization to have flourished yet, as the two men stripped away centuries of plant growth and began to draw what they saw, it rapidly became clear that this was indeed an ancient city. And it was just one of many they would visit on their expeditions to the region.

Working on the Yucatán proved exhausting and dangerous, and both men succumbed to bouts of malaria and frequent parasitic infestations in the oppressive, wet heat of the jungle. As their clothes rotted, their tools rusted and their health failed, they were eventually forced to retreat to the coast and take ship to New York where Stephens published his two-volume *Incidents of Travel in Central America, Chiapas and Yucatán*, beautifully illustrated by Catherwood. The book caused a sensation in those early days of archaeology. It told of a sophisticated civilization inhabiting complex cities in an area that had since become wild jungle. No-one could guess at the age of places like Palenque, although Stephens hazarded that they dated from before the time of European contact. Equally, no-one knew who the builders of these cities were or what happened to them.

At a time when it was commonly thought that all civilization had its origins in the Near East, elaborate theories were constructed as to how the Lost Tribe of Israel or perhaps the Egyptians had sailed across the Atlantic to found these cities. Catherwood had another idea, although it received little publicity at the time. Having spent months carefully drawing the human figures depicted on the ruins, he had noted, as had Galindo before him, that the appearance and the customs of the native guides were remarkably like those carved into the temples and palaces of Palenque. But he was unaware that he had stood within metres of the remains of the inhabitants of that city.

The 'Temple of the Inscriptions'

The pyramids at sites like Palenque baffled 19th-century archaeologists. Unlike Egyptian pyramids – tombs in which the remains of rulers and their treasures might be found – Mayan pyramids were apparently empty. Perhaps they were only used as temples and were therefore devoid of the bodies and grave goods that might give an insight into the identity of their builders. But one pyramid at Palenque was different. Catherwood and Stephens had recorded the 'Temple of the Inscriptions' in detail because its sanctuary enclosed three tablets containing the second-longest inscription in the Mayan script ever found. But what they failed to notice was the double row of stone plugs set into one of the stone slabs on the sanctuary floor.

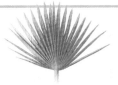

TIMELINE

THIRD TO NINTH CENTURIES The Maya rise to prominence in Central and South America

*c.*830 Mayan civilization collapses and cities such as Palenque, Tikal and Copán are abandoned

1836 Frederick Catherwood and John Lloyd Stephens first meet

1839 Accompanied by Catherwood, Stephens mounts an expedition to explore the Yucatán peninsula. They discover the ruined city of Palenque

1841 Stephens publishes *Incidents of Travel in Central America, Chiapas and Yucatán*

1949 Alberto Ruz Lhuillier visits Palenque and lifts a large stone on the floor of the 'Temple of the Inscriptions', revealing a vaulted passage filled with rubble

1952 The royal tomb of Lord Pacal the Great (603–83) is finally uncovered

In a chamber 1.5 metres (5 ft) below the floor of the 'Temple of the Inscriptions' Lhuillier found the sarcophagus of Lord Pacal the Great. Pacal came to the throne at the age of 12 and ruled over Palenque for 68 years until his death in 683.

In fact no-one took any notice of these until the Mexican archaeologist Alberto Ruz Lhuillier (1906–79) visited the site in 1949. By then much more was known about the Mayan civilization, and the neat stone floor of this building with its strange stone plugs marked it out as unusual. Lhuillier guessed that the plugs marked the lifting points where the stone had been lowered into position, implying there might be something beneath it.

Removing the stone, he found he was right. Beneath it lay a vaulted passage filled with rubble – so much of it that it took four digging seasons to clear – and it was 1952 before his team reached the bottom. Here they found their way blocked by a wall, next to which stood a stone box that proved to contain pottery jars, shells filled with red pigment, beads, jade earplugs and a solitary pearl. Having broken down the wall blocking their path they made a more grisly discovery: a chamber containing the skeletons of six human sacrifices, beyond which lay another large stone block.

A royal tomb

With some difficulty they removed the huge triangular block only to discover something unheard of in Mayan archaeology – a royal tomb at the heart of a pyramid. Through a doorway and down a flight of steps lay a chamber – 4 metres by 10 metres (13 ft x 33 ft) – covered in the mineral calcite which had been deposited by the incessant rains. Lhuillier later wrote:

> *'Out of the dim shadows emerged a vision from a fairy tale, a fantastic, ethereal sight from another world. It seemed a huge magic grotto carved out of ice, the walls sparkling and glistening like snow crystals. Delicate festoons of stalactites hung like tassels of a curtain, and the stalagmites on the floor looked like drippings from a great candle. The impression ... was that of an abandoned chapel. Across the walls marched stucco figures in low relief. Then my eyes sought the floor. This was almost entirely filled with a great carved stone slab, in perfect condition.'*

The slab covered a large, elaborately decorated sarcophagus standing on six short piers, beneath which lay pottery food dishes and two life-size stucco human heads. The lid of the sarcophagus was decorated with one of the most important scenes on any Mayan monument, a depiction of its owner, Lord Pacal the Great, falling into the underworld. He is represented as being at the centre of the universe, surrounded by images of the cosmos, and behind him stands the 'world tree' on which a supernatural bird perches and through whose branches a double-headed serpent crawls.

WHAT HAPPENED TO THE MAYA?

In a land that has over 300 centimetres (118 in) of rain a year and a tropical climate, holding back the jungle was always a problem for the Mayan architects, but for over 1000 years they managed. During that time tens of thousands of people were housed and fed, great pyramids were constructed and an empire was forged. Then, in about AD 830, Mayan civilization seems to have collapsed. Within a few years their huge cities became overgrown and were lost, and the sophisticated inhabitants seem to have simply melted back into the jungle. So what happened?

The sudden collapse of Mayan civilization is one of the most puzzling events in history, but almost as strange is the fact that it ever existed at all. Most early civilizations occurred in places where it is easy to live, particularly along the banks of large rivers in warm countries. But having fought so hard to carve their civilization from impenetrable jungle and maintain it spectacularly for 1000 years, it seems almost impossible that the Maya would suddenly give up and go away – but that is exactly what they did.

Many solutions have been put forward to explain this, but a new theory suggests that the answer may lie, ironically, in the cities' success. Many of the sites were huge – Tikal in the Guatemalan highlands covered 24 square miles (62 sq km), contained over 3000 buildings and was home to well over 45,000 people. In an area of dangerous jungle with a thin and poor soil, a huge amount of work would have been required to provide for such a large population.

The Maya created detailed and beautiful pieces of art, including terracotta sculptures depicting gods, rulers or religious scenes. This figurine is an effigy of a Mayan deity.

As the population increased, pressure mounted on the farming communities around each centre to squeeze more from the fragile soil. The Maya were not only consuming the jungle; in doing so, they were consuming themselves. By about AD 830 the years of over-expansion suddenly and catastrophically took their toll. The local ecology collapsed and crops failed, putting pressure on the labyrinthine irrigation network, which also failed.

Virgin jungle could not be cleared quickly enough and the bureaucracy was not prepared. A chain reaction began: with food and water supplies exhausted, trade stopped, and the administration ground to a halt. There was no need for astronomers or architects, and certainly no need for kings. The outside world heard nothing more from the Maya so no ambassadors went there, no shell traders picked their way through the highlands and almost overnight Mayan civilization became just a memory.

The sarcophagus lid was only the beginning. Beneath it lay the body of Pacal himself, surrounded by over 700 items carved in one of the Maya's most precious substances: jade. He wore a jade diadem, a net skirt made of jade pieces held together with gold wire, necklaces, pectoral decorations, rings, bracelets and ear-flares. In one hand he held a jade cube, in the other a jade sphere – what they signify is still a mystery.

Although the discovery of Pacal's body posed many new questions, this unique funerary collection makes one thing clear: Catherwood was right – the people of Palenque were not Egyptians or lost Israelites, but an indigenous civilization whose descendants were the bearers and guides who had first led the two explorers to this 'lost city'.

WHITE GOLD
The Salt Miners of Hallstatt, 1846

Hallstatt. Until the late 19th century this isolated community was accessible only by boat across the cold waters of a mountain lake. But this place had not always been cut off; in fact, nearly 2500 years earlier it was one of the most important trading centres in Europe, and on the high pastures above the town lies a site that has made Hallstatt one of the most important names in the prehistory of Europe.

Hallstatt's fortune has always been built on a substance that is almost as valuable as gold – salt. It is a precious commodity, an essential condiment in cooking and, in the days before refrigeration, one of the main methods of preserving food over the winter months. Although salt can be panned slowly and expensively from saltwater lakes, the mountains above Hallstatt are literally full of the mineral and it has been mined in this area for millennia. Eighteenth-century miners knew this, for they occasionally found items belonging to their counterparts from times gone by – wood and bone tools, fur clothing and lamps – that had been lost in the distant past and had been preserved where they fell in the damp, salty conditions. In 1734 they had even found the preserved body of one of their mining ancestors under an ancient rockfall and, with the respect shown by men who ran the same risks every day of their lives, the body was taken carefully down the hill and re-interred in the local churchyard.

A gruesome find
But the discovery that put Hallstatt on the map did not come from the mines. In 1846 a young engineer, Johann Ramsauer (1795–1874), took a party of workmen up to the high meadows near the mines and set them to work digging for gravel for use in road building. Within a few minutes of starting work, however, one of the men pulled something else from the pit – a human skull. Digging around the find, the men soon began to uncover other strange objects, including swords, daggers, unusual jewellery and rustic pots. Nor was this an isolated find. Just a few metres away lay another skeleton surrounded by similar artefacts. Ramsauer realized that they were digging in an ancient cemetery.

An ordinary man may have been forgiven for finding all this rather annoying. The workmen had a job to do and these burials were clearly getting in the way. But

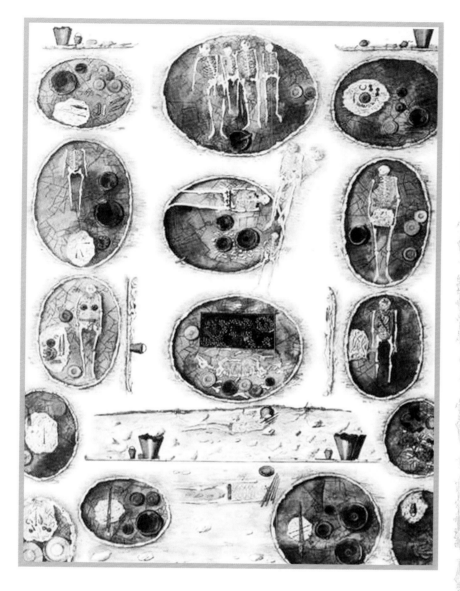

*The meticulous methods used by Ramsauer while
conducting excavations at Hallstatt included detailed
watercolour paintings of the individual graves and the
human remains and artefacts they contained.*

Ramsauer was no ordinary man. He was intrigued and, instead of shovelling
the finds to one side, he made measured drawings of each grave, packed up
the drawings with the artefacts and sent them all to his employers. From
there they made their way to the office of the Imperial Cabinet of Coins and
Antiquities in Vienna, where the keeper realized at once the value of this
strange collection. These objects of bronze and iron appeared to be from a
time before the Romans (there were no Roman finds among them), a time
that had only recently been classified into the three prehistoric ages of Stone,
Bronze and Iron. Perhaps this site could furnish the Austrian empire with
prehistoric artefacts to match those now filling the museums of Scandinavia?

TIMELINE

C.800–400 BC Hallstatt is an
important European trading centre
with a sophisticated society whose
wealth is based on salt mining

C.400–15 BC La Tène culture
flourishes

1734 Miners at Hallstatt find
a body preserved by the salty
conditions of the mountains; it is
taken down to the town and buried

1846 Johann Ramsauer's
workmen dig up bronze and iron
artefacts. Ramsauer draws and
records the finds before sending
them to his employers. He later
receives instructions to continue
excavations and state funding for
the project

1857 In the parched Lake
Neuchâtel at La Tène, Switzerland,
Hansli Kopp finds 11 wooden stakes
and about 40 iron swords

1863 Ramsauer completes his
excavations at Hallstatt, where he
has unearthed more than 1000
burials

1868 Ferdinand Keller publishes
Kopp's findings at La Tène
in his study on Swiss pile dwellings
(*Pfahlbaubericht*)

1880 Thorough investigations
begin at La Tène after deliberate
draining of the lake

The Charnel House at Hallstatt is packed with the remains of more recent citizens. Because Hallstatt lies between a mountain and a lake, land for burials is scarce, and until 1960 the occupants of the tiny cemetery were exhumed after 12 years and moved to the Charnel House. The skulls were painted with the names of the deceased.

Accordingly, orders reached Ramsauer that his brief had been changed. He was given state funding and a small team of labourers and told to continue his excavations in the Hallstatt meadows. Little did he know then that he would spend almost 20 years there unearthing over 1000 burials and cremations.

It is to his great credit and to the enormous benefit of archaeology that he proceeded to excavate each one with the same slow, methodical care as the first, measuring and drawing each find and, in an age long before that of colour photography, producing watercolours of each assemblage before it was removed from the ground. The result was probably the finest piece of field archaeology of the 19th century.

Iron Age 'type site'

To the present day more than 2500 graves have been found at Hallstatt, covering the transition from the Bronze Age into the first half of the Iron Age. So wide is the range of finds and so large their number that it has become the 'type site' for the early Iron Age, and this period is now often referred to as Hallstatt culture. Ramsauer's painstaking work revealed that the ancient Hallstatt miners had a history of elaborate burials that spanned some 400 years. The people who worked the mines during the Bronze and Iron Ages amassed great wealth from selling salt and preserved meat across Europe. With this wealth they bought the latest in fashionable jewellery and weaponry, which they no doubt displayed in life and which they certainly took to their graves with them.

This amazing collection of objects, including swords, pins, cauldrons, torcs, earrings and knives, has allowed archaeologists to build up a typological history of the end of the Bronze Age and the first half of the Iron Age, tracing the changing styles of objects and their development over time. Using this information, they have been able to date other sites yielding fewer but similar items relative to Hallstatt, and this has formed the backbone of our understanding of a vital part of European prehistory. In this way much of our knowledge of a 400-year period, from an age before written records, has been gleaned from the habits of a community of miners in the Austrian Alps.

THE LA TÈNE CULTURE

The other major type site for the European Iron Age was discovered at La Tène on the north side of Lake Neuchâtel in Switzerland. A prolonged drought in 1857 caused the water level in the lake to fall by some 2 metres (6.5 ft), and this gave Hansli Kopp his opportunity. Kopp was employed by a local colonel to find antiquities for his collection, and the receding water gave him access to previously inaccessible areas. Walking along the northern edge of the lake near the River Zihl, he stumbled upon a series of wooden stakes sticking out of the shallow water, and around them he found nearly 40 iron swords.

It was 11 years before Kopp's finds were published in a report by the Swiss archaeologist Ferdinand Keller (1800–81), who suggested that the wooden stakes were the piles for an ancient lake dwelling. Formal excavations began shortly afterwards and, in 1880, after the deliberate and permanent lowering of the lake's water level, the site finally became completely dry and could be explored thoroughly. These excavations found the remains of two bridges, each originally over 100 metres (330 ft) long, and the remains of five houses on the ancient shoreline. Among these wooden finds were also many more metal objects, and to date more than 2500 have been dug from the site, including over 100 apparently unused swords, lances, shields, brooches and even parts of chariots.

Exactly what was the original purpose of the site is uncertain, but the fact that many of the items found were unused has led to the suggestion that it was a ritual site, where valuable offerings were placed in the water. Whatever the reason for their deposition, all of these items date from after the Hallstatt period and neatly take the story of the European Iron Age from around 400 BC – the end of Hallstatt culture – to the Roman invasion of present-day Switzerland in 15 BC. The sheer number and variety of finds have made this a type site for the latter part of the Iron Age – now termed the La Tène culture – and similarities in style have helped to date and order sites as far apart as Britain and Spain.

This iron sword with bronze hilt was recovered from La Tène and dates from c.260 BC, the second period of the European Iron Age.

IN STRABO'S FOOTSTEPS
The Search for the Serapeum, 1850

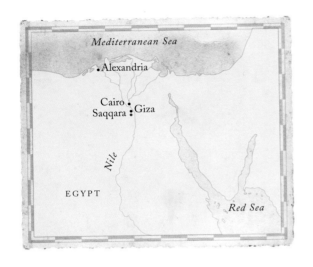

The Egypt that Auguste Mariette (1821–81) first set eyes on in 1850 bore little resemblance to the tourist destination of today. Two thousand years of neglect had left its ancient monuments buried under the encroaching desert. Apart from the pyramids, only a few fragments of the pharaonic past poked up through this sea of sand like the rotten spars of a ship, wrecked on a forgotten beach. When early archaeologists came here to dig, it was not to laboriously unearth these temples and towns but to prospect for treasure, to sift the sands for the jewels and statues that commanded a good price on the burgeoning antiquities markets. Ancient Egypt was a ruin to be plundered; its riches were waiting to be shovelled up and sold abroad.

But the young French archaeologist who arrived in Egypt that year – ostensibly as one of those colonial looters – saw something different when he surveyed the ancient sites. As a relative of a friend of Jean-François Champollion (1790–1832), the man who deciphered ancient Egyptian hieroglyphics and translated the Rosetta Stone (see pages 44–7), Mariette perceived in the ruins a story waiting to be told, the history of a nation reaching back over 5000 years. The problem in a desert land, however, was where to begin digging.

Fortunately Mariette was equipped with more than spades and baskets and workmen to put them to use. He was armed with the memory of a description written more than 1800 years earlier, a recollection that brought him in the autumn of 1850 to the necropolis of Saqqara near the ancient capital of Memphis. Two millennia before, another traveller, the Greek writer Strabo (*c*.64 BC–AD 23), had stood here and complained of a similar problem:

'One finds a temple to Serapis in such a sandy place that the wind heaps up the sand dunes beneath which we saw sphinxes, some half buried, some buried up to the head, from which one can suppose that the way to this temple could not be without danger if one were caught in a sudden wind storm.'

STRABO *Geography* (BOOK XVII CHAPTER I)

And sphinxes were just what Mariette had been noticing since he had arrived in Egypt:

'I noticed at Alexandria, in M. Zizinia's garden, several sphinxes. Presently I saw more of these same sphinxes at Cairo, in Clot-Bey's garden. M. Fernandez had also a certain number of such sphinxes at Geezeh. Evidently there must be somewhere an avenue of sphinxes which was being pillaged.'

AUGUSTE MARIETTE *Le Serapeum de Memphis* (1856)

The lost avenue of sphinxes

It was while trying to locate this rapidly vanishing avenue that Mariette had recalled the Greek traveller's words. Strabo had found a sphinx avenue half buried in sand; but the site he was visiting was not at that time entirely lost to the desert, nor were the memories of what lay at its end forgotten. It was one of the most important sites in ancient Egypt: a temple and tomb complex held in the highest regard by Egyptians; a lavish, strange monument dedicated not to a pharaoh but to an animal – the Apis bull, which

The Step Pyramid at Saqqara dominates the necropolis complex. Begun in c.2630 BC, it was the first pyramid to be built and it housed the tomb of King Djoser, who ruled Egypt during the Third Dynasty. The Serapeum lies to the northwest of the pyramid.

to the people of the Nile valley was a living god; a monument that Strabo said lay at Saqqara, part of the necropolis for Memphis.

And it was here that Mariette stumbled upon yet another sphinx, identical to the others he had seen but with one key difference. This one was clearly still *in situ*. Here was the plundered avenue he had been searching for. But could it be that this was also the processional way mentioned by Strabo as already being swamped in sand and, if so, did the tomb of the Apis bull still lie buried at its end? Mariette recorded excitedly:

> 'Did it not seem that Strabo had written this … to help us rediscover, after over 18 centuries, the famous temple dedicated to Serapis? It was impossible to doubt it. This buried sphinx, the companion of 15 others I had encountered in Alexandria and Cairo, formed with them … part of the avenue that led to the Memphis Serapeum …'

For Mariette this was a turning point. Gone were thoughts of his original mission and his hopes of a career at the Louvre Museum in Paris. In their place came a new idea, that of dedicating his life to uncovering Egypt's past – a past which now lay buried beneath his feet:

> '… undoubtedly many precious fragments, many statues, many unknown texts were hidden beneath the sand upon which I stood … and it was thus, on 1 November 1850, during one of the most beautiful sunrises I had ever seen in Egypt, that a group of 30 workmen … were about to cause such total upheaval in the conditions of my stay in Egypt.'

Furtive investigations

Mariette had to be careful. Officially he was on a mission to collect Coptic manuscripts: not only might his masters in Paris take issue with his diverting their funds away from their original purpose, but local rulers and other, more violent collectors might object to his muscling in on their business.

> 'Regardless of all risks, without saying a word, and almost furtively, I gathered together a few workmen, and the excavation began. The first attempts were hard indeed, but, before very long, lions and peacocks and the Grecian statue … together with the monumental tablets or stelae of the temple of Nectanebo, were drawn out of the sand, and I was able to announce my success to the French government, informing them, at the same time, that the funds placed at my disposal for the researches after the manuscripts were exhausted, and that a further grant was indispensable. Thus was begun the discovery of the Serapeum.'

As he continued to dig, Mariette found that the line of over 100 sphinxes led to a sand-filled courtyard in which he discovered one of the most exquisite Egyptian statues in existence: the Squatting Scribe. It stood in what must once have been an above-ground temple but which was now, as he described it:

> '… but a vast plain of sand mingled with fragments of stones scattered about in indescribable confusion.'

THE APIS BULL

Apis, the bull god of the city of Memphis, was represented by a living bull that was kept in its own temple and treated with the respect due to the earthly manifestation of a god. The Apis had been a powerful symbol in Egypt since the very first dynasties well over 2000 years earlier. Originally it had represented the power and will of the pharaoh himself and was later thought to represent the god Ptah, whose centre of worship was at Memphis.

By the Late Period (c.712–332 BC), however, the animal had come to represent Osiris, the lord of the dead, who was usually depicted in human form, wrapped and mummified for burial. According to Plutarch (46–127), the bull was the living aspect of this dead god or, as he put it:

Animal worship in Egypt dates back to the fourth millennium BC. Among the most important cults that developed were those of the Apis bull, representing the god Ptah, and the Buchis bull, the embodiment of the war god Montu.

'*… the beautiful image of the soul of Osiris.*'
PLUTARCH *Moralia, Isis and Osiris* (CHAPTER 20)

To Egyptians this creature was more holy than the sacred cows that walk unmolested through the streets of Indian cities. When the Apis bull died the whole of Egypt mourned and fasted for 70 days, during which time the carcass of the huge animal was mummified and prepared for a lavish funeral. The body was then carried down the sphinx-lined processional way from Memphis to the great funerary complex at Saqqara, where some of the earliest pharaohs had been buried. Here the line of sphinxes directed the mourners to a temple and catacomb where the Apis bull would be laid to rest. From the third century bc the chief god of this temple was Serapis, and the temple became known as the Serapeum.

After the lavish, almost pharaonic burial, word would go out to the priests that a new Apis had to be found and the Nile valley would be scoured in the search for a calf born under just the right circumstances. The Greek historian Herodotus (c.484–425 BC) says the priests were looking out for the:

'*… calf of a cow which is never afterwards able to have another. The Egyptian belief is that a flash of lightning descends upon the cow from heaven, and this causes her to receive Apis.*'
HERODOTUS *Histories* BOOK III (THALEIA) CHAPTER 27

In practical terms this meant finding a black calf with a white diamond on its forehead, an eagle on its back, a scarab mark under its tongue and twice the usual number of tail hairs. When such an animal was tracked down, the country rejoiced in the knowledge that the living god had returned to them. The calf's mother was immediately revered as the 'Isis Cow', while her calf was transported down the Nile to Memphis, housed in a golden cabin on its own barque.

From now on the bull would live like a king, appearing to an adoring public during the seven days of the annual Apis festival, when it was led through the crowds by priests. It was said that a child who smelled the breath of the Apis would be granted the gift of foreseeing the future, because the bull was an oracle. Those without access to such a fortunate child could ask the bull itself about their future by holding out food for it. If it took the offering, their future was bright, but if it refused, the omens were bad.

AUGUSTE MARIETTE

Auguste Mariette is often considered to be the founder of Egyptian archaeology, although his techniques of excavation – which included the use of high explosives – have been heavily criticized by later generations. He should, however, be judged in terms of the age in which he lived, and by those standards he was a champion of the new subject.

As a minor official at the Louvre Museum in Paris, Mariette had originally come to Egypt in 1850 with orders to find and buy manuscripts for the French national collection. The mid-19th century witnessed a 'collecting craze' among national museums, and ancient books, artefacts, art and even whole monuments were snapped up by agents in the Middle East and shipped back to European capitals.

At the heart of this trade lay Egypt. Ever since Napoleon's invasion, European imaginations had been fired by images of Egypt drawn by the legion of draughtsmen the emperor had brought to the country along with his army. Since Jean-François Champollion had deciphered Egyptian hieroglyphics (see page 47), the whole story of this ancient biblical land was being rediscovered, and European agents now swarmed over the country looking for artefacts to bring home for their wealthy clients.

Although many of these agents claimed to be archaeologists or historians, this was little more than a cover for looting, a practice which horrified Mariette. Even his masters in France, encouraged by Mariette's success in discovering the Serapeum, agreed to fund his excavation work only if he sent his best finds back to the Louvre. Despite now having the funds to work in the way he wanted, Mariette was uncomfortable at seeing Egypt's treasures uncovered only to be taken abroad. When he was offered the post of conservator of Egyptian monuments for Ismail Pasha (1830–95), the khedive who ruled Egypt, he leapt at the chance. He left the Louvre and brought his entire family to Egypt, where he intended to settle.

Working for the khedive proved more agreeable to Mariette than working for his fellow Frenchmen, but the attitude he encountered among his new Egyptian masters was not very different. Local rulers and the khedive in Cairo all saw in archaeology simply an opportunity to exploit treasure for personal profit or political advantage. A typical example of this arose after the discovery of the fabulous treasure of Queen Ahhotep (c.1560–1530 BC) by Mariette's team working near Thebes. When the queen's gilded sarcophagus was uncovered, the local potentate, the mudir of Keneh, stole it and ordered it to be taken to his harem – one of the few places beyond Mariette's grasp. Opening it to reveal the magnificent jewellery within, the mudir saw an opportunity: he packaged it up and set off by sailing boat to present the treasure to the khedive as a personal gift. But Mariette was determined not to let this one get away and set off in pursuit in his own steamer. With the advantage of steam power, Mariette soon caught up with the mudir, boarded his boat and reclaimed the treasure.

If this incident was typical of the frontier attitude towards archaeology in Egypt at the time, at least Queen Ahhotep's treasure served a greater purpose than most. Presenting the jewellery to the khedive himself, Mariette told him of the theft, the boat chase and his heroic retrieval of the treasure. Amused by the story and impressed with his conservator's tenacity, the khedive helped himself to a couple of the choicest pieces from the treasure and then ordered that the rest be placed in a specially built museum. It was the first purpose-built museum in Egypt, the first attempt to stop the tide of antiquities flowing out of the country and its first curator was Auguste Mariette. From now on only Mariette was allowed to dig in Egypt, so no more Egyptian treasures, at least for the time being, would go abroad.

Mariette dedicated the rest of his life to his adopted home, exploring the pyramid fields of Saqqara and Meidum, clearing centuries of sand from the temples of Edfu and Dendara and excavating from Tanis in the delta to Gebel Barkal in Sudan. In his spare time he even managed to fulfil the khedive's request to write a plot for an opera set in ancient Egypt. It was this outline that was worked up by Giuseppe Verdi (1813–1901) into *Aida*, and Mariette oversaw the scenery and costume design of its first performance.

Mariette died in 1881 aged 59 and was buried, like one of ancient Egypt's own, in a sarcophagus.

The necropolis of sacred bulls

It was now more than a year since excavations had begun, but one area of the courtyard had yet to give up its secrets. So it was, with a great public fanfare, that on 12 November 1851, Mariette used explosives to remove a rockfall and revealed a seemingly endless series of subterranean galleries cut into the living rock beneath Egypt's oldest pyramids. This was the last resting place of the sacred Apis bulls, perhaps the strangest necropolis on earth.

Each bull had been buried in a giant sarcophagus cut from a single piece of granite weighing between 60 and 80 tons. All 24 of the sarcophagi in the first gallery had been opened and robbed of their contents long ago. Further exploration revealed a number of undisturbed vaults, each older than the last, culminating in two huge gold-covered coffins containing the remains of bulls from the reign of Ramses II (r.1279–1213 BC). Around these lay four human-headed canopic jars in which were the embalmed viscera of the animals, and 350 small statuettes, known as *shabti* figures. Mariette was in the presence of a god, and modern Egyptian archaeology can truly be said to have begun.

Despite the activities of robbers who had plundered the Serapeum in the past, Mariette found this sarcophagus intact, containing the remains of an Apis bull and complete with the fingerprints and footprints of the workmen who had made it.

THE STONES BENEATH THE SAND

The Ancient Village of Skara Brae, 1850

The islands of Orkney off the northeast coast of Scotland receive more than their fair share of winter gales, but the storms of 1850 were particularly destructive. That winter the west coast of the islands was battered by an exceptionally ferocious storm which tore the grass from the sand dunes along the shore of the parish of Sandwick's Bay o'Skaill. By the next day the local landscape had changed and something from a lost time had emerged.

The storm had uncovered what appeared to be a series of stone circles. They intrigued the local landowner, William Watt, 7th laird of Breckness, sufficiently for him to begin excavating the sand that still surrounded them. Over the next 18 years he uncovered not stone circles but four ancient houses containing a collection of pottery as well as bone and stone tools, which he would eagerly show visitors to his home, Skaill House. What made the houses unique was that, save for the lack of roofs, they appeared completely intact, with stone floors, stone furniture and many smaller items left just as though the occupants had simply gone out.

The question that William Watt could not answer was exactly when these houses had been abandoned. The great breakthrough in 19th-century archaeology had been the development of the 'Three-Age System', which divided prehistoric artefacts into three groups and attributed them to three successive ages – the Stone Age, the Bronze Age and the Iron Age. This new classification enabled order to be brought to the mass of material that had previously been called simply 'pre-Roman'. But the spectacular excavations of Egypt and Mesopotamia had also given rise to the idea that civilization must have originated there and then spread across the world. For this reason, sophisticated buildings in distant corners such as Orkney, it was thought, must date from a later period than those in the Near East.

So the various distinguished visitors to William Watt's house perused his collection and suggested that, despite the obvious lack of metal finds, the site was clearly Iron Age, owing to the sophistication of the construction work. Others claimed the buildings to be 'Pictish houses' from the first millennium AD. But beyond that, the site known as Skara Brae (which may be a corruption of a Gaelic phrase meaning 'Hill of the

Cormorant') remained a mystery. It would take another great storm for interest in the site to be rekindled.

In 1924, nearly three-quarters of a century after the site was first exposed, another gale ripped more sand and grass from the shoreline in the Bay o'Skaill. It revealed more houses and, for the first time, threatened the survival of those already uncovered. The site clearly needed proper excavation and protection, and the person chosen for the job was Vere Gordon Childe (1892–1957).

The Pompeii of the north

Childe was an Australian archaeologist who made his name not as an excavator but as a theorist. He came to academic and public notice in 1925 with the publication of his book *The Dawn of European Civilization*; and his work comparing the spread of Indo-European languages to the spread of physical cultures made him a leading light in the

Built on the southern shore of Sandwick's Bay o'Skaill is what we now know to be the Neolithic village of Skara Brae, dating from c.3100 BC. When the storms of 1850 first revealed the ancient site, all that could be seen was four stone circles.

TIMELINE

1813 Lauritz Vedel Simonsen suggests that early humans progressed from stone and wooden tools to bronze and then iron implements

1816 Christian Thomsen organizes the prehistoric collection of artefacts at the National Museum of Denmark into three separate rooms, which he calls Stone, Bronze and Iron; within a short time other European museums followed suit, and the 'Three-Age System' of dating objects from prehistory became accepted

1850 Storms across the Orkney Islands reveal stone circles at the Bay o'Skaill

1850–68 The laird of Breckness uncovers four ancient houses containing artefacts of pottery, bone and stone

1924 Another storm reveals more houses at Skara Brae

1925 Vere Gordon Childe publishes *The Dawn of European Civilization*, suggesting European civilizations originated in the Near East and spread outwards

1927 Childe is appointed first Abercromby Professor of Prehistoric Archaeology at the University of Edinburgh

1928 Excavations by Childe at Skara Brae suggest to him that the people who lived there had a sophistication that implies a late date

1950s Carbon-14 samples from the site show that it dates from *c.*3100 BC, before the great Mediterranean civilizations

diffusionist movement, which attempted to trace human development from key centres to all parts of the globe. Now, in 1928, having been appointed as the first Abercromby Professor of Prehistoric Archaeology at the University of Edinburgh, Childe was invited to put theory aside and turn his mind to supervising the excavations at Skara Brae. What he and subsequent archaeologists discovered there – a preserved Stone-Age village – has been called the Pompeii of the North.

The complex at Skara Brae consists of seven almost identical stone houses, each dug into a midden (a rubbish dump) which provided insulation from the bitter Orkney winter, and all interconnected by deep stone passages. Their extraordinary survival owes much to the fact that nearly everything in the village is made of stone – the obvious building material on an island devoid of woodland and where the only available wood was driftwood. But these were not 'man-made caves', primitive hovels belonging to farmers eking out a poor living on a desolate land. They were homes, offering many of the things we might consider to be the conveniences of modern life.

A comfortable existence

Each house was entered through one of the dark, enclosed, stone passages that ran between the buildings, gently curved to deflect the bitter gale force winds from the doorways. At the end of the passage lay a lockable door and beyond this a single room with high stone walls and probably a thatched roof. Light in this gloomy world came from a huge fire in the central hearth that burned seaweed and bone. The food resources available on Orkney in the Stone Age, when the weather was one or two degrees warmer than today, were excellent and the diet here might even be considered luxurious by some modern standards. The first farmers to arrive on Orkney had brought with them deer to hunt and also cattle and sheep to tend, so there was plenty of meat available. The nearby sea also provided a huge variety of foods from seabird eggs, lobster, crab, whale and dolphin to huge fish – the remains of a cod weighing 34 kilograms (75 lb), which is at the limit of the modern world line-fishing record, was found here.

Opposite the door in most of the houses lay a great stone 'dresser' – a series of shelves and cupboards where, judging from its position, the most important items belonging to the family were kept. No evidence of exactly what these might have been has survived, but it has been suggested that perhaps food or religious items were kept here. Strange carved stones found during Childe's excavations may have had religious significance, although equally they could have been playing pieces for ancient games of 'jacks' and dice designed to while away the long northern winter nights. Other strange spiral carvings might have been the work of this society's shamans (priests), although deciphering the meaning of such patterns, made in an age long before the invention of writing, is far from easy.

Excavations revealed that the houses shared the same basic design: a large square room with a central fireplace, a bed on either side and a 'dresser' on the wall opposite the doorway.

THE THREE-AGE SYSTEM

The division of prehistory into three ages – Stone, Bronze and Iron – was one of the key insights in the early development of archaeology. Before its introduction in the 19th century, the curators of artefacts from times before the existence of written records had no way of knowing how to order their collections. The first suggestion that it might be possible to date objects by their material technology was made by the Danish historian Lauritz Vedel Simonsen (1780–1858), who tentatively wrote in 1813:

'The weapons and implements of the earliest inhabitants of Scandinavia were at first of stone and wood. These folk later learnt the use of copper … and only latterly, it would appear, iron.'

To be fair, it was not an entirely new idea – the ancient Greeks had suggested that there had been a time before iron was known when only bronze was used, but the thought that such an idea could be extended and applied to the chaos of antiquarian collections was novel. Vedel Simonsen's idea did not initially meet with wide acceptance, however. Most people in Europe held that prehistory must be a very short period of time, since the Old Testament, which they believed to be the true basis of early history, allowed very little room for it. Indeed, in 1650 Archbishop James Ussher (1581–1656) had counted back the generations described in the Bible to arrive at what was still widely regarded as a definitive date for creation – dusk on the evening before 23 October 4004 BC (see page 31).

In 1816, however, another Dane, Christian Thomsen (1786–1865), decided that the three-age approach might just help him with his own problem. Thomsen had been appointed as the first curator of the National Museum of Denmark and had become responsible for the museum's collection of Scandinavian artefacts. In an attempt to bring order to the collection, Thomsen set about grouping the material into stone, bronze and iron divisions. When the ever-growing number of artefacts forced a move from the University Library in Copenhagen to the more spacious apartments of the Christiansborg Royal Palace, Thomsen took the opportunity to arrange them in three separate rooms, which he named Stone Age, Bronze (or Brass) Age and Iron Age. Each age, he wrote in his guide, followed the one before.

Soon museums across Europe were trying to order their antiquities in a similar fashion. At last it was possible to create some form of relative chronology for human development in times before written records existed.

The three-age system has not survived entirely unscathed to the present day, however. As archaeologists tried to refine their chronologies further, the three ages were sub-divided until objects were being forced into chronological boxes that they simply didn't fit. It soon became apparent that not every area went through the same changes in technology at the same time, and some divisions that had been taken to be earlier or later than others were simply regional variations. Nor did the ages have discrete start and finish dates: in the early Bronze Age, for example, most tools were still made of stone as metal was not available to most people. Equally, bronze tools and weapons continued to be used long after the introduction of iron.

More recent archaeological discoveries have also shown that not every culture went through each stage. In sub-Saharan Africa there is a move from stone to iron tools without an intermediate Bronze Age. Likewise, the idea that more 'primitive' technology is associated with a more 'primitive' culture has been disproved by the discovery that in the Americas the Maya had an understanding of mathematics and astronomy rivalling that of late Medieval Europe; yet without metalworking they were theoretically a 'Stone Age' culture.

Despite this, Thomsen's system remains one of the great stepping stones in archaeology. The broad strokes of his divisions proved accurate, particularly in Europe, and allowed silent objects from an age that was previously considered impossibly distant to speak for the first time.

On the floor of the rooms lay querns – sets of stones, probably for grinding cereals to make unleavened bread (there was no yeast used in bread making at this time), or perhaps for grinding fish bones to make fishmeal as a winter feed for cattle. The rooms were also fitted with stone tanks which have been interpreted as bait stores, filled with weed and live bait ready for the next fishing trip. On the right in this central room stood a great stone bed, piled high with heather, fleeces and duck down (microscopic fragments of which survived). Stone pillars at each corner supported a canopy, like that of a four-poster bed. The animal skins suspended from these pillars no doubt helped to keep out the draughts, provided a little privacy and perhaps caught the drips from a leaky thatch. Opposite, on the left, stood another, smaller, canopied bed – near one such bed a small stone oil lamp was found.

It has been argued in recent years that the smaller bed represents the 'female' side of the house and the side with the larger bed is the 'male' side. This is based on evidence from the 18th- and 19th- century Western Isles of Scotland, when such divisions were still apparently in use. It might also explain the discovery of two necklaces of carved bone and killer-whale teeth in the niche above one of the 'female' beds. They may have belonged to the mistress of the house, although it is possible that men and children might also have worn jewellery.

A sophisticated culture

With the houses at Skara Brae packed so tightly together, drainage and sanitation was obviously important, and excavations have shown that each building was provided with drainage channels to take away surplus water. One such channel in a doorway has even been identified as a primitive indoor toilet, a convenience which would save the occupants from having to venture out in the wild winter nights.

This stone artefact embellished with spiral carvings was found at Skara Brae. These mysterious objects, whose use is still unknown, hint at the sophistication of the community that once lived there.

It is of course dangerous to draw too many parallels between the way we use things today and what they might have been used for then. This was a society that left no written record to tell us that a stone cell was a 'toilet' or that what looks to us like shelving was a 'dresser'. Just because we think an object might have been used in a certain way does not mean that our interpretation is correct.

Skara presented a problem for Childe, who had spent much of his life tracing the spread of cultures from their assumed origins in the great ancient civilizations of the Near East to the more remote and 'primitive' parts of the world. Just as William Watt's visitors had proclaimed Skara to be Iron Age or later, so the level of sophistication at the site implied to Childe that this Orkney culture must have been influenced by other, more advanced peoples and therefore be relatively late in date. In an era before carbon-14 dating, however, the only way he had of calculating dates for sites was by collecting groups of items and producing complex comparative chronologies.

Sites such as Skara Brae, which he excavated so meticulously, would, in the era of carbon dating, eventually prove his ideas wrong. More recent excavations have shown that the first houses at Skara were built around 3100 BC, before the great civilizations of the Mediterranean and the Near East had even begun. The sophistication of the people of ancient Orkney, therefore, was not an import, but entirely home grown.

THE LOST WORLD OF ALTAMIRA

The Discovery of Cave Art, 1868

During the autumn evenings of 1868 Modesto Cubillas could often be found walking the estate of Don Marcelino Santiago Tomás Sanz de Sautuola (1831–88). Not that the marquis of Sautuola was aware of this fact. Indeed Cubillas hoped very much not to meet the owner of the large estate that stretched across the hinterland of the town of Santillana del Mar in the northern Spanish province of Cantabria, for he was a poacher.

It had been an unsuccessful day's poaching, very unsuccessful in fact, because Cubillas had almost lost his dog. It had picked up the scent of a wounded fox and had chased the animal apparently off the face of the earth. After hours of searching Cubillas had heard the dog barking deep underground; following the sound, he managed to uncover a small hole in the scrub through which the fox had bolted and the dog had followed. He squeezed through the gap and found himself in the caves of Altamira – their first human visitor for perhaps 13,000 years. Only several years later did Don Marcelino learn of the uninvited guest on his estate and his unexpected discovery. The only thing that had interested Cubillas in the cave was his dog, and he had left as soon as he had found it. He had mentioned the unusual cave to friends, however, and word had eventually got back to the marquis.

Don Marcelino immediately set off to visit the site and was shown to the small cleft in the limestone bedrock. The opening to the cave system was tiny; it is possible that it was only opened to the modern world as a result of recent quarrying activity nearby. Until then it had remained sealed for millennia. But Don Marcelino ordered the opening to be cleared and widened and then, lamp in hand, he became the second modern man to enter the cave. What he saw impressed him. The floor of the cave was covered with a thick deposit of animal bones, and as he felt around in the dark he stuffed handfuls of them in his pockets to examine on his return to the surface.

Above ground, Don Marcelino looked through his finds. They were clearly not the remains of wounded foxes or other modern creatures. They were something bigger, something completely different. Seeking confirmation of his suspicions, he packaged up the remains and sent them to his old friend Juan Vilanova y Piera (1821–93), a professor of palaeontology at the University of Madrid. Piera examined the remains

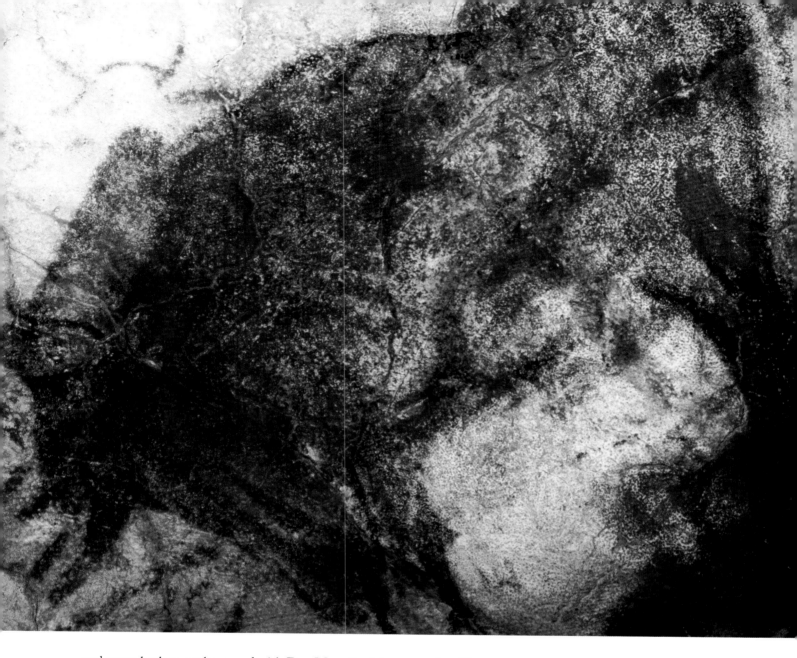

and wrote back to say he agreed with Don Marcelino's interpretation. These were ancient remains, from an age when bison, wild horses and reindeer lived in Spain. The bones had also been broken deliberately to remove the marrow, so the early humans who had hunted these animals had also been in the cave. Don Marcelino had discovered a time capsule – a window into our prehistoric past. His discoveries would turn out to be more rare and beautiful than he imagined, and so surprising that it would take 25 years for the academic community to accept their significance.

Altamira's secret is revealed

Just how extraordinary the Altamira cave was would not emerge until 1879. Don Marcelino was re-excavating in the floor of the cave following a visit to the Exposition Universelle in Paris the previous year, where he had seen a French collection of prehistoric stone tools, tools that he recognized and that he was even now uncovering on the floor of his cave. With him were his five-year-old daughter, Maria, and her little dog. Before long, Maria wandered off to explore the extensive cave system, something she could do with greater ease than her father, thanks to her small size. In the darkness behind the excavations she also did something her father had never done in those

The caves at Altamira consist of a series of rooms and passages, a number of which are decorated with ceiling paintings that remain as well preserved as the day they were made. Using just three colours – black, red and ochre – the artists expertly represented the animals they hunted, including this bison.

cramped conditions – she looked up at the cave roof. Moments later her voice rang out: *'Papá, mira toros pintados!'* ('Daddy, look at the painted bulls!').

Holding up his acetylene lamp, Don Marcelino saw the reason for her exclamation. Illuminated above him, painted on the rock face, was a herd of colourful bison stretching nearly 14 metres (46 ft) across the natural vault. Don Marcelino was initially suspicious. At that time the people who had left their tools in the cave more than 13,000 years earlier were widely thought to have been the most primitive of creatures, incapable of anything more than brutal and bloody survival. But the animals depicted so beautifully on the cave were undoubtedly the same types whose bones he was excavating nearby and they must have been caught and eaten by the makers of the stone tools he had found. He called for Juan Vilanova y Piera, who immediately came to Altamira. The professor confirmed the find and began preparing a scientific paper on the subject. The following year that paper, entitled 'Brief Notes About Some Prehistoric Objects in the Province of Santander', was published, including descriptions of the tools and bones and reproductions of paintings Don Marcelino had commissioned of the herd of bison.

If Don Marcelino had hoped for recognition for his daughter's discovery, he was disappointed. His paper was met with ridicule. What did this amateur archaeologist know about ancient humans? The 'savages' who lived in these caves, so the critics claimed, were incapable of producing art. The towering figure of French prehistory at the time, Émile Cartailhac (1845–1921), went further. He suggested that not only were the paintings unassociated with the tools and bones of the cave floor – they were a hoax. Don Marcelino was crushed by the criticism. As an amateur archaeologist, he felt unable to defend himself against such accusations. All he would say, in private, was that he was an honourable man. He died in 1888, still labelled a fraud.

Don Marcelino's reputation is restored

But his story did not die with him. Don Marcelino's friend Vilanova mounted a robust defence of the finds and, as the last years of the 19th century slipped by, more and more discoveries of Palaeolithic cave art across Europe began to suggest that the Altamira site was no hoax. In 1895 the excavation of the rock shelter at La Mouthe in the Dordogne region of southwestern France gave professional archaeologists their first chance to examine a cave that was incontrovertibly sealed in prehistory and which contained cave art just like that at Altamira.

Finally, in 1902 Don Marcelino's daughter Maria received a visitor. It was Émile Cartailhac, by now president of the Prehistoric Society of France, who wished to see the cave paintings she had discovered as a little girl. He also wanted to apologize to her and to the memory of her father for having doubted the authenticity of their claims. After seeing the caves with his own eyes he went on to produce one of the most famous academic apologies in the history of archaeology, when he published a paper in the journal *L'Anthropologie* entitled 'Les Cavernes Ornées de Dessins: La Grotte d'Altamira. Mea Culpa d'un Sceptique'. Don Marcelino's reputation was restored and the history of art had a new beginning, 15 millennia in the past.

CAVE ART

These cave paintings of hands and birds found near Río Pinturas in Santa Cruz province, Argentina, are thought to have been made between 13,000 and 9,500 years ago.

Cave and rock art is found all over the world from Australia to Finland, but the earliest examples currently known are from Europe. Most of these paintings date from a period known as the Upper Palaeolithic, the last part of the 'Old' Stone Age whose dates can be roughly given as between 40,000 and 10,000 years ago, during the last ice age.

The subject matter of cave paintings varies but common themes are the animals of the period, particularly game animals such as bison, reindeer, horses and a very large extinct type of cattle known as aurochs. These are the animals that the humans of this cold, glacial period hunted, as evidenced by the large numbers of their bones found in many cave sites such as Altamira. Some caves, for example, Chauvet-Pont-d'Arc in southern France, also depict predators from warmer times such as lions and panthers as well as non-game animals including rhinos and hyenas.

Depictions of the makers of these paintings are harder to find, however. For reasons we may never know these people did not usually choose to paint themselves into scenes or, if they did, it was in a schematic and not easily recognizable way. What we do have from many European sites are hand prints, made either by placing an inked hand on the wall to make a positive print or by placing the hand against the rock and spitting a fine spray of pigment over it to leave a negative impression. Some of the tools used by these early humans to make their paintings have also been found in the back of the caves where they left them, as at Altamira. Here too have been found shells used to hold the pigments – most commonly ochre, charcoal, haematite and manganese oxide – and even stone oil lamps that illuminated the cave interiors as they worked.

Dating such work has been controversial ever since the days of Don Marcelino. Whilst the paintings are now universally agreed to be prehistoric, dating pigment on a rock face is not a precise science, and radio-carbon samples from caves containing material of different ages can be easily contaminated. Often the best estimate of the age of a painting is gauged by comparing the animals depicted to the known extinction dates for those species in various areas. The oldest cave art discovered so far is at Chauvet-Pont-d'Arc, which has been tentatively dated to 32,000 years ago, although the accuracy of this date is still hotly debated.

Controversy also surrounds the purpose of cave art. Because many scenes show images of game animals, it has been suggested that the pictures were a form of ritual carried out to ensure a successful hunt. More recent theorists propose that because much of the painting lies in the deepest, most inaccessible parts of caves, where no natural light ever reached, it was created by shamans. In this view, which draws heavily on anthropological studies of more modern peoples, the shamans retired into dark interiors, where they communed with the spirits of the animals they depicted on the cave walls. Whether we will ever understand what motivated our Palaeolithic ancestors to create this art remains debatable, but it offers us a glimpse of an ice-age world that is far removed from the brutal savagery imagined by people in the 19th century.

'MEN OF FLESH'
Schliemann Excavates Troy, 1870

'*The heroes of the Iliad and Odyssey have become to us men of flesh and blood; we can watch both them, and older heroes still, in almost every act of their daily life …*'

A.H. Sayce, Preface to Heinrich Schliemann's
Troja und seine Ruinen (1875)

After a highly successful but not always thoroughly scrupulous career in business, the German treasure hunter Heinrich Schliemann (1822–90) had retired early. Now in his mid-forties, he set himself the task he had first dreamt of as a child – to take the characters and places from Homer's account of the Trojan War out of the realm of fiction and place them firmly in a real archaeological past. In short, Schliemann's abiding ambition was to prove that Homer's epic tales were history, not fable, an idea widely ridiculed in the 19th century. But it was one that brought him in 1868 to a farm owned by the English archaeologist Frank Calvert (1828–1908), on the slopes of the hill of Hissarlik in northwestern Turkey.

Frank Calvert had himself been excavating the site for over 20 years and may well have been the (uncredited) originator of the idea that this dusty mound concealed the remains of legendary Troy. Schliemann brought with him two things that Calvert lacked, however: a fervent and well-publicized belief that Homer's stories were fact not fiction, and the very large amount of money needed to prove it.

The burning of Troy, as depicted by the 17th-century Dutch painter Pieter Schoubroeck. Homer's epic tales of the Trojan War and the siege and eventual fall of the city were long consigned to the realm of legend, until Schliemann and his successors uncovered no fewer than nine cities built on top of one another at the supposed site of Troy in northwestern Turkey.

So it was that in 1870 Schliemann set his 150 workmen the task of cutting away the millennia of human debris on the hill to uncover the city of King Priam which he was convinced lay dormant beneath. His methods were crude and have since been widely criticized but they were not particularly unusual for their day. Instead of carefully peeling away the layers of soil one at a time, a huge trench was dug through the centre of the site to enable the excavators to get quickly to the bottom of the mound, where Schliemann believed Homer's Troy lay. In the process, centuries of material, whole histories of the waxing and waning of this city's fortunes, were simply discarded, and only four main superimposed cities were identified.

It was when Schliemann reached the second city on the site that he believed he had found what he was looking for. Here was a great city apparently destroyed by fire, its mud bricks scorched by the flames, its roofs collapsed and their rafters carbonized. Surely this was Homer's Troy, where Paris, King Priam's son, brought the beautiful

TIMELINE

*c.*3000 BC Troy founded in what is now Çanakkale province in northwestern Turkey; it becomes a thriving trading city during the Bronze Age

*c.*1300 BC The late Bronze Age city of Troy is destroyed by an earthquake

1184 BC Traditional date for the destruction of Troy as described in Homer's *Iliad*

1868 Heinrich Schliemann makes his first visit to Troy and teams up with Calvert to investigate the site

1870 Schliemann undertakes his first excavation, digging down through the upper layers to reach fortifications that he believed represented Homeric Troy

1873 A cache of gold and other artefacts ('Priam's Treasure') – whose authenticity is later disputed – is 'discovered' and smuggled away by Schliemann

1875 Schliemann publishes the results of his excavations at Troy in *Troja und seine Ruinen* ('Troy and Its Ruins')

1876 Banished from Turkey, Schliemann begins excavating shaft graves at Mycenae on mainland Greece, finding gold grave goods

1878 Schliemann resumes work at Troy, undertaking three further excavation campaigns there (1878–9, 1882–3, 1888–90)

1890 Schliemann dies in Naples on his way back to Athens and Troy

Helen, inciting the warlords of Mycenaean Greece to cross the sea and lay siege to the city for ten years. This rubble was surely the remains of the great fire that swept through the city after the Trojans fell prey to the stratagem of the Trojan Horse and unwittingly let their enemy into the stronghold. Schliemann surmised that the burn marks evident at the site must have been caused by the fires lit by Agamemnon's heroes.

Of course, Schliemann was well aware that scorched bricks and blackened wood were not the stuff of newspaper headlines and were unlikely to capture the world's imagination. Not content with discovering Troy, he was also extremely eager to let the world know that he had found the city; accordingly, to ensure that public interest did not flag, he sent regular dispatches to *The Times* and *The Daily Telegraph* newspapers, reporting on his discoveries. This search for publicity would lead him into one of the most questionable episodes of the entire campaign.

'Priam's Treasure'

Schliemann reported that on 31 May 1873, as he was excavating one of the gateways of what he claimed was King Priam's palace, he noticed the bright green corrosion on a copper object and the gleam of a piece of gold between two ruined walls. Calling for an early lunch, he cleared the site of workmen and, with his wife Sophia, set about uncovering the objects. What they found, or at least what Schliemann said they found, was a treasure trove packed in a rectangular shape, suggesting it had once been enclosed in a box that had long since decayed. There were gold diadems, earrings, metal vases, bronze weapons, human figurines and peculiar quartz crystal 'lenses'. As each fabulous treasure came to light it was quickly wrapped in Sophia's shawl, away from prying eyes, and the whole hoard was then secretly removed from the country, pending Schliemann's great announcement.

When that announcement came, it caused more of a stir than even Schliemann may have bargained for. The Turkish authorities, which owned the half of the site that did not belong to Frank Calvert, were incensed that the treasure had been smuggled out of the country and that they had been robbed of their share. Legal proceedings were begun and Schliemann was forced to pay a large fine as well as a 50,000-franc fee to become the legal owner of the items. It also seemed unlikely that he would be permitted to return to Troy again in the near future.

Nevertheless, for Schliemann the financial cost of this escapade was well worth bearing, and indeed was easily borne by a man of his great wealth. In his eyes and in the eyes of the general public who avidly devoured his reports, he had uncovered a unique moment in history. Here were King Priam's most precious possessions, which he had packed in a box and hidden in the walls of his palace even as the Trojan War raged all around him. As far as Schliemann's public was concerned, these were the earrings and diadems that had once framed the 'face that launched a thousand ships', the jewellery of Helen of Troy herself. Schliemann reinforced this impression by publishing photographs of his wife wearing the artefacts. Troy, it appeared, had risen from the ashes.

HEINRICH SCHLIEMANN

Heinrich Schliemann remains one of the most controversial figures in the history of archaeology. Born in northeastern Germany in January 1822, his childhood was blighted by a series of misfortunes, beginning with the death of his mother when he was just nine years old. He had only completed a year of preparatory schooling when his father, a Protestant minister, was accused of embezzling church funds and was forced to transfer his son to the free local school. This institution provided vocational training, so the opportunity to learn classical languages or history evaporated overnight and instead Heinrich was prepared for life as a tradesman.

The roots of the adult Schliemann's obsession with proving the historical truth behind Homer's *Odyssey* and *Iliad* are unclear. His own account of his life is larded with fantasy and conveniently glosses over its more dubious episodes. His preferred claim was that his interest was sparked by his father's Christmas gift to him in 1829 of Georg Ludwig Jerrer's *History of the World*.

Having left school at 14, Schliemann served as an apprentice grocer before moving to Hamburg. There, he set sail on a ship bound for Venezuela, only to be shipwrecked off the Dutch coast. Turning to business, he used his remarkable facility for languages (he spoke over a dozen) to build a fortune as an importer. After a spell as a company agent in St Petersburg, Russia, he sailed for the United States where he set up a bank in the California gold fields, buying gold dust from prospectors to sell on the bullion markets. In just six months he made $1.3 million profit. He abruptly abandoned this lucrative trade in 1852; rumour had it that he had defrauded his business partner and needed to make a quick exit.

He resurfaced in Russia, where he met Katerina Lyshina, the daughter of a wealthy friend. They were soon married, but from the start his wife complained

'Priam's Treasure', the hoard of metal artefacts and semi-precious stones allegedly discovered at Troy by Schliemann. Archaeologists now suspect that he assembled this hoard from disparate finds.

that he did not keep her in the style to which she was accustomed. Keen to make amends, he augmented the wealth he had amassed from gold speculation by cornering the indigo market. Then, in the Crimean War, the fortune he earned as a military contractor to the Russian government finally enabled him to retire and indulge his passion for archaeology.

Schliemann duly embarked on his travels. His wife, who did not share her husband's interests and was disaffected with their marriage, flatly refused to accompany him. His response was typically ruthless and devious; while visiting the United States, Schliemann took US citizenship and three days later took advantage of the state of Indiana's liberal divorce laws to annul the marriage. He subsequently found a more sympathetic companion in the 17-year-old Greek Sophia Engastromenos, whom he married just a year later.

Now began the most fruitful but also the most controversial period of Schliemann's life, in which he located and excavated many of the great sites of Bronze Age Greece. Once again, he was not averse to employing dubious methods – fabricating evidence, rewriting his diaries and spiriting away treasures from sites. Even so, his endeavours provided firm proof that the cities of Homer's tales were not mythical sites but real places rooted in history.

During Schliemann's last campaign at Troy in 1890 an ear infection forced him to return to Germany for surgery. This was unsuccessful, but he ignored his doctor's advice to rest and immediately set off back to Turkey. He only made it as far as Naples; after visiting Pompeii to witness the uncovering of another lost world, Schliemann collapsed on the Piazza della Carità on Christmas Day, and died the following morning in his hotel room.

STRATIGRAPHY – PEELING BACK THE LAYERS

A criticism regularly levelled at Schliemann is that in his search for Homer's Troy he recklessly dug through layers of soil representing thousands of years of valuable, irretrievable archaeology. There is some truth in this. Archaeological digs are, uniquely, unrepeatable experiments. In order to dig down into a site, the later, higher layers must be excavated. Unearthing each new, earlier level involves destroying the level that lies on top of it. Once a site has been dug it can never be dug again.

One of the great challenges in the development of archaeology has been finding ways to ensure that each layer in an excavation is at least identified and fully recorded before it is removed. Archaeological stratigraphy – the study of the layering of successive levels of soil on a site – has been central to this. Assuming the site is undisturbed, the law of superposition, which states that the oldest layers are at the bottom and the newest at the top, holds true. As archaeologists dig down through a site they try to follow the stratigraphic sequence, removing the layers one at a time, starting with the most recent and working back to the most ancient.

Schliemann sketching the ruins at Troy. The Homeric city that the amateur archaeologist thought he had excavated has since been shown to lie several strata higher.

The value of stratigraphy lies in more than simply providing a rigorous method of excavation, however. Because layers lie in chronological order, it is possible to give relative dates to objects found in each layer. Hence a coin found in a layer above a pot in a lower layer must have been deposited there at a later date. In the same way, pots found at a certain level on one site and therefore attributed to a particular period may allow archaeologists to date layers found at another site to the same period.

Of course this dating system is only relative. A pot in a higher layer of earth than a ring in another layer can only be said to be more recent than the ring – no absolute date can be given. Even in cases where objects carry dates, such as coins, the presence of a coin in a layer only tells us that the layer was deposited sometime after the coin was minted. However, by building up large numbers of comparative collections of objects from stratigraphic sequences and with the aid of modern scientific dating techniques such as carbon-14, it has been possible for archaeologists to build detailed typological sequences of artefacts that demonstrate the development of material culture and technology.

In Schliemann's day little was known of stratigraphy, so it is perhaps unfair to criticize him unduly for his excavation methods at Troy. In fact, it was only in his early work there that Schliemann cut through the mound; an approach very similar to that of European barrow openers who dug straight into the middle of a barrow, which they believed was the most likely place to find the grave goods.

In Schliemann's later campaigns at Troy he sought the advice and assistance of Wilhelm Dörpfeld (1853–1940), a pioneer in stratigraphy, who persuaded him that his early work had damaged many important layers of archaeology. This advice, together with Dörpfeld's continuing help, prevented the further wholesale destruction of the site. From this point on, the excavations at Troy became some of the more advanced of their day and in this, at least, Schliemann should be considered a pioneer.

The truth as we know it today is rather different. We now understand that the second city of Troy, the one Schliemann identified as Priam's city, was destroyed hundreds of years before the Trojan War can possibly have taken place. Nine successive cities have now been identified on the site, with the most likely candidate for Homeric Troy being City VIIa. Indeed, the suggestion that Schliemann had dug straight through the city he was looking for, destroying much of it in the process, had been made as early as 1872 in a paper published by Frank Calvert, which led to a rift between the two men.

Priam's Treasure presents even more of a problem. Arguments continue over whether the treasure was all found in one place or was gathered together by Schliemann to corroborate his claim that he had made a spectacular 'discovery'. It is certainly odd that the hoard was excavated secretly, and we know that Sophia was not even at the site at the time and so cannot have wrapped it in her shawl and spirited it away as he stated. One of Schliemann's workmen also later claimed to have discovered some of the pieces at an entirely different location. It is also doubtful whether it is even a royal treasure, since the find includes small gold ingots and may in reality represent a craftsman's scrap metal collection ready for recycling.

Excavations at Mycenae

All of these modern doubts have tended to cloud the memory of Heinrich Schliemann and the discovery of Troy, yet he undoubtedly deserves a place among the founders of archaeology. Having been forced out of Turkey for a time, he turned his attention to the citadel at Mycenae in Greece, the legendary home of King Agamemnon, where he uncovered a Bronze Age palace and the famous shaft burials with their golden masks. It was after seeing one of these for the first time as it emerged from the earth that he cabled the Greek king saying he had 'gazed upon the face of Agamemnon'. While this was perhaps too optimistic a claim, these excavations, along with those at Troy, did prove that a lost Mycenaean civilization – the setting for Homer's tale – had flourished in Greece and the Aegean and had come into conflict with the Hittite cities on the Turkish coast. In proposing a hypothesis about an age before written history and trying to prove it using the scientific techniques of archaeology, Schliemann was one of the pioneers of archaeological theory.

Although in his haste he may not have been as methodical as he ought to have been, and despite the fact that he sometimes fabricated evidence to suit the story he wished to tell, Schliemann brought the Mycenaean Bronze Age out of mythology and into the light of history. The city of Troy and the treasure he found there may not have been what he thought it was, but if ever King Priam lived it was at Hissarlik. Even if Priam is a mythological hero, Schliemann proved that the story told by Homer was not a fantasy but the memory of a distant time and half-forgotten rivalries fought out in the age of bronze.

This finely crafted gold funeral mask – popularly known as the 'Mask of Agamemnon', was found during excavations of shaft graves at Mycenae by Schliemann in 1876. Controversy still surrounds this artefact, with some authorities claiming that it does not date from the 16th century BC, but rather was made at Schliemann's request to enhance his reputation for spectacular archaeological finds.

SEARCHING FOR THE LOST TEMPLE OF SOLOMON

Great Zimbabwe, 1871

'*Among the gold mines of the inland plains between the Limpopo and Zambezi rivers there is a fortress built of stones of marvellous size, and there appears to be no mortar joining them ... This edifice is almost surrounded by hills, upon which are others resembling it in the fashioning of stone and the absence of mortar, and one of them is a tower more than 12 fathoms [22 m] high. The natives of the country call these edifices Simbaoe, which according to their language signifies "court".*'

VIÇENTE PEGADO, Captain of the Portuguese garrison of Sofala (1531)

The antiquarians of the 19th century differed from modern archaeologists in one crucial respect. As explorers and adventurers they often set out with a fixed idea of what they were looking for. They were impelled by a desire to locate the ruins of cities and temples mentioned in ancient texts, and no text held a greater fascination than the Bible.

Karl Mauch (1837–75) was just such a man. When he landed on the coast of southern Africa in 1865, he carried with him not a map but a copy of the Old Testament. Mauch was in Africa for two reasons. The principal reason was to prospect for gold, which he found but could not persuade the local tribes to mine. And so he turned his attention to his second goal – the search for the biblical city of Ophir. Mauch took his cue from the Book of Chronicles, which made mention of an ancient gold prospector:

> *'And Huram sent him by the hands of his servant's ships, and servants that had knowledge of the sea; and they went with the servants of Solomon to Ophir, and took thence four hundred and fifty talents of gold, and brought them to King Solomon.'*
>
> 2 CHRONICLES 8:18

In search of the lost city

Ophir, where Solomon had found his great wealth, had never been identified, but Mauch believed that it was close at hand. In 1867, rumours of a lost city between the Limpopo and Zambezi rivers led him to speculate that this might be the place he was looking for. The journey north was beset with difficulty. The chiefs of each area he

The tower in the Great Enclosure at Great Zimbabwe. Mauch thought it was a defensive fortress, though it is more likely to have been a granary.

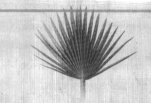

TIMELINE

*c.*1000 Several Shona chiefdoms rise and fall between the Limpopo and Zimbabwe rivers. Mainly agricultural, these cultures also mine, smelt and trade iron, copper, chrome and gold

*c.*1200 The Munhumutapa empire emerges, centred on the site of Great Zimbabwe

*c.*1450 Great Zimbabwe is abandoned, only 50 years or so after its heyday. Its decline may be due to dwindling resources or to the rise of the rival state of Mwene Mutapa

1871 Karl Mauch, searching for the lost biblical kingdom of Ophir, is the first European of modern times to visit and describe the ruins

1905 The first properly scientific archaeological investigations of Great Zimbabwe are carried out by the British scholar David Randall-MacIver (1873–1945)

1929 Gertrude Caton-Thompson determines that black Africans built Great Zimbabwe

1980 In honour of the indigenous culture that built the site, the former white supremacist state of Rhodesia is renamed Zimbabwe when it gains its independence. An image of one of the soapstone carvings of birds found at the site is incorporated as a symbol on the nation's new flag

1986 Great Zimbabwe is made a UNESCO World Heritage Site

passed through required gifts in return for safe passage, or refused passage altogether. His only clothing, a leather suit, provided some protection from thorns and insects but was heavy and stifling in the tropical heat. Nor did he get on well with his travelling companions. Mauch disliked most white people, particularly expatriates living in southern Africa, but his feelings were no more generous towards the black population who provided him with his essential guides, translators and porters. His poor treatment of this group ultimately led to the dire situation in which he found himself on 26 August 1871 – alone in the bush, surrounded by hostile tribes and unable to progress any further, his entire party having abandoned him.

Mauch eventually ended up as a captive of a local chief, but through an extraordinary stroke of luck came to hear about another white man living in the area – Adam Renders – who had apparently 'gone native', leaving his wife and moving in with two local women. Mauch's disapproval did not prevent him from writing a letter to Renders begging for help.

THE REAL GREAT ZIMBABWE

Great Zimbabwe, as the site is now known, has been subject to many archaeological investigations since Mauch's day, none of which have revealed any biblical connection. Instead they have proved the existence of an indigenous African civilization that no 19th-century European would have believed possible. Great Zimbabwe was not the home of a white Semitic people but the capital of a Medieval empire created by the ancestors of the Shona. Their Munhumutapa empire had probably begun to emerge in the 11th century and reached its height in the 1440s. It is thought to have derived its great wealth initially from cattle and later from controlling gold exports to Arab traders via the Atlantic port of Sofala in Mozambique.

The site is one of several stone settlements, the Shona term *Zimbabwe* ('building made of stone') denoting a court or chieftain's house. Great Zimbabwe is by far the largest and most impressive. Built in the 13th to 14th centuries, it covered some 730 hectares (1800 acres) and comprised three main areas: an enclosure on the plain (the largest ancient structure in sub-Saharan Africa), a valley complex and a hill complex. The hill site seems to have been home to the king and his family, while the enclosure area held houses for the royal wives along with grain stores. The common people lived in the valley.

The city's massive, sinuous walls were made of local granite, cut into blocks and locked together without mortar. Ranging from 1 to 5 metres (3 to 16 ft) thick, these structures were so well built that in Mauch's day many were still complete and displayed fine herringbone decoration along their tops. The walls had originally connected dwellings made

of *daga* – a thick adobe – which have long since disappeared but which at the city's height were home to some 12,000 to 40,000 people.

Since the people of Great Zimbabwe left no written record we do not know why it was abandoned. By the mid-15th century trade had shifted north, perhaps as the result of a growing scarcity of local gold and salt deposits, and firewood. In the following century the Portuguese increasingly pressured the Munhumatapa empire, while the growth of the slave trade factionalized and impoverished the area. By this stage, Great Zimbabwe was long since derelict.

A century of archaeology finally disproved the myth that the Shona city was once the home of the queen of Sheba. One of the site's greatest excavators, Gertrude Caton-Thompson (1888–1985), wrote in 1931:

'*Examination of all the existing evidence, gathered from every quarter, still can produce not one single item that is not in accordance with the claim of Bantu origin and Medieval date. The interest in Zimbabwe and the allied ruins should, on this account … be enhanced a hundredfold; it enriches, not impoverishes, our wonderment at their remarkable achievement … for the mystery of Zimbabwe is the mystery which lies in the still pulsating heart of native Africa.*'

Great Zimbabwe's true significance was finally commemorated in 1980; when black majority rule came to Southern Rhodesia in that year, the nation that was home to this greatest of African sites changed its name to Zimbabwe.

Renders heeded Mauch's plea and bought his freedom. Together, they then explored the uncharted region inhabited by the Banyai, a sub-group of the Shona people of Zimbabwe. The Banyai told Mauch that white men had once lived in the area. They also recounted a legend that the nearby Ghost Mountain was home to a magical, walking cooking pot that maimed anyone who saw it. Mauch, ever the intrepid explorer, climbed the summit; his effort was rewarded not with the sight of a magic pot, but something far more real:

' "*Bravo*", I exclaimed, "*that is what I have been seeking since 1868. What luck! And how unexpected! Only a few days before, occupied with serious thoughts of death, and today standing before the most brilliant success of my travels. God be praised!*" '

What Mauch had seen from the mountaintop lay in the plain below – a vast ruin, apparently of a city. The site of the ruin was owned by a tribe that was hostile to Mauch's presence, so he had to proceed carefully. On the morning of 5 September he crept secretly into the site to discover broken-down walls made from mortarless granite blocks. Moving through the overgrown ruins, he came to an enclosure containing:

'... a tower-like structure ... It stood there apparently quite undamaged. Altogether it rose to a height of about 30 feet. The lower 10 feet are cylindrical with a diameter of 15 to 16 feet, the upper 20 feet are conical with a diameter of about 8 feet at the top.'

The appearance of the local chief abruptly ended this first visit, but did help to thaw relations. Two days later Mauch was back on the site, this time with the owners' permission. He climbed to the citadel above the strange tower, which he decided was an ancient fortress. But what really fascinated him was the enclosure on the plain, which he believed corresponded with certain passages in the Old Testament. He scrambled up the tower, clinging to the vines that encircled it, and discovered that it was solid.

The House of the Great Woman

Mauch learned from the local people that this 'city' had a name – 'Zimbabye' and that they referred to the enclosure as 'The House of the Great Woman'. Mauch's mind was made up: this was the land of Ophir, and the enclosure was a model of Solomon's temple in Jerusalem built by the queen of Sheba, who is mentioned in both the Old and New Testaments and the Qur'an as the ruler of an unidentified but hugely wealthy land. On hearing of Solomon's great wisdom she had travelled to Jerusalem, bringing with her 4.5 tons of gold as a gift. Now Mauch believed he had archaeological flesh to put on the bones of the story.

When Mauch eventually returned to Europe in 1872 he brought with him his carefully drawn plans and news that he had found archaeological proof of another part of the Old Testament. In an era when the remains of Ur and Nineveh were bringing to light records of biblical rulers, the discovery of the queen of Sheba's kingdom did not seem fanciful. His news caused a sensation. As the European powers scrambled for control of Africa's resources, the idea that this gold-rich area of southern Africa had once been home to a biblical (and white rather than black) African people seemed to justify the bloody land-grab that was already under way. Indeed, as late as the 1970s, the myth that Great Zimbabwe was the former home of a Semitic Middle Eastern people and not the remains of a black African civilization was still widely taught in white-ruled Rhodesia. But by then proper archaeological investigations at the site had uncovered the truth.

For Mauch, however, the romantic notion that he had found a lost city from the Bible was unassailable. As an antiquarian rather than an archaeologist, he had gone looking for a dream and forced his discovery to fit it. His endeavours had brought an ancient civilization to light but archaeology would disprove his theories. Mauch never returned to Africa; his eight years there had ruined his health and deepened his misanthropy. Aged 37, he fell from a window and died, in a delirium probably brought on by malaria.

The wall around the Great Enclosure is some 250 metres (800 ft) long and 10 metres (30 ft) high. Mauch's mistaken belief that he had stumbled upon the ancient home of the queen of Sheba later inspired Henry Rider Haggard's adventure classic, King Solomon's Mines *(1885).*

THE COWBOY ARCHAEOLOGIST

Richard Wetherill in the Midwest, 1884

The American Midwest of 1884 offered little scope for archaeology. Yet, unlike most of the white settlers who were busy colonizing this supposedly 'virgin' territory, the Wetherill family, including Richard (1858–1910), his four brothers and their father John, knew that this was not a pristine, empty environment but an ancient settled land. They had mediated in disputes between new settlers and the indigenous peoples of Texas and Oklahoma, and as pacifist Quakers who only ever carried guns for hunting, had earned the respect of native Americans.

Life had been hard on the Wetherills in what was still very much the Wild West. After early attempts at farming in Kansas and Missouri, the family had moved to Colorado to join in the silver rush, but had never struck lucky. By 1880 they were destitute and so took their wagons back east to the area known as the Four Corners, where the states of Colorado, Utah, Arizona and New Mexico meet, to try their hand at ranching. The place they chose was a little oasis in a barren and desolate landscape. The Mancos valley was one of the few regularly green areas in a land of table mountains and deep canyons, which was bone dry in the summer and subject to flash flooding and blizzards in winter. Much of the landscape was so harsh that even the local indigenous peoples – the Navajo, Hopi and Ute – did not venture there. Thanks to the good relations between the Wetherills and the native Americans, however, the latter let their new cowboy neighbours graze cattle on their land.

The land in question was the Mesa Verde, a stone plateau some 1.5 miles (2.5 km) above sea level cut through with deep, winding gorges. The terrain provided a tenuous habitat for the cattle to graze and a thousand opportunities for them to get lost or fall to their death. It was here, in the dying days of 1884, that Richard Wetherill and his brothers established a winter camp from which to watch their cattle.

The winter of 1884–5 was dull and cold in Johnson Canyon, and the brothers occupied their time by exploring the gullies and ravines in which the native Americans told them the spirits of their ancestors dwelt. Here they would often find pottery and stone tools

The most prominent structure at the Mesa Verde site is Square Tower House. This dwelling is thought to have been occupied between around AD 1200 and 1300.

scattered around small buildings clinging precariously to the valley walls. Collecting these artefacts soon became both a pastime and the source of a small additional income: the objects would be sent via their father to a Denver bookseller who sold native American curios. It was small-scale looting, no more, but as the brothers explored deeper into the valley systems, encouraged by the reports from indigenous peoples of amazing sights there, one find would change everything.

A city in the rock

On 18 December 1888 Richard Wetherill and his brother-in-law Charlie Mason were picking their way through the snow of Cliff Canyon, looking for stray cattle. It is possible that the snow helped to highlight the details of the cliff face ahead of them, or perhaps a stray animal simply tempted the two cowboys further into the canyon system than usual, but when Richard Wetherill glanced up he saw an extraordinary sight – a huge cave in the rock face, filled with buildings.

Working their way around the gully, the two men managed to gain access to the site, which Richard named Cliff Palace, and walked into a lost world. The cave seemed to hold an entire city of beautifully constructed stone buildings, reaching from floor to ceiling. As they walked from room to room, they found the floors strewn with stone tools and broken pottery. In the dry cave air, even the remains of food had been desiccated and preserved. Wetherill wrote:

> 'It appears as though the inhabitants had left everything they possessed right where they had last used it.'

Other finds proved more unsettling. The wooden rafters and floor joists of the buildings had been ripped away, causing many rooms to collapse, and in the rubble they found caches of 'hidden' valuables covered by the skeletons of the inhabitants.

With a few hours of daylight left the two men decided to split up and explore the rest of the valley; before nightfall Richard had found another site, even better preserved, which he called Spruce Tree House. As snow was falling and the light fading, he simply made a mental note of where it was and turned back to meet Charlie. The next day he tried to retrace his steps but the snow had transformed the appearance of the valley and the two men missed their turn. They set off down another ravine where, under a rocky overhang, they discovered yet another complex, Square Tower House – a building of some 70 rooms.

After returning to the ranch, Richard assembled a small team and headed back into the canyon to explore the ruins more thoroughly. For a month, five cowboys camped in Square Tower House, uncovering black and white painted pottery, stone arrow tips, shells, beads and even fabrics. The arid environment had acted as such an effective preservative that the bodies of the inhabitants of the site were naturally mummified. They survived, tucked in the darkest recesses at the back of the cave, their skin stretched like parchment across their dry faces and their clothes still wrapped around their skeletal forms.

VANDAL OR VICTIM? THE CONTROVERSY SURROUNDING RICHARD WETHERILL

When Richard Wetherill first began exploring the sites of the ancient pueblos he was filled with a mixture of fascination for the unknown past and the thought that his finds might help supplement his family's precarious income. As Charlie Mason, the man who rode with him on the day of his first find, wrote shortly before they returned to the site:

'Our previous work had been carried out to satisfy more our own curiosity than for any other purpose but this time it was a business proposition.'

The Wetherill family's first 'excavations' were little more than treasure hunts and certainly did a great deal of damage to some sites as the men searched for suitable artefacts to sell, initially to the Colorado Historical Society. But as time went on the silent ruins of the pueblos began to excite a deeper interest in Richard, and his focus shifted from treasure hunting to trying to understand more about the people who had lived in these places.

In 1893 a visit by Wetherill to the Chicago World's Fair, where some of his Mesa Verde finds were displayed, brought him into contact with the wealthy Hyde brothers, who offered to sponsor his next expedition, to Grand Gulch. The meticulous preparations Wetherill made for this venture, including a plan for recording the orientation of every artefact and the depth at which it was discovered, indicate clearly that the treasure hunter had by now given way to the serious archaeologist.

At Grand Gulch Wetherill discovered and named the Basket Maker culture. The term was derided by professional archaeologists as a marketing gimmick, but has since been shown to be correct. He was not trying to hoodwink collectors; he had simply dug, as a modern archaeologist would, one by one through the layers of soil and debris to identify an earlier culture beneath that of the pueblo builders.

Suitably impressed, the Hyde brothers agreed to fund an expedition in 1896 to Chaco Canyon in New Mexico, where there was rumoured to be a pueblo dwelling of some 650 rooms (compared to the 217 at Cliff Palace). Even so, the Hydes effectively demoted Wetherill by appointing a professional archaeologist to lead the team. Wetherill's tireless work at the site, which yielded one of the largest caches of pottery ever found in the United States, was not even acknowledged by a mention in the official report.

As the century drew to a close, Wetherill found himself mired in debt – the family ranch was struggling and the Hydes failed to pay him regularly. He decided to move permanently to Chaco and set up a store, where he and his family made a modest living trading goods for Navajo blankets which were sold in New York. But the political tide was already turning and in 1900 the Hydes were ordered to stop work pending an investigation into charges that they were simply looting and destroying sites.

Although Wetherill and the Hydes were cleared of any misconduct, they were refused permission to continue excavating. At the same time the Indian Commission accused Wetherill of mistreating the native Americans who worked for him and stealing from them. A government inspector reported:

'The more I know of Wetherill the more I am convinced he is a man without principle. He boasted to me that he was known as "the vandal of the Southwest".'

This was a gross calumny; there was no denying that the Wetherills had financed their expeditions by selling artefacts, but this was standard practice at the time, as the collections of many European national museums demonstrate. But the untutored Richard Wetherill made an easy scapegoat. Sadly, he would not live long enough to clear his name. On 22 June 1910, he was shot dead as he rode to his store in Chaco Canyon. One of the Navajo men who had worked with him for years and who was known to owe him money was arrested and tried, but got off with a derisory sentence. Richard Wetherill had been born a cowboy and had died a cowboy, but much of his life had been spent as one of America's first great archaeologists.

What Richard Wetherill – who was not a trained archaeologist – had discovered was the remains of a sophisticated civilization that had grown, flourished and disappeared many centuries before the arrival of Europeans. It was a civilization that gave the lie to the idea commonly held at the time that native Americans were 'primitive' people whose lands could be taken from them without conscience. From now on, uncovering just who these people were would become Wetherill's life work, and the cause of his death.

In 1891 Wetherill's expedition was joined by a Swedish mineralogist, Baron Gustaf Nordenskiöld (1869–1928), the son of a famous arctic explorer. He introduced Wetherill to the new European methods of excavation, using a pointing trowel to remove each layer of earth rather than the shovel he had been wielding. Nordenskiöld also made the first attempt at dating the sites – something which was a complete mystery to Wetherill – counting tree rings at Spruce Tree House to prove that the settlement was at least 162 years old (we now know it was many hundreds of years older than that). Wetherill also started making meticulous notes of the debris that had previously been shovelled away, including the remains of food, from which he reconstructed the diet of the Pueblo peoples, and clothing, which he used to make comparative studies between the two distinct cultures he believed he was uncovering.

Earthenware from Chaco Canyon, such as this pot, is typically decorated with a variety of monochrome geometric designs. Pottery, which is indicative of a settled lifestyle, is thought to have supplanted baskets for culinary use at this site between AD 400 and 750.

Basket makers and cave dwellers

Over the next 22 years Wetherill excavated numerous sites in the Mesa Verde, at Grand Gulch 100 miles (160 km) to the west in Utah and at Chaco Canyon in New Mexico; in doing so he began to uncover a story that few white settlers would have believed. The sites he found had belonged to two peoples. Their first occupants were what he called the 'Basket Maker' people, who had settled the area of the Four Corners perhaps as early as 1200 BC. They had begun the cultivation of crops, including maize (corn) and squashes, and hunted game with stone-tipped spears, thrown using a notched stick known as an *atlatl*. They did not use pottery but instead made baskets so finely woven that they could be used to carry water; this distinctive feature provided Wetherill with his name for the culture.

Wetherill often found Basket Maker sites underneath later buildings, partly because these peoples dug bottle-shaped rooms known as pit houses. Later peoples unwittingly built over the concealed entrances of these rooms. Inside he found not only Basket Maker artefacts but, as he recorded in his letters, the remains of the people themselves:

> 'In these pot holes of caches are found the bodies of all ages and sexes – sandals upon the feet – human hair, gee string, cedar bark breech cloth. Beads around their necks. All wrapped in a blanket of rabbit … Over the head is a small basket – flat – about 20 inches in diameter, usually found in good condition; Apaches make a similar one today.'

Around AD 750 this culture began developing into what Wetherill called the 'Cave Dweller' people – the civilization that had built the cliff dwellings he had stumbled upon. They lived in above-ground 'pueblos', sometimes up to four storeys high, just one of which (Pueblo Bonito) was home to between 2000 and 5000 people. These people also grew squashes, corn and now beans (which had been introduced to the area through trade with Central America) and had domesticated the turkey. The pit house of the Basket Maker people also developed under the Cave Dwellers into ritual *kivas*, sunken ceremonial halls which could hold up to 500 people.

However, their greatest achievement was the management of water resources. The area around the Four Corners is very dry in summer, and although winter can bring violent storms and heavy snowfall, the water that results is unpredictable and quickly drains away into the sandy soil. To make long-term habitation there possible, the Cave Dwellers built elaborate irrigation systems, damming seasonal rivers, terracing hillsides and digging cisterns to catch and conserve their erratic water supply. Managing this required more social cohesion and central control, so towns like Cliff Palace grew up.

By the time Richard Wetherill came across these sites the people who had lived there were long gone. His first thought, as he surveyed the wreckage of houses and spear points embedded in bones, was that this culture had been wiped out in a catastrophic war. Modern archaeologists are less certain. The arrival of more nomadic peoples from the 13th century onwards may have increased the pressure on the Cave Dwellers, but climate change also probably played a part. Some of the skeletons Wetherill found bore injuries that showed signs of healing, suggesting they had survived attack, while many others simply represented formal burials. Equally, the dismantling of the buildings may have had as much to do with a shortage of wood as with wanton destruction.

In fact the pueblo builders may simply have moved on to areas of more reliable rainfall. The Hopi, whom Wetherill knew well, still built religious *kivas* and modern Pueblo peoples live today in Arizona and New Mexico. The cave settlements may have been long abandoned by the time Europeans found them, but the descendants of their builders were still all around.

Ancient kivas *at Pueblo Bonito in Chaco Canyon. These underground rooms were a common feature of many ancestral Pueblo societies, and were used as places to conduct religious ceremonies.*

HORIZON OF THE SUN
The Forgotten City of the Sun Pharaoh, 1887

On the east bank of the Nile in Middle Egypt, some 200 miles (320 km) south of Cairo, lies a flat desert plain surrounded by a high cliff. No-one lives in this inhospitable landscape today, but for centuries visitors to the region have been aware that this was not always the case. For high up on the cliff face, in almost inaccessible locations, 11 huge stelae (stone inscriptions) are carved into the rock, bearing writing in the ancient script of Egypt – hieroglyphics.

In the 19th century local people in the nearby villages of El-Til el Amarna and El-Hagg Qandil had another reason to suspect people had once lived there, for the plain was a source of *sebakh* – decomposed mud brick – that was used as a fertilizer. It was in 1887 that a local woman digging for *sebakh* near the centre of the plain came across something else. Under the decayed mud and straw lay what looked like a complete brick; on removing it, she saw that the baked clay was inscribed with some form of ancient writing. As she widened the hole, many other tablets soon came to light, hundreds of them, all inscribed with the same strange arrow-shaped markings.

But if they were treasure they were not an obvious one and the woman took little interest, destroying a number of the tablets before selling the rest – more than 300 – to her neighbour for 10 piastres. Her neighbour, however, had an eye for the unusual and recognized that there was a market for such ancient relics and so they came into the possession of the antiquities dealers of Cairo and Alexandria and from there began trickling into the museum collections of Europe and America. At first the almost perfectly preserved tablets were dismissed as fakes until E.A. Wallis Budge (1857–1934), an assistant curator at the British Museum in London, acquired a number of them. Wallis Budge was a brilliant linguist and immediately recognized that the script on the tablets was cuneiform and the language Akkadian – the international diplomatic language of the Mediterranean Bronze Age. Translating the writing, he noted:

'on the largest and best written ... I was able to make out the words "A-na Ni-ib-mu-a-ri-ya", i.e., "To Nibmuariya," and on another the words "[A]-na Ni-im-mu-ri-ya shar matu Mi-is-ri," i.e., "to Nimmuriya, king of the land of Egypt". ... I felt certain that the tablets were both genuine and of very great historical importance.'

On this stone stele relief, Akhenaten and his family are shown worshipping Aten, the giant disc of the sun. The 'Great Hymn to the Aten' composed during Akhenaten's reign refers to the deity as 'O Sole God beside Whom There is None'.

THE AMARNA LETTERS

Since the initial discovery of about 300 tablets in 1887, a thorough search of museum collections, dealers' catalogues and a series of further excavations at Amarna have located a further 82. Together these form the official copies of the 'Foreign Office' correspondence of Akhenaten and his father Amenhotep III with many of the major rulers of the Middle East and their replies. The collection gives us a unique insight into the world of Bronze Age diplomacy in an era before the Trojan War.

This was a time when the Egyptian New Kingdom was wealthy and relatively peaceful and its interests extended well into the Middle East – it was Egypt's age of empire. This prosperity brought with it power and in these carefully worded letters we can build up a picture of who was who in the ancient world.

Written in the international *lingua franca* of the day – Akkadian – the letters were sent with gifts to friends and allies by couriers and included requests for goods, offers of diplomatic marriages and, of course, veiled threats to potential enemies.

One of the pharaoh's main objectives in writing was to secure diplomatic brides for his harem. Populated as it was by the daughters of kings of Mitanni, Babylon and Arzawa, the harem represented a cross section of the civilized peoples of the ancient world. Foreign wives provided a useful bargaining tool for both sides in the deal, demonstrating an alliance between states, giving the wife's country a presence at a foreign court and providing that court with cultural and political intelligence on the state from which she came.

The pharaoh's letters to the kings of the Middle East promised wealth in return for such alliances:

'The gifts I send are trivial compared with what I will send if you let me have the woman I want.'

Not every king was so easily bribed, however.

The king of Babylonia, Kadashman-Enlil, wrote in reply:

'You are asking for my daughter in marriage now, but my sister whom my father gave you was there with you and no-one saw whether she is still alive or whether she is dead.'

It is evident that Kadashman-Enlil took a dim view of the family news that was filtering through to him from Amenhotep's court. The pharaoh, however, was not a man to be crossed lightly and his response was unsympathetic:

'But have you ever sent a man here ... who knows your sister, and could speak to her and identify her?'

It seems that even the king of Babylonia was not in much of a position to bargain. He soon relented, as he knew he must, to the demands of an all-powerful Egypt:

'... As for my daughter ... about whom you wrote to me for marriage, she has become a woman; she is nubile. Just send a delegation to collect her.'

In return, he put in a bid to receive an Egyptian bride for himself:

'When I wrote to you about the possibility of my marrying your daughter you wrote to me as follows: "For ever, no daughter of a king of Egypt has been given to anyone." Why not? You are a king and do what you like. If you give her, who will say anything? ... Did you not seek brotherhood and friendship and did you not write to me about marriage so that we could become closer to each other?'

The answer was negative and the Babylonian king was realistic enough to modify his request:

'... Send me a beautiful woman as if she was your daughter. Who will be able to say "This is not the King's daughter?"'

The Amarna Letters reveal that *realpolitik* in the Bronze Age was little different from today.

Wallis Budge did not err in his assessment of the significance of these finds. What the *sebakh* digger had stumbled upon was the archive of two of ancient Egypt's greatest pharaohs, the 18th-Dynasty rulers Amenhotep III (r.1391–1350 BC) and his son Akhenaten (r.1350–1336 BC), buried in the ruins of the records office of a city which had been lost to the sands for over 3300 years. These were copies of letters written by the pharaohs to other potentates in the Middle East and their replies.

The sun king

Over three millennia earlier, Amarna had been the site of an astonishing city, Akhetaten – the 'Horizon of the Aten', as the boundary stelae called it.

Pharaoh Akhenaten had come to the throne of Egypt as Amenhotep IV in the 13th century BC at the height of a period of Egyptian civilization known as the New Kingdom (*c.*1550–1070 BC). But this pharaoh was an iconoclast and believed in a single god – the Aten, or sun disc. Accordingly, he instituted a new religion in honour of this deity in the fourth year of his reign (1346 BC).

To mark his break with thousands of years of Egyptian tradition he changed his name from Amenhotep IV to Akhenaten ('one who is effective for Aten') and, with his beautiful wife Nefertiti, founded a new city far away from the old religious centre of Thebes. He chose a virgin site where his people would be able to worship the new and singular god he had revealed to them.

On this baked clay tablet is inscribed one of the renowned Amarna letters. Written in Akkadian cuneiform script, the universal language of diplomacy at that time, it is a letter from Akhenaten to a Canaanite ruler.

German and British excavation teams have worked at the site since 1891, when the pioneering Egyptologist Sir William Flinders Petrie (1853–1942) first began to recover the plan of the city from the sand. Their work has shown that for just a few years this was an extraordinary place. Running along the Nile for 8 miles (13 km), it was nearly 3 miles (5 km) wide at its central point and was divided down the middle by a grand processional road. Its focus was the Great Temple, a unique building in Egyptian history – unlike the dark and mysterious temples of the past it was open to the air so that the sun god might shine his rays down upon the

TIMELINE

*c.*1346 BC Akhenaten and his wife Nefertiti found the religious cult city of Akhetaten (the modern city of Amarna) on the banks of the Nile 250 miles (400 km) north of Thebes (Luxor)

*c.*1338 BC Nefertiti disappears from the historical record, never to be heard of again

*c.*1336 BC Death of Akhenaten. Shortly thereafter, the Aten religion falls into disuse and the city of Akhetaten is abandoned, with the court returning to Thebes

1887 A cache of over 300 baked clay tablets inscribed in cuneiform is discovered at Amarna in Upper Egypt

1891–2 Sir William Flinders Petrie investigates the Great Temple of the Aten at Amarna

1907 The *Deutsche Orient-Gesellschaft* (German Oriental Society) under the leadership of Ludwig Borchardt begins excavation of the city of Amarna (to 1914), finding the bust of Nefertiti

1921 British archaeologists from the Egypt Exploration Society begin work at Amarna. Their investigations continue to the present day

The bust of Queen Nefertiti from the workshop of the sculptor Thutmose, housed in Berlin's Altes Museum. It is the most copied of all ancient Egyptian artefacts.

believers. Akhenaten also moved his government to the city and built a bureaucratic area which included the 'House of Correspondence', where the Amarna letters were uncovered. Further out were the suburbs where the citizens lived, rich and poor, all together without any apparent segregation. Closer to the mountains a purpose-built workmen's village housed the tomb builders whose job it was to cut suitably lavish tombs into the living rock of the cliff and then decorate them.

Nothing, however, could compete for sheer splendour with the four palaces. The royal estates of Akhenaten covered an area greater than the extravagant French châteaux at Fontainebleau and Versailles combined. The floors and walls of the palaces were decorated with images of flowers and birds, families taking lunch, fathers playing with children and lovers courting in the shade of sweet-scented incense trees.

Praise to the new deity

In the palace halls a new form of poetry could be heard, devised – some claimed – by the king himself. Its stanzas praised the one god and rejoiced in the natural world he had created, in tones which echoed down through the centuries to find expression again in the biblical song of Solomon. For example the 'Great Hymn to the Aten' reads:

'When you rise from the horizon the earth grows bright ...
When your rays gleam forth, the whole of Egypt is festive.
People wake and stand on their feet
For you have lifted them up ...

... All the cattle enjoy their pastures,
Trees and plants grow green,
Birds fly up from their nests
And raise their wings in praise of your spirit.
Goats frisk on their feet,
And the fluttering and flying things come alive
Because you shine on them ...'

However, the city of Akhetaten was to be a short-lived dream. The pharaoh's new religion was not the popular success he had hoped for. The old gods of Egypt and the wealthy temple institutions that promoted them were not easily set aside in this very conservative civilization. After the pharaoh's death his religion, his city and even his memory rapidly began to collapse. In a violent backlash against his faith, his name was hacked off the monuments, his temples were razed to the ground and his city was abandoned, its inhabitants drifting back to the old capital at Thebes. Here a new young pharaoh was busy restoring the old order (or at least having the old order restored in his name). His name was Tutankhamun (see pages 134–41).

LUDWIG BORCHARDT AND NEFERTITI

In early December 1912 a German archaeologist and founder of the German Archaeological Institute in Cairo, Ludwig Borchardt (1863–1938), was supervising excavations in a then unidentified area of Amarna.

On 6 December his foreman, Mohammed Ahmes es-Senussi, was digging in room 19 on grid square P47 (the whole site had been laid out in a grid to assist in mapping) when he noticed a patch of bright blue and yellow in the pit beneath him. Brushing away the sand, he discovered what appeared to be part of a carved and painted necklace. Borchardt was not on hand, although accounts vary as to whether he was away from the site or simply sleeping off his lunch in a hammock in his site hut, so Professor Ranke, who was supervising in his absence, scrawled a note and ordered it dispatched to Borchardt at once.

When Borchardt arrived, his foreman had uncovered what was clearly an intact limestone bust, about 50 centimetres (20 in) tall, buried head down. As the sand was removed, the bust was finally lifted into the foreman's hands and photographed for the first time. What that photograph captured was the first glimpse for over 3000 years of what many people claim is the greatest work of art surviving from the ancient world – the bust of Nefertiti. Borchardt was speechless. That night he simply wrote in his diary:

'Description is useless – see for yourself.'

Three millennia earlier, room 19 on grid square P47 had been the workshop of the master sculptor Thutmose. Here, in around 1345 BC, he had carved this exquisite image of his queen, inlaid her necklace with lapis lazuli and her eyes with rock crystal and then painted the stone with such life-like brilliance that she appears to have stepped, living, from the deep past out into the modern world.

Quite why this beautiful work of art was buried remains a mystery. In the dark days following the disappearance of Nefertiti from history and the collapse of the city of Akhetaten perhaps it was a dangerous possession to have. There is also evidence that the bust was not finished, the missing inlay in the left eye apparently never having been fitted. Its subsequent arrival in Berlin, where it remains to this day, is also the subject of controversy: it has been

suggested that Borchardt deliberately underplayed, perhaps even disguised, the find to ensure that the Egyptian antiquities service would allow him to take it out of the country.

But a far greater mystery is the woman the bust depicts. Nefertiti, whose name means 'a beautiful woman has come', was the 'great wife' of the iconoclast pharaoh Akhenaten, but she was far more than just another royal queen. The intimacy of surviving depictions of Akhenaten and Nefertiti hints that theirs was more than a royal marriage of convenience. Akhenaten referred to his wife as 'sweet of love' and said 'she contents the Aten with her sweet voice'.

In the grandiose surroundings of the northern apartments of the palace, Nefertiti brought up her children. She is seen in reliefs here in happy times – playing with them and kissing them – and in the depths of despair at the funeral of a daughter. No other queen in the ancient world seems so real, so human, and no other queen's subsequent disappearance could be more mysterious.

All seemed well at Akhetaten after 12 peaceful years had passed. Year 12 itself was to be one of celebration in the city. The pharaoh's mother Queen Tiye, still one of the most important people in Egypt, was to pay a state visit, and an international pageant was to be held.

As the ambassadors arrived from around the world, Akhenaten could be confident that Egypt was still an international power. Envoys from Africa brought gold, ivory, leopards and monkeys. From the ancient African kingdom of Punt came incense, musk and sandalwood. Syrians brought chariots engraved in gold, antelope, a lion and an oryx, whilst the Minoans paraded with rows of extravagantly decorated amphorae. The Nubians were there, as were the Libyans and the Mittanians. And so was Nefertiti, sitting beside her husband, depicted now not as just a Great Wife, but a co-regent, his equal. There had never been a partnership like it.

Then, sometime in Year 12, at the height of her powers, Nefertiti simply vanished from history. Soon Atenism had crumbled, the city was gone and even the image of the beautiful Nefertiti lay face down and forgotten in a sculptor's rubbish pit.

THE SEARCH FOR THE MISSING LINK

Eugène Dubois Meets Java Man, 1890

Charles Darwin's *On the Origin of Species by Means of Natural Selection*, published in 1859, provided a biological counterpart for the works of the early geologists and archaeologists who had become convinced that the earth must be far older than was claimed in the Bible. It also presented them with an intriguing possibility. If humans really did share a common ancestor with the great apes, then was it possible to find a fossil of early human-like creatures halfway between the two? This search soon became known as the hunt for the 'missing link'.

Although ancient human remains had already been found in Europe, these were (in so far as they were identifiable at the time) still of anatomically modern humans – *Homo sapiens* – or Neanderthals (whose exact relationship to modern humans is still debated). A young Dutch anatomist, Eugène Dubois (1858–1940), was convinced that if a real 'missing link' was to be found it would not be in the relatively challenging, cold climate of Europe but in the warmer conditions of the tropics. So, in 1887, he resigned his post as an anatomy lecturer in Amsterdam and took a job as a medical officer with the Dutch army in colonial Indonesia.

Dubois and his young family arrived in Sumatra in December of that year and he immediately set about using every moment away from the hospital to search for fossils, becoming in the process the first person to go looking systematically for human ancestors. Sumatra proved a difficult hunting ground, however, covered in dense jungle and poorly mapped as it was. Even after being assigned two engineers and 50 forced labourers to work with him, results were meagre; one of his engineers died and many of the unwilling workmen ran away.

A species in-between

In 1890 Dubois therefore moved his operations to Java where, he had heard, a human skull had been found by a mining engineer in 1888. Having recruited two more engineers and a labour gang made up of convicts, he began searching the area where the first skull had been found and soon began to locate small quantities of

human remains. Then in September, along the Bengawan Solo River at Trinil, he hit a much richer seam, uncovering the right side of a human-like chin and jaw with three teeth still attached. Searching the gravel of the Solo River was painfully slow and it was the following August before another molar was uncovered and a further two months before the skullcap that would become known as Java Man was uncovered just 1 metre (3 ft) away. Another ten months would pass before an almost complete left thighbone was found at the same site.

An illustration of what was once thought to be the 'missing link' following the discovery of 'Neanderthal Man' in 1856. It was, in fact, a species of Homo *that lived 24,000 years ago.*

101

PILTDOWN MAN AND THE MISSING LINK

The search for the human 'missing link' was a direct product of Darwin's publication of his theory of natural selection and led to one of the greatest archaeological hoaxes of the 20th century.

Charles Dawson brought the Piltdown Man fossil to world attention at a meeting of the Geological Society of London in 1912. He claimed that a workman from the Piltdown quarry near Uckfield in Sussex, southeast England, had handed him a fragment of a skull in 1908 and that he had visited the site and found further pieces. He had shown them to the keeper of the geological department at the British Museum in London and the two men had returned to the site, where they found yet more pieces of the skull and half of the lower jaw.

When the bones were reconstructed at the museum they found that the skull case, although fragmentary, seemed to be about two-thirds the size of a modern skull but the jaw, despite its human-like molar teeth, was otherwise very similar to that of a chimpanzee. This should perhaps have come as a surprise to the members of the Geological Society and anyone else interested in human evolution, but it did not. In fact, it was exactly what they had been looking for. The theory of the day suggested that human evolution was led by an increase in brain capacity, so a creature with a large brain but a primitive jaw filled the role of 'missing link' perfectly.

Not everyone was happy with the discovery, however. Many of the important diagnostic parts of the skull, such as the articulations between jaw and skull base, were missing, making it difficult to see how such a 'primitive' jaw had attached to a large skull. Furthermore, a reconstruction of the badly damaged skull case by the Royal College of Surgeons produced a skull not two-thirds the capacity of a modern one, but almost indistinguishable from a modern one. That the debate raged over the Piltdown fossil for so long

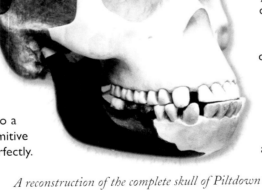

A reconstruction of the complete skull of Piltdown Man. The authenticity of Dawson's 'discovery' was challenged almost from the outset, but it took more than 40 years to prove that is was a fraud.

is partly to do with the lack of scientific techniques available at the time of its discovery and partly to do with people's reluctance to give up on something they had been seeking for so long.

It was 1953 before proof that the find was a forgery was published. It had been observed that one of the molar teeth sloped at an angle different from the others; examination under a microscope showed that it had been filed down. Piltdown Man had not been found, he had been created. Carbon-14 dating has since shown that the jaw was that of a 500-year-old orang-utan from Sarawak on the island of Borneo, the teeth were from a fossil chimpanzee and the skull was a Medieval human specimen. Where the pieces fitted badly – for example the teeth, which were a different shape from a human's – they had been filed to fit and crucial areas that would have easily identified the fraud, such as the jaw articulation, had simply been snapped off. The whole 'fossil' had then been stained in iron solution and chromic acid to give it a unified appearance.

The forger's identity remains a mystery and no-one has ever claimed responsibility. Charles Dawson is an obvious suspect, as are some of his collaborators. The discovery in 1970 of a trunk left in storage at the Natural History Museum in London by the palaeontologist Martin Hinton (1883–1961) has added to the puzzle. It contained animal bones filed and stained in a manner similar to the Piltdown remains, so Hinton has also come under suspicion. Why the hoax was perpetrated is even less clear. It may have been a practical joke, aimed at the establishment, which got so far out of hand that no-one dared own up. What it has shown is that archaeologists and anthropologists should be wary of developing ideas and then looking for evidence to prove them; rather, they should allow the finds to speak for themselves.

Dubois realized that the remains he had, albeit fragmentary, represented neither a modern ape nor a modern human but were, in his words:

'a species in-between human and apes.'

He was soon convinced that he had found exactly what he had been looking for, his 'missing link', and when he published his results in 1894 he gave the creature the Latin name *Pithecanthropus erectus*, meaning 'the upright apeman'. The following year he returned to Europe and set about publicizing his discovery, lecturing widely on the fossils, but he was met with what seemed to him an incomprehensible indifference. To many of the archaeologists, anthropologists and anatomists of Europe his finds were too fragmentary to be definitive. Some argued that they were clearly the remains of some form of giant ape, others that they were obviously human. Despite Dubois arguing that this difference of opinion rather proved his point, the controversy failed to die down and his ideas only found limited acceptance. In particular, he was unable to prove that the pieces of bone taken from the river gravel belonged to the same animal, and even today there are still arguments over how many individuals (of how many different species) are represented by the group he collectively called *Pithecanthropus*.

Discoveries at Dragon Bone Hill

Dubois eventually became disillusioned with the debate and in 1900 abruptly withdrew from it, locking the fossils away in his home and preventing any further access to them. It was 1923 before he grudgingly brought Java Man back into public view, just as a new spate of discoveries was about to be made. That year in China, excavations in limestone caves at Dragon Bone Hill at Zhoukoudian, near Beijing, began unearthing human-like bones. Over the next 13 years more than 40 specimens, including six nearly complete skullcaps, were excavated at the site and given the name *Sinanthropus pekinensis*. The work here only ceased in 1937 with the Japanese occupation of Beijing, the year after another fossil attributed to *Pithecanthropus* was unearthed in Java.

Many archaeologists and anatomists now began to note similarities between these new specimens and those of Dubois, but by then the world-weary Dubois seemed reluctant to accept the late recognition. He even went to great lengths to try to prove that the new Chinese and Javanese specimens were not *Pithecanthropus*. In his mind, only his precious fossils were the real thing.

Eugène Dubois died in 1940, still adamant that he had not received the official recognition he deserved. Since then his finds, along with the later Javanese fossils and those from Dragon Bone Hill, have been reclassified – just as Dubois believed – as belonging to *Homo erectus*, an extinct species of the genus *Homo* to which modern humans (*Homo sapiens*) belong. Exactly how *Homo erectus* fits into human evolution is still debated, with two schools of thought arguing over whether modern humans replaced *Homo erectus* populations or developed locally from them. What is beyond dispute is the importance of Dubois's work in bringing these early hominids to world attention; in particular, his discovery of Java Man provided the first vital fossil evidence corroborating Darwin's theory of natural selection in ancient humans.

TIMELINE

1859 Charles Darwin's publication of *On the Origin of Species by Means of Natural Selection* revolutionizes understanding of human evolution. His work implies that humans must share primitive ancestors with the apes

1891 Eugène Dubois discovers the fossil remains of an early hominid, which he names *Pithecanthropus erectus*, at Trinil on the banks of the Bengawan Solo River on Java. His discovery is largely ignored

1912 The discovery of a supposed early hominid fossil at Piltdown in southern England seems to prove the link between humans and apes, but is later unmasked as a hoax

1923–7 Excavations at Zhoukoudian in China unearth another example of the early hominid species *Homo erectus*. This find is popularly referred to as 'Peking Man'. Anthropologists begin to realize Java Man may be an early human ancestor

1924–5 Fossil evidence begins to come to light, in southern and eastern Africa, of an even earlier ancestral genus for modern humans, *Australopithecus*

1959 The Leakey family of anthropologists (Louis, Mary, Richard and Meave) embarks on a remarkable series of discoveries of hominid fossils up to 1.75 million years old in the Great Rift Valley in Kenya and Tanzania

1973 The remains of *Australopithecus afarensis*, the earliest hominid to date are found in the Afar region of Ethiopia. They take the human family tree back to around 3 million years ago

'THE MOST BEAUTIFUL WOMAN IN THE WORLD'
Unearthing the Lady of Elx, 1897

At 11.15 on the morning of 4 August 1897, the pickaxe wielded by Manuel Campello Esclápez hit something hard. It had already been a difficult morning's work at L'Alcúdia, just south of the city of Elx in Valencia, eastern Spain, and with the sun rising ever higher Esclápez was not looking forward to hauling out another boulder. Yet further digging revealed not a boulder but a semicircle of stones; as he cleared the sand from between them, a face stared back at him.

The area where Esclápez and his fellow farm labourers were digging that day had an archaeological pedigree. It had once been the site of the Roman settlement of Illici Augusta Colonia Julia, and from time to time small Roman artefacts were thrown up by ploughing, earning a few pesetas for the finder from local antiquarians. This was something special, however, and Esclápez was keen to discover just what it was he had found. The face, clearly a stone sculpture, had been placed in a semicircular stone box or cist, which had been filled with beach sand, making the digging easy and preserving the object wonderfully. But when he eventually hauled out the 0.5-metre- (1.6-ft-) tall bust, it was not the Roman statue he had hoped for. It was much more. This was a face from an earlier time – the fifth or fourth century BC – when the area had been known as Helike to the Iberian tribes who had settled there.

The discovery of this extraordinarily well-preserved bust caused an immediate furore. Just two weeks after being unearthed it was sold for the princely sum of 4000 French francs (about £20 today) to the French collector Pierre Paris, and 12 days later it was packed aboard a steamer and dispatched to the Louvre Museum in Paris. Spain would not see the Lady of Elx, as the bust had become known, for another 44 years.

The Second World War finally brought the Lady of Elx home to Spain. Removed from display in the Louvre as the Nazis invaded Paris, the bust was taken south and hidden in the unoccupied, Vichy-governed part of France. In 1941 that government decided to return the Lady to Spain in exchange for a tapestry and two paintings by Velázquez and El Greco. But the statue did not return to Elx; until 1971 it was held in Madrid's Prado Museum before moving to the National Archaeological Museum, also in the capital.

The Lady of Elx. Some people have argued that she is, in fact, a man, while others insist she is an Art Nouveau fake, but the prevailing view is that she is that rarest of things – a face from Spain's pre-Roman past.

TIMELINE

100 BC The Greek traveller Artemidorus visits Spain and describes the surviving pre-Roman culture of its people

AD 1897 (4 August) Farm labourers unearth a beautifully preserved ancient polychromed limestone Iberian bust. It is initially dubbed *La Reina Mora* ('The Moorish Queen') but later rechristened the Lady of Elx (*La Dama de Elche*)

1897 (30 August) Pierre Paris ships the sculpture to France, where it is displayed in the Louvre in Paris

1941 (27 June) The Lady of Elx, repatriated to Spain by the government of Vichy France, is installed at the Prado Museum in the Spanish capital Madrid

1971 The bust is given a permanent home at the National Archaeological Museum in Madrid

1995 John Moffitt questions the authenticity of the bust in his work *Art Forgery: The Case of the Lady of Elche*

2006 The Lady of Elx is put on display from May to November in the town near where she was found. A ongoing campaign aims to have the sculpture returned to Elx permanently

Priestess or aristocrat?

Throughout this time, academics had been pondering the identity of the Lady of Elx. Because she was found in the course of farm work and not on an excavation there is very little archaeological evidence to provide more clues.

The slight asymmetry in the face, which was once brightly painted but now retains only a hint of red on the lips and clothing, suggests that the bust was modelled on a real woman, perhaps a priestess or member of a royal family. The back of the statue contains a circular cavity, which has been interpreted as a place for offerings or possibly even for the ashes of the woman depicted.

Yet the most notable thing about her is her headdress, and it is this that may reveal her identity. On either side of her head are carved what appear to be large, hollow drums which probably held her hair, plaited and coiled into spirals. When the Roman geographer Strabo (*c*.64 BC–AD 23) was describing Spain he mentioned in passing something the Greek traveller Artemidorus had apparently noticed when he visited the country in around 100 BC:

> '*One might also class as barbaric in character the ornaments of some of the women, of which Artemidorus has told us. In some places, he says, they wear round their necks iron collars which have curved rods that bend overhead and project far in front of their foreheads; and at will they draw their veil down over these curved rods, so that the veil, thus spread out, furnishes a sunshade for the face; and all this they consider an ornament. In other places, he says, the women wear round their heads a 'tympanium', rounded to the back of the head, and, as far as the ear lobes, binding the head tightly, but gradually turned back at the top and sides; and other women keep the hair stripped from the forepart of the head so closely that it glistens more than the forehead does; and still other women put a rod about a foot high on the head, twist the hair round the rod, and then drape it with a black veil.*'

The Spain that Artemidorus visited was already part of the Roman world, but the culture he described had a longer pedigree and the Lady of Elx seems to be wearing an early version of the elaborate headdresses he describes. She is thought to have hailed from a period when the only visitors to Spain's shores were Phoenician and Carthaginian merchants. Her elaborate clothing, her jewellery and the fine headdress (which probably would have been metal) suggest she was a member of the élite from one of the Celtiberian tribes. These people had arisen from an intermingling of native Iberian cultures and Celtic invaders who had been moving into the area from France since the Bronze Age. Each group seems to have been based around an aristocratic warrior élite who controlled each area from a fortified hilltop known as a *castro*. Some of these fortresses later developed into larger cities of the type Artemidorus visited and where he perhaps encountered the descendants of the Lady of Elx.

Beyond that, her identity remains a mystery, although few in Spain would disagree with surrealist artist Salvador Dalí's simple assessment:

> '*She is the most beautiful woman in the world.*'

WHO OWNS THE PAST?

The quick sale and removal of the Lady of Elx from Spain highlights one of the most difficult questions in archaeology – who owns the past? The Lady of Elx was found on private land and thus the owner had, under the laws of the day, every right to sell her to whomever he chose, whether inside or outside Spain. In this case, after the export of the bust the governments of France and Spain agreed to a 'swap' to return national treasures to their homelands, but even now many of the people of Elx feel 'their' lady should be on permanent display in their city rather than in the National Archaeological Museum in Madrid.

Arguments over where archaeological artefacts belong reach far beyond Elx, however. The world's museums are full of artefacts from other countries, some bought, some donated and some taken as the spoils of war. In a few cases these items might have perished had they remained *in situ*, or may never have come to light in the first place. But the question of who owns them, who has the right to buy and sell them and where anything actually 'belongs' remains a controversial issue.

Perhaps most famously, the pediment statues, metope panels and frieze from the Parthenon in Athens (sometimes known as the Elgin Marbles) have been a source of some tension between the UK and Greece ever since Lord Elgin removed them from Athens to London in 1806. From Elgin's point of view he had every right to take them, for he had authority to do so from the (then Turkish) authorities in Greece. But even in England their arrival was not universally welcomed, the poet Lord Byron writing:

*'Dull is the eye that will not weep to see
Thy walls defaced, thy mouldering shrines removed
By British hands, which it had best behoved
To guard those relics ne'er to be restored.'*
BYRON, *Childe Harold's Pilgrimage* (1812–18)

The argument is never simple. From the perspective of the British Museum in London, where the marbles are currently displayed, their return might set a precedent whereby all artefacts taken from other countries have to be returned, making comparative collections such as theirs impossible. The museum's cases would be left with just British artefacts, and the Egyptian mummies, the 'Benin bronzes', the Greek vases and Roman mosaics that make it one of the greatest collections on earth would all be gone. The museum authorities regard their holdings as a 'world heritage collection', a single resource where works from many countries can be studied and cross-referenced.

There is also the question as to what would happen to the marbles if they were returned, or indeed what would have happened to them had they never been removed. Those parts of the frieze that were left in place have been badly damaged by the polluted atmosphere of Athens, a fate that has not befallen the panels in London. Even if they were to be returned now, they would have to be placed in a museum near the Parthenon, not back in position – an event for which the Greek government is already planning. Finally, the British Museum points out that the legal terms of its charter prevent it from returning anything currently in its collection (with the exception of human remains which can be repatriated for interment). All of this, however, has to be weighed against Greece's strong moral claim to a work of art created in and intended for that country.

The claims on artefacts taken from their homelands in the past are perhaps matters for politicians to decide, but modern archaeologists must deal with the ownership of items they uncover. The best model for this was set early on in the history of archaeology: in 1875 the Greek and German authorities agreed that Greece would keep any items found during German excavations at Olympia but that the excavators would retain the right to publish their findings. Today the finds from Olympia can be seen in a purpose-built museum on site, while the results of the excavations there are available in libraries around the world. In this case certainly, few would disagree that this is the best solution.

THE REALM OF THE MINOTAUR

Arthur Evans at Knossos, 1899

The north entrance to the Palace of Minos at Knossos on Crete. This part of the complex is an extreme example of the speculative reconstruction work undertaken by Arthur Evans, which was sometimes based on no original evidence.

'*Pasiphae gave birth to Asterios, who was called Minotauros. He had the face of a bull, but was otherwise human. Minos, following certain oracular instructions, kept him confined and under guard in the labyrinth.*'

APOLLODORUS, *The Library* 3.8-11

Excavations at Troy, Mycenae and Tiryns by Heinrich Schliemann (1822–90) had brought to light a previously unknown late Bronze Age civilization that pre-dated classical Greece and given it a name – Mycenaean (*c.*1600–1100 BC). (See pages 78–83.) But as is so often the case in archaeology, finding an answer to one question only succeeded in giving rise to another – namely, what had Mycenaean civilization developed from?

Crete holds the key

Schliemann himself believed the answer might lie on the island of Crete, home to the legendary King Minos and the Minotaur. His particular interest focused on a site at Kephála discovered in 1878 and partially excavated by the Cretan merchant and antiquarian, Minos Kalokairinos. This work had revealed a long room filled with huge storage jars (*pithoi*) and pottery of a type similar to that found at Mycenae. Schliemann had even got a permit to excavate here but had been frustrated by the exorbitant fees charged by the site owner. And so, on his death in 1890, Kephála remained an enigma.

Moreover, Crete at this time was an island in crisis as it struggled to break away from Ottoman Turkish rule. A further eight abortive attempts were made to dig there before Arthur Evans (1851–1941), then curator of the Ashmolean Museum in Oxford, England, arrived in the newly independent country in 1899 and began work. Evans had been fascinated by a number of seal stones found in Crete bearing an untranslated script that he believed might be the language of the earliest Greek civilization. At Kephála he hoped to find evidence of this culture. He was not to be disappointed.

Evans's excavations proved spectacular from the start. In the first nine weeks he uncovered over 0.8 hectares (2 acres) of a massive palace complex – the centre of an almost entirely forgotten civilization. The only clues to just who these people were had come from the dimly remembered stories and legends of ancient Greece. In deference to these myths, Evans named the building he had uncovered 'the palace of Minos'.

THE MINOANS

Despite a century of archaeology, the Minoans remain elusive. Their language is still undeciphered and we do not even know what they called themselves (though contemporary Egyptian records call Crete 'Keftiu'). Foreign records and finds of Minoan pottery in Egypt, Cyprus, Syria, mainland Greece and Spain suggest they were a trading people, and extensive archaeological work on the island has shown that their culture was based around a number of 'palace' complexes. Who ruled these palaces and whether, as Evans believed, Knossos was the dominant site is unknown.

Minoan civilization flourished in the Aegean Bronze Age (c.2800–1100 BC) and much of its wealth came from trading tin (which alloyed with copper made bronze) and other prestigious commodities such as saffron.

Frescoes and statuary found at Knossos show Minoan men wearing loincloths and short kilts, while women wore short-sleeved robes with flounced skirts and fitted bodices adorned with colourful geometric designs. Art seems to have played an important part in Minoan life, with walls and pottery often highly decorated. Early designs generally comprised spirals and zigzags, but these were later supplanted by more naturalistic portrayals of animals, plants and sea creatures such as octopuses, dolphins and fish.

Paintings also give some clues to the beliefs of the Minoans. The famous bull-jumping frescoes show young men and women vaulting over the horns of a bull. Despite the excellent state of preservation of Knossos, no building that can be definitively called a temple has been found there. Instead, a large number of votive offerings have been found in caves around the island. The vast majority of the statues found at such sites are of

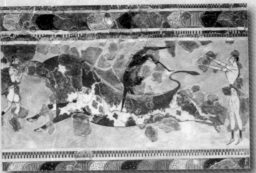

A fresco from Knossos showing bull jumping. This dangerous activity, thought to have been part of a religious rite, may have taken place in the open courtyards of the palace complexes.

female figures, suggesting that the Minoans worshipped a Mother Goddess or a pantheon of female deities. More contentiously, the discovery of four bodies – one apparently bound – in the 'temple' at Anemospilia near Heraklion, which seems to have collapsed in mid-ritual during an earthquake, has led to speculation that the Minoans practised human sacrifice. The bones of four children from the North House at Knossos also bear butchery marks which have been cited as further evidence that humans were sacrificed and eaten. However, at Anemospilia it has proved impossible to show that the 'victim' was not another celebrant who died, like the others, from the collapse of the building, while the children at Knossos may have had the flesh removed from their bones after death as part of their funerary rite.

The decline of Minoan civilization is also shrouded in mystery. At several points in their history, the palace complexes on Crete suffered devastating damage – possibly caused by earthquakes resulting from the eruption of Thera, or by invading forces – but each time they were rebuilt. Around 1420 BC there is evidence for Mycenaean influence in Crete. Certainly, from this period onwards, the Linear A script of the Minoans is taken and used for Linear B – the Mycenaean Greek language.

The final decline of the Minoans took place in the following century, however, and may have its roots in economics. As the new iron technology spread across the Mediterranean, the Minoan tin trade grew progressively less viable. For a civilization whose rise had depended upon its control of a vital constituent of bronze, the demise of the Bronze Age and the dawning of the Iron Age may have done more to end the palace era than any invasion or natural disaster.

When Evans published his first findings in 1901, it seemed in the popular imagination as though the legend of the Minotaur had come to life. The ancient Greek myth told of a ferocious beast – half man and half bull – that inhabited a labyrinth built by the architect Daedalus under the palace of King Minos. Each year (or, in some versions, every nine years) the people of Athens were forced to send seven boys and seven maidens to be devoured by the beast, until one year the hero Theseus came and slew the creature with a magic sword, escaping the labyrinth by retracing a thread given to him by Minos's daughter Ariadne.

The labyrinthine home of the Minotaur

Now here at Knossos was a palace so large and strangely laid out that is appeared to many to be a labyrinth. Even the term 'labyrinth' seemed particularly apposite here, since the word derived from the Lydian *labrys* – meaning 'double-headed axe' – a symbol that appeared frequently on the plastered walls Evans found in the palace. And this was by no means the only wall decoration.

On the rubble-strewn floors of many rooms, Evans found fragments of brightly painted plaster. With the help of the Dutch artist Piet de Jong, it proved possible to piece these together into whole scenes, although just how accurate some of these reconstructions are is still a matter of debate. Evans's conduct at Knossos was not uncontroversial and his passionate, single-minded approach sometimes antagonized his peers. He argued with and eventually fired his assistant Duncan Mackenzie (1861–1934), hastening his most dedicated supporter's sad decline into mental illness. When his fellow archaeologist Alan Wace (1879–1956) refused to accept Evans's ideas that there was a single timeline for the rise and fall of the civilizations that preceded classical Greek culture, Evans used his influence to end his digging career in Greece. In addition to restoring the frescoes, he also insisted on reconstructing parts of the site using concrete where the original construction was no longer present. Aside from causing manifold conservation problems, as the reinforced concrete deteriorates, this led to accusations that he had 'Disneyfied' Knossos – letting his imagination take the place of strict archaeological evidence. However, the day books that were meticulously kept by Mackenzie, plus Evans's own extensive publication of the site, generally allow us to separate the facts from his occasional flights of fancy. One can perhaps also forgive a man who dedicated his life to uncovering a lost civilization for wanting to allow visitors to Knossos to imagine themselves walking through the labyrinthine home of the Minotaur.

Despite the more fanciful reconstructions, the frescoes Evans found provided a fascinating new insight into the culture of the ancient inhabitants of Knossos. Some frescoes, for example, showed young men and women involved in a ritual known as 'bull jumping' – seizing a bull by the horns and vaulting over its back. Was the legend of the Minotaur perhaps a half-forgotten memory of this strange bull cult celebrated in the maze-like rooms of Knossos?

The striking similarity to the legend of King Minos brought immediate recognition for Evans's work and even gave a name to this previously

TIMELINE

*c.*2800 BC Minoan civilization emerges in the Mediterranean

*c.*1600 BC Minoan civilization flourishes on Crete and surrounding islands in the Aegean Sea

*c.*1350 BC The spread of ironworking around the region heralds the demise of Minoan civilization, which gained its wealth from exporting tin for use in the alloy bronze

AD 1883 German archaeologist Arthur Milchhöfer is the first person to suggest the existence of an advanced Bronze Age civilization on Crete

1894 Minos Kalokairinos, who had been investigating the site at Knossos since 1878, unearths two storerooms of the palace. Arthur Evans makes his first journey to Crete and meets Kalokairinos

1900 (23 March) Evans begins his excavations of the palace ruins at Knossos, discovering some 3000 clay tablets with inscriptions, plus many other artefacts

1901 Evans publishes the first findings from his archaeological work at Knossos, in *Scripta Minoa* (Volume 1)

1952 Michael Ventris deciphers Linear B, the written language of the Mycenaeans

A 'Snake Goddess' figurine found by Arthur Evans in the storehouse of the central sanctuary at the Palace of Minos at Knossos. Made of faience, this artefact dates from around 1600 BC.

unknown civilization – Minoan. But there was more to Knossos than just giving a location to a myth. The 'Great Palace', as it became known, had clearly been the centre of a unique culture with a long history. Its 1300 rooms, covering 20,000 square metres (215,260 sq ft), had been constructed between 1700 and 1300 BC and displayed evidence of a high degree of sophistication. The whole palace complex was equipped with its own terracotta plumbing and sewerage system and included a theatre, a room with an exquisite gypsum chair that Evans called the 'Throne Room' (but which may have had a religious use), grain mills, oil and wine presses and huge 'magazines' of storage *pithoi*. In places the structure was five storeys tall, supported on painted columns and fitted with ingenious air ducts to allow cooling sea breezes to penetrate into the heart of the palace in hot Mediterranean summers.

A female-dominated society?

Frescoes and finds in the rooms afforded further glimpses into the lives of the people of Knossos. There is very little evidence of warfare in their art, and the walls and even the pottery were decorated not with military processions – as in many contemporary Near Eastern societies – but with scenes of sea creatures, fishing and flower gathering. For example, a fresco from the Aegean island of Santorini (Thera) north of Crete shows Minoan saffron gatherers. The fact that women are depicted in Minoan art more frequently than men, along with Evans's discovery of a female figure holding two snakes (which he identified as a Minoan goddess) has led to suggestions that this was a female-dominated society, or at least one in which the status of women was far higher than elsewhere in the ancient world.

The Minoans were also clearly literate, as Evans had suspected, and he uncovered over 3000 clay tablets inscribed with scripts similar to those he had first seen on the seal stones. These inscriptions were written in two distinct languages, known as Linear A and Linear B, the latter being the early Greek script of the Mycenaeans and the former the language of the Minoans themselves. Sadly for Evans, Linear B was not deciphered in his lifetime, so their accounts of Mycenaean rule at Knossos remained unknown to him. To this day, Linear A has still not been fully deciphered.

Unlike Schliemann, Evans was not put off by the costs of excavating Knossos. Indeed, he purchased the entire site in 1901 to guarantee its preservation. His own excavations there continued for eight full seasons, followed by many more smaller campaigns. By the end of his work in Crete he had established the continuous occupation of Knossos from the Neolithic (New Stone Age) through the rise and fall of the Bronze Age Minoan civilization and its Mycenaean successor to Roman occupation of the area – a timespan of over 4000 years. He had also restored to the world a civilization that had drifted into myth even by the time of the classical Greeks and named it Minoan in recognition of the myth that had preserved the last memory of this culture.

MICHAEL VENTRIS AND THE DECIPHERMENT OF LINEAR B

The saddest part of Arthur Evans's career was that he died still unable to translate the strange glyphs that had first brought him to Knossos and which he later found inscribed on thousands of clay tablets at the site. It was during one of his lectures on this most stubborn of mysteries however that a 14-year-old English schoolboy, Michael Ventris (1922–56), decided to try to solve the puzzle that eluded Evans all his life.

Ventris did not intend to become an archaeologist or linguist but pursued the decipherment of the language Evans called Linear B as a hobby. His first venture into the subject came just four years after Evans's talk when, still only 18, Ventris wrote an article for the *American Journal of Archaeology* suggesting the language might be related to Etruscan. The Second World War interrupted his work, however, and after serving as a navigator in the Royal Air Force he returned to his chosen career as an architect.

Nevertheless, Ventris did not neglect his hobby, and corresponded with academics all over the world on the subject of Linear B, issuing monthly reports on his own laborious work on the script. With the publication in 1951 of a large number of Linear B tablets found at Pylos in Greece, Ventris suddenly found himself with a great deal more material at his disposal. He developed a grid into which he began inserting the 90 or so syllabic signs of the language, looking to connect them and showing that many shared the same vowels – although he had no way of saying what sound that vowel made. It was painfully slow work, but with the connections in place all Ventris needed was to know the value of a few signs and the rest could be inferred from his grid of connections. When Ventris finally identified a group of signs as Cretan place names, he had the key he was looking for and could begin to crack the code.

To his great surprise what he found was that Linear B was not related to Etruscan but to an early form of Greek. The Mycenaeans who used it – the people described by Homer – were indeed the Greek-speaking ancestors of the classical period. After tentatively suggesting this revolutionary decipherment in a private letter in June 1952, his confidence rapidly grew and a month later he announced his theory publicly. Aware that he was not a professional linguist, and with great modesty, he immediately set about contacting Greek scholars for help, including the young Cambridge academic John Chadwick (1920–98) and the two published their decipherment in 1953. Initially the work was greeted with scepticism but the publication the following year of another tablet which could immediately be read using Ventris's technique brought general acceptance from the academic world that one of the greatest problems in ancient studies had finally been solved – and by an amateur at that, albeit an astonishingly gifted and patient one.

With the language of Homer's heroes now deciphered, a new era in Greek studies opened up. The reading of Linear B forced a radical reinterpretation of the relationship between Crete and mainland Greece as well as giving new insights into the operation of Mycenaean palaces, agriculture and trade. Ventris was awarded the OBE and an honorary doctorate but tragically he would not live long enough to receive the acclaim his brilliant work deserved. Michael Ventris died alone in the early hours of 6 September 1956 in a car accident outside Hatfield in Hertfordshire. He was only 34 years old.

In 1924 Evans donated Knossos to the British School at Athens, which he had helped found, his villa on the site becoming the home of the curator. Back in England, his discoveries brought him wide acclaim. He was the fourth successive generation of his family to be elected a fellow of the Royal Society and he received honorary degrees from Dublin, Edinburgh and Berlin as well as a knighthood. Filled with boundless energy for most of his life, his travels were curtailed in 1938 following an operation, after which he contented himself with archaeological investigations closer to his home of Youlbury near Oxford. He died there in 1941, three days after his 90th birthday.

A CLOCKWORK UNIVERSE

The Recovery of the Antikythera Mechanism, 1900

'*Why, if any one were to carry into Scythia or Britain the globe which our friend Posidonius has lately constructed, each one of the revolutions of which brings about the same movement in the sun and moon and five wandering stars as is brought about each day and night in the heavens, no one in those barbarous countries would doubt that that globe was the work of intelligence.*'

CICERO *On the Nature of the Gods* 2.34

South of the Greek mainland, between the Peloponnese and Crete, lie the islands of Kythera and its smaller neighbour Antikythera. Lying in the open waters of the Ionian Sea, Antikythera suffers the full wrath of the spring storms that appear seemingly from nowhere in this region and which have carved out its rocky and precipitous coast.

A chance discovery

Yet Antikythera is not unvisited; when the spring storms rage, it offers the only safe haven for ships in this region. So it was that, in October 1900, Captain Dimitrios Kondos and his crew of sponge divers found themselves sheltering there on their way back from Africa. As the weather cleared, the crew decided to make the most of their unplanned visit and dive for sponges and rare black coral. It was a risky dive, to a depth of over 33 fathoms (61 m/220 ft), using old-style diving suits with bronze helmets and a hand-pumped air supply, but as Aristotle had noted two millennia before, the best sponges are to be found in the deepest and most dangerous waters. The first man to dive was Elias Stadiatos, an experienced crewman, but when he resurfaced, he began babbling about horrific sights in the deep – heaps of dead women lying scattered on the sea floor.

But Stadiatos was not suffering from delirium brought on by the deep dive, so Captain Kondos ordered another man down to investigate. This second diver returned to report that what Stadiatos had seen were classical statues, the precious cargo of a centuries-old ship that had come to grief on Antikythera's wild shores.

It is unclear whether the sponge divers took any of the smaller pieces from the wreck that year, but there were reports of bronze statues of great quality suddenly coming on the market in Alexandria the following spring. Moreover, the ship's lead anchors (a vessel this size would have had five) were never found – lead is a precious commodity for divers. Yet Captain Kondos did inform the Greek authorities of his find when he next docked on the mainland and was rewarded with a government contract to return to the site and salvage it for the Greek nation.

During the summer of 1901 amazing treasures were recovered from the Antikythera wreck. There were thousand of coins, jewellery, painted Greek vases and silver dinner services. There were storage jars from ancient Rhodes, cooking utensils and even a bronze lyre. The huge boulders that lay strewn across the site proved to be marble and bronze statues, encrusted with marine growth, their exposed surfaces etched by centuries of sea water and the action of marine animals.

By 1902 investigations had yielded a lot more information about the Antikythera wreck. Pottery on board revealed it to be a first-century-BC merchant ship that had sailed from the Greek islands of Rhodes and Kos to Rome with a priceless cargo of Greek art. It has been speculated that this cargo may have been part of the booty taken by the Roman general Sulla when he sacked Athens in 86 BC. Certainly the date would fit.

Initially ignored as a shapeless lump of bronze, the Antikythera Mechanism would prove to be possibly the most extraordinary object to have survived from the ancient world.

An extraordinary find

Among the priceless treasures there was also an apparently formless lump of bronze. This odd item, with wooden panels clinging to its corroded surface, was put to one side and soon forgotten. Eventually Valerios Staïs (1857–1923), an archaeologist at the National Museum of Greece, decided to investigate the object. By now the wooden 'case' that had once enclosed it had crumbled away. What remained was a series of metal plates covered with writing. Staïs called in a specialist in Greek inscriptions, who confirmed that the script was from the first century BC. Moreover, all the legible words seemed to refer to astronomical or zodiacal terms. Beneath the inscribed plates lay something even more fascinating. Peering inside, Staïs saw what looked like intricately interconnected wheels and cogs. This forgotten lump of bronze was some sort of ancient machine.

The announcement that an ancient machine had been found on the Antikythera wreck initially provoked little more than ridicule. Kinder critics suggested that the device might be a primitive astrolabe – an astronomical navigation device known to have been in use since the seventh century BC.

TIMELINE

C.86 BC A Roman cargo ship founders and sinks off the Greek island of Antikythera

AD 1900 (October) Dimitrios Kondos and his team of sponge divers discover an ancient wreck off the island of Antikythera

1901 They begin salvage operations, bringing to the surface a large hoard of artefacts, including bronze and marble statues and a bronze lyre

1902 (May) Valerios Staïs notices that a hitherto unidentified lump of bronze and wood lifted from the wreck has a gear wheel embedded in it. Decades of study ensue on the 'Antikythera Mechanism'

1951 Derek de Solla Price publishes a paper that reveals the Antikythera Mechanism to be an ancient form of analogue computer

1974 De Solla Price publishes *Gears from the Greeks*, which proposes a model of how the mechanism may have functioned

1978 The celebrated French undersea explorer Jacques Cousteau dives the Antikythera wreck to try and find more parts of the mechanism, but is unsuccessful

2006 (30 November) Michael Wright publishes a new reconstruction of the Antikythera Mechanism based on x-ray tomography. This confirms that the mechanism could have been used to predict the positions of heavenly bodies

A diver investigates pots from a ship sunk off the coast of Turkey. The Mediterranean has yielded many archaeological treasures from the vessels of the ancient mercantile nations that once plied the region's waters.

Others dismissed the item as a Medieval instrument, lost off a much later ship that had by chance foundered near the ancient wreck. But even from the little that Staïs could make out, the object was far too complicated to be a simple astrolabe and the ancient Greek inscriptions on its face were clearly not the work of a Medieval craftsman.

It would take another 50 years for the answer to be found and then not by an archaeologist but by an English physicist. Derek de Solla Price (1922–83) began investigating the mechanism in the early 1950s. In June 1959 he published his initial findings in a paper in *Scientific American* which stunned historians and left classicists in a state of sheer disbelief. The article was entitled 'An Ancient Greek Computer'.

His paper was a sensation. What de Solla Price's reconstruction suggested was that this device was an analogue computer, easily the oldest known from anywhere in the world, which could be used to calculate the motions and positions of the stars and planets. Furthermore, the device could ascertain the rising and setting times of constellations and planets, and the phases and movements of the moon. By turning a crank handle on the outside of the wooden box, it was possible to work out the time, the day, the month, season and year. A special 'slip dial' on the mechanism even corrected for errors in the old Egyptian calendar which, without leap years, lost a quarter of a day each year.

In the early 1970s, gamma and x-ray analysis enabled de Solla Price to look deep into the mechanism, corroborating his initial hypothesis. Further studies by Michael Wright of Imperial College, London have allowed a 3D computerized model of the machine to be constructed, which suggests that it was even more sophisticated than de Solla Price had thought – in fact a fully working mechanical model of the solar system.

This device was therefore more valuable than all the rest of the cargo. It could calculate exact dates and times and model the movements of the heavens, making its owner a master of time itself. If only his ship had ever come in.

MARINE ARCHAEOLOGY

Marine archaeology is a relatively new subject that has grown out of the age-old business of salvage. At the time the Antikythera wreck was discovered, little attempt was made to explore fully or record the remains of the ship on the seabed, and the divers simply recovered whatever objects they could from the cargo. In an age before SCUBA equipment and in very dangerous diving conditions, there was little option but to salvage what could be had before the autumn storms came, with no regard to exactly where each object was found or what its relationship was to the rest of the wreck.

Back on the surface, there were several trained archaeologists on hand from the Greek antiquities service ready to identify, catalogue and attempt to preserve the items. However, the science of conservation was still in its infancy and there were many items that could not be saved. In these early years of archaeology the study of what happens to long-buried objects when they are exposed to light and air was only just beginning and the chemistry behind the processes involved was all but unknown.

Underwater sites provided an even greater challenge. Sea water has a powerfully corrosive effect on many objects, while its electrolytic properties eat away at metals. The flora and fauna of the sea bed also take their toll. Teredo worms can bore centimetre-wide holes in ships' timbers, and bacteria can quickly turn solid wood into a wet sponge of empty cells. Even the marble statues from the Antikythera wreck were attacked, not just by marine encrustations, but by shellfish slowly dissolving away the calcium in the rock to form their shells.

Modern marine archaeology has come a long way since the days of the Antikythera wreck. Shipwrecks differ from land-based archaeological sites in one crucial respect – they are the product of a moment, not years or centuries of accumulation. As such, there is rarely any stratigraphy to a shipwreck site but this does not mean that valuable archaeological information cannot be recovered from it. The spread of debris can provide important clues to the layout of the vessel and, as in a crash scene investigation, can even yield information about the ship's last moments. Today an ancient shipwreck site would be fully surveyed, photographed and perhaps even modelled in 3D on computer before any items were removed. The entire site would also be covered in a measured grid made from plastic piping to ensure that the exact location of each object was mapped before it was removed.

Modern marine archaeologists also do not have to wait on the surface for professional divers to recover items. SCUBA equipment means that they can excavate in person on the sea bed, using compressors to power air probes and vacuums to remove silt, metal detectors to locate buried items, and then airlifts to gently bring objects and structural pieces to the surface. For very deep sites beyond the reach of divers, manned or remotely operated submersible vehicles (ROVs) are now routinely used to examine and explore wreck sites.

Back on the surface, the world of conservation has also been revolutionized. In recent years, it has been possible to lift and preserve not just objects from wrecks but the ships themselves, such as the *Vasa* in Stockholm, Sweden and the *Mary Rose* (see pages 180–3) in Portsmouth, UK. Small wooden items can now be preserved by freeze drying, using the same techniques used in dried food production. Large-scale timbers can now be sprayed (in the cases of the *Vasa* and *Mary Rose* for many years) with a solution of the synthetic wax polyethylene glycol, which slowly replaces the water in each cell in the saturated wood, drying and stabilizing it in the process.

However, there is no room for complacency, as much information is still lost in every shipwreck excavation and even modern conservation techniques may not preserve our heritage as completely as was once hoped. Before we criticize Captain Kondos and his divers, we might well stop to think what the archaeologists of future centuries will say about our work.

FROM THE BOWELS OF THE EARTH
Malta's Hidden Prehistory, 1902

In 1902 a gang of builders were digging a well for a new housing development at Hal-Saflieni in the town of Paola on Malta. Malta and its smaller neighbouring island of Gozo are made of limestone, a rock that naturally forms underground caverns. And so, when the base of their trench collapsed, the workmen assumed they had hit upon just such a cave.

For the builders, this was a stroke of luck. Malta is the most densely inhabited part of Europe and waste disposal has always been a problem. With a handy rock cavern beneath the site, they could now dispose of their building rubble easily. But a problem immediately came to light – this supposedly 'natural' cavern was actually man-made.

An underground necropolis

Nearly three years passed before news of the find leaked out and the ethnographer and Jesuit priest, Father Manuel Magri (1851–1907) was asked to investigate on behalf of the Museums Committee. What he discovered was one of the most remarkable prehistoric sites in the world. Cut into the rock beneath Paola lay a 'hypogeum', a subterranean religious centre and burial ground. It had been cut from the living rock in imitation of temples above ground, complete with door lintels and roof beams. A complex of 20 chambers – some smoothed natural caverns, some carved from scratch – was found, descending in three levels, and with each room connected to the next by sinuous passageways.

The uppermost level lay only 10 metres (33 ft) below the surface and consisted of a series of manually enlarged natural caverns. Far back in antiquity this had become full (the remains of some 7000 people were found in the structure) and so a second level had been excavated beneath it. This was a *tour de force* of ancient engineering and has provided researchers with an unrivalled example of prehistoric architecture. The main feature of this second level was a central chamber, a roughly circular room carved out of the bedrock, whose walls were originally washed with red ochre. A number of doorways appeared to lead off from this room; some were real, while others were just carved into the stone. This main chamber housed a remarkable figure reclining on a couch, today known as the 'Sleeping Lady'. The statuette is of a woman with a tiny head and very large body, who may represent an unknown goddess from Malta's prehistoric past.

The Middle Chamber at the hypogeum of Hal-Saflieni. The stone carving here replicates architectural elements found at prehistoric temple sites above ground elsewhere on the islands of Malta and Gozo.

118

The rooms off this central chamber have all been given modern names that may or may not reflect their past use. There is the 'Oracle Room', a rectangular space painted with ochre spirals and with a small side chamber which produces a haunting echo throughout the hypogeum – hence its name. The 'Decorated Room' has further spiral patterns painted on it and an image of a human hand carved into the rock. In the 'Holy of Holies', a circular hole in the rock has been interpreted as a libation place for sacrifices, while steps in the 'Snake Pit' lead to a third level of smooth-walled caverns.

Such a find anywhere in the world from any period would be impressive enough, but what makes the Hal-Saflieni hypogeum so important is its age. At the time of its discovery, it was widely believed among archaeologists that all civilization had originated and spread out from a single source – probably in Egypt or the Middle East. The Hal-Saflieni hypogeum, however, is part of a complex of structures on Malta that have disproved this theory.

Ancient Neolithic temples

Malta is not just famous for its subterranean archaeology: 23 ancient temple sites have been found here and on Gozo. These huge stone structures were built to a common 'clover-leaf' plan and appear to have had a ritual use. They are built on a massive scale, using single stone blocks of up to 50 tons in weight, and include complex architectural features such as stone doorways, 'windows' carved in solid rocks and, at Tarxien, the remains of a female statue that must originally have stood over 3 metres (10 ft) tall. The problem with these undeniably impressive sites was that no-one knew how old they were. Clearly they were ancient, but were they the work of a 'primitive' Iron Age culture, or the first attempts at architecture to reach Malta from the Middle East? It was carbon dating that finally answered the question and its results changed our ideas about prehistory. The Malta temples and the hypogeum are not Bronze or Iron Age – they are Neolithic, and their story starts 1000 years before the Great Pyramid in Egypt. In fact, the temple at Ggantija is the oldest free-standing stone building anywhere on earth.

The realization that the civilization on a small Mediterranean island was older than that of Egypt or anywhere in the Near East has forced a radical rethink of how culture and civilizations spread. Before the Egyptian Old Kingdom had even begun, here was a culture with a unified religion (judging from the common features of the temples), which must have been trading extensively with other Mediterranean peoples.

Discovered in the main chamber on the second level of the hypogeum, the small terracotta sculpture of the Sleeping Lady shows a reclining figure with abnormally large limbs.

CARBON AND TREE-RING DATING

Radiocarbon dating, the technique used to date the Maltese temples and many other archaeological sites, was invented by Willard Frank Libby (1908–80) in 1949 and won him the Nobel Prize for Chemistry.

The concept behind the technique is as simple as it is elegant. Carbon in the biosphere usually occurs in its stable Carbon 12 (12C) form, but the action of cosmic rays on nitrogen in the upper atmosphere produces a tiny but steady amount of the radioactive Carbon 14 (14C). All living things take in carbon during their lifetime and hence the carbon in their bodies also maintains this same ratio of 12C to 14C. When a plant or animal dies, however, it stops taking in carbon and the radioactive 14C in it begins to decay back to nitrogen. This occurs at a steady exponential rate known as the half-life (the time it takes half a given quantity of a radioactive element to decay), which in the case of 14C is 5730 years. By measuring the ratio of 12C to 14C in a dead plant or animal it should be possible to see how much 14C has decayed and so work out how long it has been dead.

But not long after carbon dating was introduced it became clear that the system was not this simple. Beyond the innate statistical errors that can occur in measuring the amount of 14C, some items that could be accurately dated by other means were proving to have wildly inaccurate 14C dates. Clearly the proportion of 12C to 14C in the biosphere had not always been the same and some form of calibration was needed.

The answer came from the study of tree rings – dendrochronology. Many trees grow one ring a year and therefore by counting the number of rings between the sapwood and the middle of the trunk it is possible to find out the age of the tree. As the width of each ring varies depending on the climate in a given year in a particular region, a unique pattern forms, and this can be matched to similar patterns in the remains of older trees found in the archaeological record. Tree-ring lines can thus be extended back longer than any one tree has lived. In the case of the Californian bristle-cone pine, one tree can survive for up to 5000 years, so tree-ring chronologies for this plant extend back over 10,000 years. By taking samples of wood from the rings of such trees and carbon dating them it has been possible to calibrate the decay curve.

Today carbon dating is often carried out by accelerator facilities which actually count the proportion of 14C atoms in a sample rather than estimate their number from their radioactive decay. This produces a raw 'date' given as 'radiocarbon years BP' (Before Present) where the 'present' is set at 1950 (to ensure consistency). When the date has been calibrated it can then be expressed as real years before present (calBP) or converted into the AD and BC system and written calAD or calBC.

The value of 14C dating can hardly be over-emphasized. Not only is it now a standard tool for archaeologists to date organic remains but it has revolutionized our ideas about the past and provided whole new chronologies for events. Carbon dating has shown that civilization did not start in one place in the Near East and spread across the world, it has been used to unmask hoaxes such as Piltdown Man and has confirmed the date of spectacular finds such as the Dead Sea Scrolls. More than any other innovation, 14C has helped to disentangle the mass of archaeological evidence uncovered by excavators.

The temples and caverns were cut with picks made of local bone and antler but also axes fashioned from flint and greenstone, neither of which occurs naturally on the island. The architecture that grew up here must either be a local tradition or come from somewhere other than the traditional 'origins' of civilization. Most archaeologists now think that civilization, in the form of complex buildings, language and centralized administration, did not derive from a single source but emerged many times over in many parts of the world. Humans everywhere are ingenious and adaptable creatures and the work of those mysterious prehistoric temple builders on Malta does not need to be attributed to outside helpers. The people of Malta were quite capable of starting a complex civilization on their own.

THE WITCHERY OF THE JUNGLE
Machu Picchu, Outpost of the Incas, 1911

'*There is the fascination of finding here and there under swaying vines, or perched on top of a beetling crag, the rugged masonry of a bygone race; and of trying to understand the bewildering romance of the ancient builders who, ages ago, sought refuge in a region which appears to have been expressly designed by nature as a sanctuary for the oppressed, a place where they might fearlessly and patiently give expression to their passion for walls of enduring beauty.*'

HIRAM BINGHAM *Lost City of the Incas* (1948)

In late 1908 the 33-year-old academic Hiram Bingham III (1875–1956) was selected by Yale University to attend the First Pan-American Scientific Congress in Santiago, Chile. Bingham was an ideal choice as a delegate – a man born to missionary parents in Hawaii who loved adventure, but who also had the solid academic credentials to make the most of such a long and potentially hazardous trip.

Man on a mission

Having completed his work in Santiago by December, Bingham characteristically decided against returning straight home, but chose instead to explore further. Taking the old Spanish trade route from Buenos Aires, he made his way to Lima, the capital of Peru, and from there on to the ancient city of Cuzco, capital of the Inca empire before Europeans came to South America. As a lecturer in South American history, Bingham was fascinated by this country's pre-Columbian past and a casual mention by the prefect of the region that the Inca site of Choquekirau could be visited by those willing to undertake a reasonably arduous mountain climb inspired him. Bingham believed this might be the famous 'last refuge of the Incas' – Vilcabamba – the city hidden in the Andes to which the Incas retreated after the Spanish conquest of Cuzco, and when he returned to Cuzco in July of 1911 it was with a fully funded expedition and a definite mission. The 17th-century Spanish chronicles of Fernando de Montesinos and Antonio de la Calancha made mention of two 'lost' Inca cities in the region – Vilcabamba and Vitcos – both hidden high in the mountains. Bingham was determined to find them.

The terraced settlement of Machu Picchu is perched high on a mountainside above the Urumbamba Valley in Peru. Its remote location is thought to have preserved it from discovery and destruction by Spanish forces when they overran the Inca empire in the mid-16th century.

From Cuzco, which itself lies 3350 metres (11,000 ft) above sea level, he travelled by mule and on foot higher into the Andes into the Urumbamba gorge. On the night of 23 July the team camped on the banks of a river on the land of a local farmer, Melchior Arteaga. As was Bingham's custom, he asked the local man, through his police escort and translator, if there were any ancient ruins in the vicinity. Arteaga could not think of anything on the scale Bingham was looking for, but said he did have two friends who lived on the Old Mountain and farmed some ancient terraces there. If Bingham wanted to look at these old walls, he would take him up to meet his friends the next day. However, the following day dawned grey, cold and wet and Arteaga was reluctant to keep his promise of the previous evening. As Bingham put it:

'I offered to pay him well if he showed me the ruins. He demurred and said it was too hard a climb for such a wet day. But when he found I was willing to pay him a sol, three or four times the ordinary daily wage, he finally agreed to go. When asked just where the ruins were, he pointed straight up to the top of the mountain. No-one supposed that they would be particularly interesting, and no-one cared to go with me.'

Eventually just Bingham, his police escort and Arteaga set off through the dense fog, crossing rotting rope bridges and scaling precipitous cliffs, until they finally arrived, exhausted, at the huts of Melquiades Richarte and Anacleto Alvarez on the Old Mountain – or 'Machu Picchu' in the local language. Over a drink the two locals explained how they had come to the area about four years before and discovered beneath the undergrowth a series of stone terraces, which they decided to clear and replant with their crops.

It was not a particularly unusual story in a mountainous region where terraces were always being cut into the mountainsides and abandoned when they became overgrown or exhausted, but Bingham insisted on seeing the fields for himself. Unwilling to waste their own time on such a futile exercise, the local men left the visitors in the care of one of Richarte's sons and told him to take them to the top of the hill.

A lost world rediscovered

Had it not been for the diligence of the local farmers, neither Bingham nor any other archaeologists or historians might ever have found what lay outside these huts. Richarte and Alvarez, however, had worked hard and as Bingham looked up the hill he saw over 100 cleared and renovated terraces leading up to the still-forested summit of the hill. Plunging into the trees, Richarte's son was eager to show them something that appealed more to him than the terraces. Here in the undergrowth was a children's playground of ramshackle buildings and finely jointed stone walls, all covered with centuries of forest growth. Richarte and Alvarez might have discovered a lost farm, but their children had discovered a lost city – a city of the Incas.

Bingham could not stay long at Machu Picchu – he was still looking for Vilcabamba – but after leaving, he sent a survey team back to draw it and, inspired by their extensive plans of the largely hidden site, he arranged a further expedition for the following year funded by Yale University and the

THE RISE AND FALL OF THE INCAS

The Inca people first emerged as a small city-state at Cuzco in Peru around the late 12th century and remained simply a localized tribe for the next 150 years. In 1438, however, the Incas began an aggressive expansion under their leader Sapa Inca Pachacuti whose name means 'world-shaker'. He is probably the man responsible for the building of Machu Picchu.

Conquering much of what is present-day Peru and Equador, Pachacuti reorganized the Incas into a federal empire of four parts, the corners of which territories all met at his capital Cuzco (which literally means 'navel of the world' in the native Quechua language). Although, under his successors, the empire continued to grow through military conquest, most of the land that fell under Inca rule was actually incorporated without a fight. The Inca emperor would traditionally send messages to the rulers of lands he coveted, offering extravagant bribes and playing up the financial rewards of being able to tap into the Inca trade and exchange system. Rulers who agreed to join would then send their children to Cuzco to be educated and indoctrinated in 'Inca' ways, in much the same way that the sons of local colonial leaders in the British empire were sent to British public schools to be educated. For those who refused willingly to join the Inca family, the option of invasion always remained.

The lure of gold drew Spanish conquistadors to the Andes. The Spanish melted down into ingots most of the gold objects that they found, and this figurine is one of few such Inca artefacts to survive.

Under Pachacuti's son and grandson the empire rapidly expanded until it included large parts of modern Equador, Bolivia, Argentina, Peru and Chile, making it the largest empire in South American history and at the time one of the largest on earth. Its decline however was even more rapid than its rise. In 1526 the Spanish conquistadors under Francisco Pizarro (c.1475–1541) reached Inca territory and noted its wealth and sophistication. By the time he returned in 1532 he also saw an opportunity. The great-grandsons of Pachacuti were now involved in an internecine power struggle that had fatally weakened central control of the empire, while the arrival of smallpox from Central America had decimated its population and the economy. With a force of just 180 men, 27 horses and one cannon, Pizarro invaded the Inca territories and, following a skirmish, agreed to parley with the new emperor Atahualpa, whose own army numbered 80,000 men.

The meeting was one of the most confusing in history, partly due to the problems of translation and partly to the unclear intentions of both parties. Pizarro began with the ambitious gambit of demanding that the Inca empire immediately subjugate itself to Spain. Then, during a discussion of the nature of Christianity, some confusion arose, leading to a scuffle, in which Atahualpa was taken prisoner. This may, of course, have been Pizarro's intention all along. For his part, Atahualpa offered to ransom himself for a room filled with gold, an offer which inspired the stories of El Dorado. His prison cell was duly filled with gold but the Spanish reneged on the deal and, instead of releasing Atahualpa, executed him.

A pro-Spanish puppet ruler, Manco Inca Yupanqui, was quickly installed on the throne although he later rebelled during a period of Spanish in-fighting. After briefly recapturing Cuzco, he was forced to retreat to the legendary Vilcabamba, where he and his son ruled for another 36 years. In 1572, however, the Spanish discovered this final 'hidden' Inca city and captured and executed its last ruler. The Inca empire was finally at an end.

HIRAM BINGHAM III

Hiram Bingham III has been claimed as the model for Hollywood's favourite fictional archaeologist Indiana Jones – certainly, his life was not that of an average academic. Bingham was born to missionary parents in Honolulu, Hawaii in 1875. After attending school on the island he travelled to the United States, taking a succession of degrees at Yale, Berkeley and Harvard, where he later taught history and politics. During this period he also met and married Alfreda Mitchell (1874–1967), the heiress to the Tiffany & Co. fortune, thereby finding a place at the heart of the American establishment. In 1907 he was appointed Professor of South American History at Yale, a post that led to his famous expeditions in search of lost Inca cities.

The publication of his 'discovery' of Machu Picchu (which carefully glossed over any earlier visitors to the site) in the *National Geographic* magazine in 1913 made Bingham a household name. With war in Europe looming, Bingham joined the National Guard in Connecticut in 1916, but his sense of adventure drew him to the relatively new field of military aviation. In the following year he joined the US Army Signals Corps aviation section and went on to command the flight instruction centre at Issoudun in France as well as organizing the United States Schools of Military Aeronautics.

After the war Bingham turned to politics, being elected lieutenant-governor of Connecticut in 1922 and governor in 1924. Having been elected as a Republican senator in that same year, he only held the governorship for one day before resigning to take his seat in the Senate. Life in politics was turbulent and in 1929 he was censured for allowing a lobbyist to sit in on a closed committee meeting. In 1932 he lost his seat following the Democrat landslide in the wake of the Great Depression.

In the Second World War Bingham lectured at various naval training schools while compiling the materials for his most famous book *Lost City of the Incas*, in which he narrated his discovery of Machu Picchu. He died on 6 June, 1956 and was buried in Arlington National Cemetery. In his honour the winding road that today takes thousands of tourists from the Urubamba Valley to the Inca site was renamed the Hiram Bingham Highway.

National Geographic Society. During this expedition much of the top of the mountain was cleared to reveal the site we see today. Here, all made in perfectly fitted granite blocks, were roads and watercourses, baths, shrines and temples and the living quarters of the royal family and their retainers. The discovery made Bingham's name, with *National Geographic* magazine hailing his discovery as 'one of the most remarkable stories of exploration in South America in the past 50 years'.

Just what it was that he had found, Bingham never quite decided. Machu Picchu was certainly an Inca site and probably the most spectacular one at that, but it has since been shown that it is not the legendary Vilcabamba (which was identified in the 1960s as another site visited by Bingham). Bingham also toyed with the idea that this was the first Inca city, Tampu Tocco, mainly because of the presence of a temple with three windows that seemed to him to resonate with the Inca legend that their ancestors had emerged from a cave with three windows. Sadly, this has also since been shown to be unlikely. In fact, Machu Picchu is known to be nothing more than a royal Inca estate, peacefully tucked away in the mountains, far from the troubles of the empire. It is undoubtedly one of the finest examples of Inca architecture and perhaps a hint of what

had been lost elsewhere. Its true attraction, however, comes not from its history but from the location which first encouraged an Inca emperor to build there. As Bingham wrote:

'In the variety of its charms, the power of its spell, I know of no place in the world which can compare with it. Not only had it great snow peaks looming above the clouds more than two miles overhead; gigantic precipices of many-coloured granite rising sheer for thousands of feet above the foaming, glistening, roaring rapids, it has also, in striking contrast, orchids and tree ferns, the delectable beauty of luxurious vegetation and the mysterious witchery of the jungle.'

The Inca capital of Cuzco, from a German engraving of 1576. This city was the hub of a highly organized empire that expanded rapidly from 1438 onwards.

127

IN THE LAND OF ABRAHAM
The Great Death Pit of Ur, 1922

'*Our object was to get history, not to fill museum cases with miscellaneous curios, and history could not be got unless both we and our men were duly trained.*'

Sir Leonard Woolley

By the time the British archaeologist Charles Leonard Woolley (1880–1960) arrived in Mesopotamia in the 1920s, the ancient civilizations of Assyria and Babylonia that had once thrived there had already captured the public imagination. Excavations at Babylon, Nineveh and Nimrud had filled the museums of the West with monumental gateways, dramatic reliefs and thousands of clay tablets bearing the cuneiform text of these people.

But just how civilizations had arisen between the Tigris and Euphrates rivers had been largely overlooked. Experts on cuneiform noted that the script derived from some earlier source and was written in an earlier language, but who these people were, and how they lived, remained largely unknown.

The city between the rivers

The site Woolley had come to investigate was located near the city of Nasiriyah, south of Baghdad, and stood, in antiquity, by the mouths of the Tigris and Euphrates rivers. Tell el-Mukayyar was a 'tell', one of the artificial mounds that so often indicate the position of an ancient city. It had been known about since the 17th century, when the Italian traveller Pietro della Valle (1586–1652) had visited the site and noted the piles of ancient brickwork printed with strange writing. In 1854 the British consul carried out small-scale excavations there to reveal that the central mound was in fact a huge ziggurat – a type of stepped pyramid – and concluded that the site was rich in antiquities and a prime candidate for full excavation. Yet full investigation had to wait until 1922, when Leonard Woolley arrived to begin what would be 12 years of work.

It is perhaps fortunate for Ur, and our knowledge of the Sumerians who built it, that the site was relatively untouched until Woolley began work. Woolley was a new breed of archaeologist, trained in stratigraphic excavation and with the patience to glean every scrap of information he could from each layer of earth rather than driving on down in the search for treasure. And the story he uncovered at Ur is one of the longest and strangest in archaeology.

Woolley's excavations revealed the remains of a city whose origins dated back nearly 7000 years, as revealed in the crushed remnants of reed houses buried underneath a huge layer of sediment that Woolley maintained was evidence of the biblical flood. On top of this lay the ruins of many cities, of which he excavated whole neighbourhoods dating from the foundation of Mesopotamian civilization, through the era when this city was the home of the biblical patriarch Abraham to its remodelling at the time of Nebuchadnezzar and its final decline in the years before the birth of Christ. But it was the early history of Ur that seized his imagination and, in a mound of refuse by the great ziggurat, that imagination was brought to life.

This area of rubbish had first been excavated soon after his arrival but the discovery of delicate gold leaf and precious stones (which led his excavators to call it 'the gold trench') worried Woolley. His excavators were still inexperienced and he was aware that

Ur is mentioned in the Book of Genesis as being the homeland of the Old Testament prophet Abraham. The site of the ancient city-state remained unidentified until the mid-19th century. In this photograph looking across the royal tombs, the 4000-year-old great ziggurat can be seen in the distance.

129

in these early days they might destroy more than they found. To howls of protest from his team, he ordered the trench closed and moved excavations to other areas of the site.

It was five years later when Woolley finally allowed excavations around the site of the 'gold trench', and his patience was richly rewarded. The rubbish dump had later been used as a cemetery and here he found 1850 grave pits, mostly modest affairs, their occupants buried with a few pieces of pottery, or in some cases some jewellery and precious stones that testified to the relative wealth of their owner in life. But in one section of the site there was something different. Here the graves were not simply pits but tombs, each consisting of one or more chambers with a ramp leading down to them. In these were buried what Woolley believed were the rulers of ancient Ur, the kings and queens of the Sumerians he sought.

In total 16 'royal' tombs were found, and although most had been robbed in antiquity, the few items the robbers left behind still formed a unique treasure. In one four-roomed tomb, close to the remains of a man who seems to have been wearing a beaded cap, a jumble of small pieces of lapis lazuli and shell was uncovered. Realizing that this was the inlay from some wooden box that had long since rotted away in the soil, Woolley ordered the pieces covered in beeswax, which was then backed with cloth. When the cloth was lifted the pieces came away in exactly the same orientation they had been in the ground and could be taken back to Woolley's workroom to be reconstructed.

One of the two main panels on the Royal Standard of Ur, which dates from around 2600 BC. The scene depicted, dubbed 'Peace', shows servants parading animals and goods in front of feasting dignitaries. A companion scene of 'War' is on the other side of the standard.

SIR CHARLES LEONARD WOOLLEY

Charles Leonard Woolley, known as Leonard, is one of the most important figures in the history of archaeology. Having originally intended to follow his father into the church, he was persuaded while at Oxford University to embark on a career in archaeology. After taking two degrees and studying modern languages abroad he was appointed by the Ashmolean Museum as assistant to Arthur Evans (1851–1941), the excavator of Knossos.

Woolley excavated in Egypt and Italy before taking over the major site of Carchemish in Syria. Here he was joined by a new assistant, T.E. Lawrence (1888–1935), who later achieved almost legendary status as 'Lawrence of Arabia'; they went on to survey the area south of the Dead Sea as part of the Egypt Exploration Fund's plan to map the entire Holy Land. This work would be of great use to the British during the First World War. In the war Woolley joined the intelligence service in Cairo before being captured by the Turks after his ship was sunk in the eastern Mediterranean. In prison he seems to have developed his love for recounting stories of ancient civilizations.

In 1922, after years of vacillation, the British Museum agreed with the University of Pennsylvania to begin excavations at Ur and Woolley was named director. He was ahead of his time in his methodical approach, never rushing to find treasure, refusing to dig promising areas until he and his workforce were trained well enough to tackle them and insisting that his discoveries were published promptly. Yet his use of local labour rather than qualified archaeologists for excavating harked back to an earlier age and attracted much criticism.

When not digging, Woolley was a tireless promoter of archaeology, writing popular accounts of his work to complement his academic publications. Indeed, so popular did his work become that it inspired Agatha Christie to write *Murder in Mesopotamia*, a story based on his work at Ur. She later married his young assistant Max Mallowan.

In the 1930s, Woolley undertook excavations in Syria and India. After serving in the Second World War as a lieutenant-colonel, Woolley returned to the Syrian Bronze Age site of Tel Atchana, where he unearthed a sequence of palaces and temples. His archaeological results and a popular account of them (*A Forgotten Kingdom*) were all published within six years of the work finishing – a publication record that has rarely been surpassed. He continued to write and lecture into his seventies, and died on 20 February 1960.

His hunch had been correct. Under the pieces attached to the wax lay the back of the box and this too was lifted. When reconstructed what lay on the workbench was one of the most important artefacts to come down to us from Sumeria – what Woolley called the 'Standard of Ur'. This box-shaped structure, 22 centimetres (9 in) high by 50 centimetres (20 in) wide, which may once have been attached to a pole as some form of standard, showed the people of Ur. Here were scenes of banqueting, processions, ranks of soldiers, war chariots and columns of dejected prisoners – faces from 4500 years ago.

Victims of the 'Great Death Pit'

But the Royal Standard was not the only great find. One miraculously unrobbed grave included seals bearing the name Pu-abi which may have belonged to the woman, possibly the queen, who still lay on her bier at the far end of the tomb. Around her were ten rings of gold and lapis lazuli, strange amulets and strings of beads. Elsewhere in the grave were metal and stone vessels, golden chisels, a gold and lapis drinking straw and a lyre. Almost in the middle of the complex was something more shocking. Pressed into the earth, Woolley saw the remains of a wooden sledge that had once pulled the tomb's occupant. It had clearly been drawn by two oxen, and the bones of the animals still lay to either side. But next to these remains lay other bones, human bones, apparently the skeletons of the two grooms who had led the oxen into the grave. Nor were these the only other occupants of the tomb. Neatly arranged all in the same posture, as though asleep, were the richly adorned bodies of 12 women.

If this find led Woolley to speculate on the darker funeral rites of the Sumerians, the contents of 'Private Grave 1237' confirmed them. This tomb was badly damaged, indeed the grave of the owner could not even be found, but the main chamber still contained a peculiar gold leaf and lapis statue of a ram standing upright with its front hooves in the branches of a thicket along with the remnants of two lyres. But that was not what attracted the attention of the excavators, for lying between these objects were the remains of 74 people. Sixty-eight of them were women, all lying on their sides in neat rows and each with a small cup that probably once held the poison they willingly (or otherwise) drank as the tomb was sealed behind them. Woolley named the tomb the 'Great Death Pit of Ur' and concluded:

> *'The burial of the kings was accompanied by human sacrifice on a lavish scale, the bottom of the grave pit being crowded with the bodies of men and women who seem to have been brought down here and butchered where they stood.'*

The contents of the Sumerian royal graves, with their strange juxtaposition of delicate jewellery and apparent mass slaughter, greatly disturbed Woolley. The rulers of this sophisticated state seemed to have chosen to take many of their servants with them into their shadowy afterlife, although whether they went willingly or were forced, he was unable to say. What was certain was that, in opening the tombs, he had re-opened a new chapter in the history of Mesopotamia, a formative era in which beauty and brutality apparently existed side by side.

THE SUMERIANS OF UR

The civilization of Sumer was the first to appear in the region between the Tigris and Euphrates rivers known as Mesopotamia and was the first urban civilization on earth. The Sumerians, who called their land *ki-en-gir* (the Land of the Civilized Lords) had settled the region in what is today southern Iraq in the sixth millennium BC. They brought with them a knowledge of irrigation – indeed the Sumerian language is full of terms for dam, reservoir, and canal – which enabled them to practise agriculture in a desert landscape using water from the two great rivers.

Despite their dependence on agriculture, most Sumerians were city dwellers living in one of a dozen or so city-states. Each city had its own god, who was worshipped in a central location often in the form of a ziggurat – a series of square terraces forming a stepped 'pyramid' with a temple on top. Around this lay the palaces of the dynastic rulers and the houses of the ordinary citizens, all made of mud brick; there was no stone and very little wood available on the Tigris–Euphrates plain. The relative softness of this building material meant houses often had to be rebuilt on earlier foundations, a process that over time made their cities into man-made hills, known as 'tells'.

Objects such as the Standard of Ur and Sumerian inscriptions suggest that the rival dynasties of Sumer were often at war. Cities were frequently besieged by armies drawn from citizen levies. For those who died in battle, or indeed anywhere else, Sumerian mythology offered a decidedly depressing afterlife as a *giddim*, or ghost, in a gloomy underworld.

The sophistication of the Sumerian agricultural system and the location of its cities allowed their inhabitants to create a surplus that could be sold; the Sumerians are some of the first international traders known to history. Finds suggest that trade links extended to

The elaborate gold and lapis lazuli headdress and jewellery of a lady of the Sumerian court, found by Leonard Woolley on one of the bodies in the Great Death Pit of Ur.

Afghanistan and the Indus Valley, to Bahrain, the Persian Gulf and the Mediterranean coast. The fact that we know so much about their civilization is probably also down to trade, since Sumerian, the first known written language, is thought to have developed from the need to keep accounts. Yet Sumerian literature, recorded in cuneiform script on clay tablets, contains much more than financial information. The *Epic of Gilgamesh*, which tells of a (possibly real) king of Uruk in the 26th century BC, is the earliest surviving written story, and includes what may be the original source for the flood myth in the Bible.

Trade stimulated new technologies, and Sumerian civilization is credited with many innovations. They were the first people to use the wheel, write down their language, codify a legal system (with case records, courts and prisons) and develop a system of arithmetic. Their sexagesimal (base 60) counting system, which they used to devise the first means of timekeeping, is still used today and is the reason why a minute consists of 60 seconds, an hour consists of 60 minutes and a year contains 12 months.

Sumerian civilization lasted for more than 1000 years, but was over by the time Hammurabi founded the Babylonian empire in c.1780 BC. Its decline was gradual; for centuries Semitic peoples had been moving into the region, changing the culture of some cities. The area also suffered invasions. King Sargon the Great of Akkad had absorbed Sumer into his empire and on the collapse of this, another people – the Gutians – had taken control. Their expulsion led to a brief Sumerian renaissance under the Third Dynasty of Ur, but Sumerian culture and language were already in decline. By the time the Third Dynasty was destroyed by another Semitic people, the Elamites, Sumerian culture was the preserve of a small priestly caste who continued to use the old language much in the way Latin survived in Medieval Europe.

A SEALED DOORWAY

Howard Carter in the Tomb of Tutankhamun, 1922

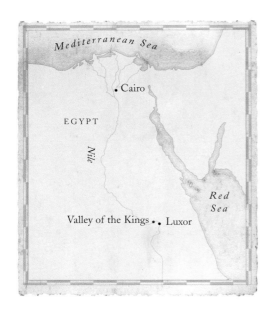

'A sealed doorway – it was actually true, then! Our years of patient labour were to be rewarded after all …'

HOWARD CARTER *The Tomb of Tutankhamun* (1923)

Howard Carter (1874–1939) arrived at Luxor on 28 October 1922 and immediately began enrolling workmen. It was to be his last season digging in the Valley of the Kings, the end of a six-year search in the burial place of the pharaohs for something that nearly every other excavator in Egypt believed wasn't there. Now even his funding was drying up, although his patron, Lord Carnarvon (1866–1923), had reluctantly agreed to one last season's work. Carter wasted no time. By 1 November he had the men he needed, and work began close to the tomb of Ramses VI. Three days later he arrived on site to find his workmen standing in silence around the excavation. There in the rubble beneath some ancient huts was the clear outline of a step.

A dream fulfilled

What Carter and his diggers had spent so many years searching for was a tomb – specifically that of an 18th-Dynasty boy pharaoh who had died some 3300 years earlier. Very little was known of this short-lived king but a few years earlier, excavators in the valley had discovered inscriptions of his name in three places – on a cup hidden in a crevice, on some gold foil in a pit and on the seals of some jars that held floral collars and other materials usually used in ancient Egyptian funerals. For Carter these discoveries meant only one thing – somewhere nearby, this pharaoh had been buried and no recent excavator had ever found him. Regardless of whether or not the tomb had been robbed, no modern eyes had seen it and Carter intended his to be the first. Now he was standing on the top step of what he hoped was the entrance to his dream – the tomb of Tutankhamun.

For the whole of the next day the excavators feverishly dug through the rubble, revealing step after step and, as they came down to the level of the 12th step, the top of a door, Carter momentarily stopped, the thought dawning on him that by far the most likely outcome would be to find that the tomb had never been finished and was empty. He had been in that situation before.

As the excavators cleared the bottom of the stairwell, however, they uncovered not an empty tomb but a sealed doorway. Carter scrambled down to inspect. There, across the

The spectacular death mask found on Tutankhamun's mummy has become the quintessential symbol of the pharaonic era in ancient Egypt. The mask is made of gold inlaid with glass and semi-precious stones; on the headdress are images of the vulture and the cobra, emblems of the lands of Upper and Lower Egypt.

top of the door, stamped into the wet clay that had been used to close it was the seal of the keepers of the Theban necropolis – the ancient guardians of the pharaohs' tombs. Carter recorded the moment that night in his diary:

> 'It was a thrilling moment for an excavator. Alone, save for my native workmen, I found myself, after years of comparatively unproductive labour, on the threshold of what might prove to be a magnificent discovery.'

However, work could not proceed immediately. First Carter had to send for Lord Carnarvon, who would take two weeks to arrive from England. In the meantime, the site was completely backfilled to protect it from modern tomb raiders. Carter had nothing to do but bide his time, and, during that wait, doubts began to creep into his mind again. The only seals Carter had seen were those of the Theban necropolis – no royal seals suggesting who might be buried there. The doorway they had found was also unusually small, not like that of a pharaonic tomb at all. More likely this was just a cache of goods like many others in the valley, the remnants of funerals and the broken fragments of grave goods gathered together from looted tombs. And even this cache, he told himself, had probably suffered looting.

Evidence of tomb robbers

On 23 November, 1922 Carnarvon arrived in Luxor in the company of his daughter, Lady Evelyn Herbert. By the afternoon of the following day, the staircase had been cleared once more – 16 steps in all – and the whole sealed doorway was visible. As Carter and Carnarvon stood before the door and examined it in its entirety for the first time, they were filled with both joy and dread. The wonderful news was that, just below the Theban seals that Carter had previously uncovered, there were other impressions that bore the unmistakable name of Tutankhamun. Dispiritingly, though, the doorway also showed clear signs of having been resealed twice by the guardians of the necropolis, which could only mean that the tomb beyond had been robbed.

The next day, the seals having been photographed and drawn, the blocking in the doorway was removed. Beyond was a passageway that had been glimpsed by Carter two weeks earlier, when he found he could not resist cutting a small peephole in the doorway to see what lay beyond. Another day passed while the rubble and broken pottery were removed. Of the next day, Carter later wrote:

> 'The day following was the day of days, the most wonderful that I have ever lived through, and certainly one whose like I can never hope to see again.'

The job of clearing rubble from the passageway continued until mid-afternoon. Some 9 metres (30 ft) down from the first door they came to another doorway, also sealed and bearing the marks of the Theban necropolis and the pharaoh Tutankhamun. It too had been resealed, so robbers had been through here as well, but clearly something was on the other side, since the keepers of the necropolis had bothered to repair and reclose it. But was it just a cache or could it be a tomb?

With the doorway cleared and photographed the time had come to see what lay beyond. Carter took a chisel and:

> 'With trembling hands I made a tiny breach in the upper left-hand corner. Darkness and blank space, as far as an iron testing-rod could reach, showed that whatever lay beyond was empty, and not filled like the passage we had just cleared. Candle tests were applied as a precaution against possible foul gases, and then, widening the hole a little, I inserted the candle and peered in, Lord Carnarvon, Lady Evelyn and Callender [Carter's assistant] standing anxiously beside me to hear the verdict. At first I could see nothing, the hot air escaping from the chamber causing the candle flame to flicker, but presently, as my eyes grew accustomed to the light, details of the room within emerged slowly from the mist, strange animals, statues and gold - everywhere the glint of gold. For the moment – an eternity it must have seemed to the others standing by – I was struck dumb with amazement, and when Lord Carnarvon, unable to stand the suspense any longer, inquired anxiously, "Can you see anything?" it was all I could do to get out the words, "Yes, wonderful things". Then widening the hole a little further, so that we both could see, we inserted an electric torch.'

This photograph, taken in November 1922, shows the south side of the antechamber discovered by Howard Carter. This storage room contained a jumble of 171 objects, including dismantled chariots, pieces of furniture, hunting equipment and games.

What Carter could see was an antechamber filled with the most astonishing collection of ancient Egyptian artefacts ever discovered. There were painted boxes, graceful statues, gilded beds, inlaid chairs, faience necklaces and heavy gold rings – a complete suite of items fit for an Egyptian king. This tomb might have been robbed but clearly the thieves got away with precious little. The air that now wafted past

HOWARD CARTER

Howard Carter was born in Brompton in London on 9 May 1874. He was a sickly child and so his father, an artist, sent him to live with two maiden aunts in Swaffham, Norfolk, in eastern England. In the countryside Carter received a modest private education, supplemented by the painting and drawing lessons that his father gave on his regular visits. By the age of 15 Carter had started to make a living as a painter, making watercolours and chalk portraits of pets for wealthy patrons. It was during this time that a British archaeologist working at Beni Hasan in Egypt, P.F. Newberry, asked some friends in Norfolk if they knew of a good artist who could come to Egypt to help him ink in the thousands of pencil drawings he had made of the site, and Carter's name was suggested.

Carter was duly engaged as a trainee draughtsman at the British Museum. Shortly thereafter, the Egypt Exploration Fund agreed to finance his first trip to assist Newberry. In Egypt his reputation for painstaking and accurate work soon spread and in 1892 he came to the attention of one of the great pioneers of modern archaeology, Sir Flinders Petrie (1853–1942). Joining Petrie at Amarna in Middle Egypt, Carter was now expected to dig, a skill that Petrie did not believe he possessed. But even great archaeologists can be wrong, and he later admitted that Carter quickly became a skilled excavator.

A succession of job offers followed and Carter first returned to Beni Hasan as draughtsman to the archaeological survey department of the Egypt Exploration Fund before starting six years' work on the temple of Hatshepsut at Deir el-Bahri, near the Valley of the Kings. Here, he also took time to learn colloquial Arabic, a skill that kept him on good terms with his workforce during the long years searching for Tutankhamun.

Carter's meteoric rise came to the attention of the Director-General of Antiquities and in 1899 he was appointed inspector-in-chief of the monuments of Upper Egypt and Nubia, based at Luxor (ancient Thebes). This gave him his first opportunity to investigate the Valley of the Kings on the opposite bank of the Nile. His success here led to his appointment as inspector of Lower and Middle Egypt in 1903 but here his career dramatically stalled. During an argument between his guards and a drunken party of French tourists at the Serapeum at Saqqara, a melée ensued in which one of the Frenchman was injured. Ordered to apologize by the British consul-general, Carter refused and was sidelined to a minor posting in the Delta from which he promptly resigned.

After making a meagre living as an artist, Carter returned to the Valley of the Kings three years later to work alongside Theodore M. Davis (1837–1915), an American lawyer and archaeologist. It was at this time that he first came across artefacts from the valley marked with the name of the mystery pharaoh Tutankhamun, which convinced him that his undiscovered tomb lay nearby. This period also saw his first encounter with the wealthy George Herbert, 5th Earl of Carnarvon, a keen amateur archaeologist who would be his close friend and sponsor from that time on.

After eight years' excavating and collecting at various sites, in 1915 Carter finally managed to persuade the director-general of antiquities to grant him a concession to dig in the Valley of the Kings. These once highly prized concessions were now becoming easier to obtain, largely because most archaeologists in Egypt believed the Valley of the Kings was worked out. Only Carter disagreed.

Disappointment followed disappointment, however, and in 1922 Carter's patron warned him that the returns on the investment did not warrant continuing the work. When Carter offered to fund the next season himself – something he could barely afford – Carnarvon relented, but announced that this would be the last season.

That autumn changed the lives of Carter and Carnarvon, and the discovery of the virtually intact tomb of the boy pharaoh made both men celebrities. It would also prove to be both men's last excavation. Carnarvon died of pneumonia in 1923 while Carter spent the next ten years just cataloguing the huge number of finds from the tomb and researching his book. After this, and in failing health, he retired from archaeology and took to collecting and lecturing. He died of Hodgkin's lymphoma at his flat in Kensington, London, on 2 March 1939.

Carter's candle, making the shadows in the chamber beyond dance, had last been breathed more than 3000 years earlier.

The doorway was now carefully cleared in order to enable the excavators to step into the antechamber. For Carter it was the moment of a lifetime, filled with a combination of excitement, trepidation and awe. He later wrote:

> 'Three thousand, four thousand years maybe, have passed and gone since human feet last trod the floor on which you stand, and yet, as you note the signs of recent life around you – the blackened lamp, the finger-mark upon the freshly painted surface – you feel it might have been but yesterday. The very air you breathe, unchanged throughout the centuries, you share with those who laid the mummy to its rest. Time is annihilated by little intimate details such as these, and you feel an intruder.'

Had this room been all there was in the tomb, it would still have ranked as the greatest archaeological discovery in Egyptian history, but there was more to come. Almost as soon as Carter entered the room, he noticed two life-sized statues in gilded kilts standing to either side of another sealed doorway. But for now that would have to wait. Carter was an archaeologist, not a tomb robber, and he knew that many long weeks of painstaking work now lay ahead, in which all the objects in this room would have to be carefully drawn, photographed, conserved and packed before any thought could be given to investigating what lay inside the next chamber.

Anticipation mounts

It was mid-February 1923 before the antechamber was finally cleared. In the process another room, known as the annexe, had come to light. This had also been broken into by tomb robbers and ransacked. Clearing these two rooms was likened by Carter to an enormous game of spillikins (jackstraws); the added difficulty here was that every piece was unique and priceless and some, such as the funerary wreaths, so delicate that a mere breath could reduce them to dust.

Friday 17 February was the date appointed for opening the next room, the burial chamber itself, and Carter went to great lengths to prepare for the occasion. By this time news of the find had spread around the world and the names of both Tutankhamun and Howard Carter were on everyone's lips. For the opening Carter had erected a small podium, to allow him to reach the top of the doorway, and arranged chairs for the large number of Egyptian and English dignitaries and reporters who were to witness the event. Electric lighting had also been installed so no-one need strain their eyes in the flickering light of a candle.

Carter began very slowly to remove the blocking at the top in order to prevent pieces falling into the room beyond and damaging whatever lay there. After about ten minutes he could contain himself no longer and he shone his torch through the small hole he had made:

Howard Carter (kneeling), his assistant A.R. Callender and an Egyptian workman ease open the door to the burial chamber of Tutankhamun's tomb in February 1923. Carter exposed this event to the full glare of publicity.

Like most of the treasures found in the tomb, Tutankhamun's throne is now displayed in the Egyptian Museum in Cairo. The decoration on the seat-back, which shows the Aten sun disc, indicates that this piece was made when the pharaoh was still very young, before the cult of Aten fell out of favour.

'An astonishing sight its light revealed, for there, within yards of the doorway, stretching as far as one could see and blocking the entrance to the chamber, stood what to all appearance was a solid wall of gold.'

Carter's dream really had come true. This wasn't just a cache of objects. There, in the light of his torch, almost filling the room, stood an immense gilt shrine and in another little room off to the side was the Treasury – a collection of treasures that made what Carter had found in the outer rooms seem positively mundane. Inside was a dazzling array of equipment and goods meant to support the deceased pharaoh in the afterlife. These included gilded boats and figures, along with the canopic chest containing several of the embalmed inner organs of the dead ruler. This chest was protected by the gilded figures of four goddesses, while the door of the room was guarded by an effigy of the jackal-headed deity Anubis.

Face to face with the boy king

Only one question now remained. Was the shrine intact, and did it contain the body of the pharaoh Tutankhamun? Having removed all the blocking, the outer doors to the shrine were slowly unbolted and the doors opened. Inside stood another set of doors and on its bolts a seal that was still perfectly intact. The robbers had never penetrated this far. Somewhere beyond was the body of the pharaoh.

Once again, it would be many months before the shrine itself could be opened. All the artefacts that had been discovered had first to be drawn, photographed and conserved so that no information was lost. The last people to enter this room before Carter were the ancient Egyptians themselves. Never had modern people been so close to these objects, and so it was vital that everything was meticulously recorded.

The following season, Carter was finally able to cut the cord holding the seal on the shrine doors to discover another shrine inside. In all, there were four shrines and behind the sealed doors of the fourth a huge yellow quartzite sarcophagus with a red granite lid. After installing blocks and tackle the lid was eventually raised, in the last great formal opening ceremony that Carter would perform.

'I gave the word. Amid intense silence the huge slab, broken in two, weighing over a ton and a quarter, rose from its bed. The light shone into the sarcophagus ... a gasp of wonderment escaped our lips, so gorgeous was the sight that met our eyes: a golden effigy of the young boy king, of the most magnificent workmanship, filled the whole of the interior of the sarcophagus.'

Howard Carter had come face to face with the man he had spent so many years searching for. Holding the torch over the coffin he finally gazed into the inlaid eyes of Tutankhamun.

THE TUTANKHAMUN MYSTERY

Despite the amazing finds from Tutankhamun's tomb (which number 32,000) we still know surprisingly little about the pharaoh himself. What we do know is that he lived at a time of great turbulence in Egypt. His predecessor, possibly his father, was the heretic pharaoh Akhenaten, who had replaced the millennia-old Egyptian religion with a cult of sun worship (Atenism) centred on a new capital city at Amarna.

Amarna was where Tutankhamun had spent his youth, although at the time he had been known as Tutankhaten. Sometime after the mysterious death of Akhenaten, he had came to the throne and taken a new name, Tutankhamun, confirming that the experiment with Atenism was over.

The country was now in chaos and needed firm guidance, but the king was only nine years old. This situation gave the most influential man in the kingdom, the vizier Ay, a long-standing adviser to Akhenaten, the chance to step in as regent, styling himself 'The God's Father'. Ay now set about expunging every last vestige of Atenism – Akhenaten, Nefertiti and Amarna slipped into obscurity, while Amun and Thebes were restored. By the time Tutankhamun was 19 and able to rule in his own right, everything seemed to have returned to normal.

In that year, the boy-king died. With Akhenaten no more than a distant and painful memory, perhaps the boy who had been born Tutankhaten was just too uncomfortable a reminder of a time best forgotten. Now a new pharaoh would rule – Ay himself.

Tutankhamun's strange and tragic life may explain why Howard Carter found the tomb and its contents so disturbing. No archaeologist can ever have been more delighted than Carter was on finding the tomb, but something about it didn't make sense. From the day it was uncovered, he was concerned that the space was simply too small to be a pharaoh's last resting place. By the great shrine, Carter had also found a pile of debris which suggested that the sarcophagi inside had been cut down to fit – implying they had originally been made for someone else. Moreover, many of the items in the tomb seemed out of place. Some showed Aten, a god wholly discredited in Tutankhamun's reign, and much of the assemblage, about 80 percent, had

little connection to the boy king. Even the famous gold funerary mask has a solder line running inside the face, suggesting that it had originally been made for someone else and that Tutankhamun's face had later been grafted into it. Carter concluded that Tutankhamun had been buried with a 'job lot' of other people's possessions. For a pharaoh this would have been unthinkable.

It was an essential tenet of Egyptian belief that a pharaoh had to be buried with his own possessions in the tomb he had prepared for himself. All of these things, the Egyptians believed, were necessary for the king's happiness in the next life and many rulers, and indeed many commoners, spent much of their lives preparing for this. But Tutankhamun, who had died young, had not had decades in which to prepare a lavish tomb, let alone to commission the objects with which he would need to stock it for the afterlife. This left the vizier Ay in a quandary. In order to succeed, as he intended, he had to complete the proper funerary rites for his predecessor, but nothing was ready. Ay would simply have to make do.

Taking another smaller and less elaborate tomb, possibly prepared for a noble, he had it quickly reworked as a royal tomb. To stock it with grave goods, he turned to the only ready supply – the funerary items prepared for Akhenaten and his family at Amarna. The king's body was then placed under a reused mask and lowered into a sarcophagus with the wrong lid. Around it were packed the items from Amarna, before the whole thing was sealed up. Shortly thereafter, robbers broke in and took some of the smaller items but the theft was discovered and the tomb resealed. Some years later, the builders of another tomb erected their workmen's huts over the tiny entrance to Tutankhamun's final resting place and the whole site was forgotten.

Until 1923, that is. In that year, Howard Carter became the first man in 3300 years to set eyes on the treasures of the pharaoh – a ragtag of assorted items packed around a second-hand sarcophagus. What is astonishing is that this hurried and ill-assorted collection for a relatively unimportant and short-lived pharaoh is still one of the greatest and most beautiful treasure troves ever found on earth.

THE MOUND OF THE DEAD

Discovery of the Indus Valley Civilization, 1924

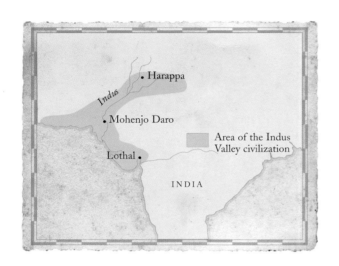

The common view held by European and American archaeologists at the beginning of the 20th century was that there were two centres of prehistoric culture – Europe and the Near East. Even in British India, a country which clearly had a long and complex history, the director-general of the Archaeological Survey, Sir John Marshall (1876–1958), could complain in 1922 that there was no evidence for the subcontinent's early prehistory. Just two years later that had all changed.

In truth there was no lack of evidence for the early civilizations of India, it was simply that it had never been recognized as such. Travelling through the Punjab, Charles Masson (1800–53) had recorded in *Narrative of Various Journeys in Balochistan, Afghanistan and The Panjab, 1826–38*, that he had come across '… *in Harappa a ruined brick castle with very high walls and towers, built on a hill'*.

Legend told that the 'castle' belonged to an evil rajah whom the gods had punished by burning down his home, since when it had become a playground for local children. What remained of Harappa when Masson visited we will never know, because in 1857 the builders of the East Indian Railway took the opportunity to rob the site of bricks to provide over 100 miles (160 km) of ballast on which to set the railway tracks. The site had, however, come to the notice of Marshall's predecessor, Sir Alexander Cunningham (1814–93), who made a few small excavations there in 1873 and recovered strange stone seals engraved with what looked like a form of ancient writing. They were despatched to the British Museum in London but no further action was taken until 1921, when the British government hired an Indian archaeologist, Daya Ram Sahni, to investigate.

A city beneath the mound

Digging a trench through the 'castle mound', Daya Ram Sahni came across more stone seals engraved with the strange writing. But, more importantly, as he dug he discovered this was not one large building but the remains of hundreds of houses buried one below the other in seven or eight distinct phases. He wrote to the Archaeological Survey announcing that Harappa was not a castle but an entire city from a previously unknown civilization, with a history stretching back as far as any then known. At about the same time another Indian archaeologist, R.D. Banerji, had begun excavations at a site 400 miles (640 km) to the south, known as Mohenjo Daro – the Mound of the Dead – which local people believed was an ancient burial ground. Digging through later historic periods, Banerji also arrived at what appeared to be large numbers of houses, some of which contained stone seals almost identical to those at Harappa. Here was another city from an age before the earliest Indian texts, an India that had been written off as nonexistent.

So, in 1924, two years after complaining that Indian prehistory was simply 'missing', Sir John Marshall could write an article for *The Illustrated London News* entitled 'First Light on a Long-Forgotten Civilization', announcing a discovery which, he said, was as great as the discovery of Troy. The Indian subcontinent's ancient history had been recovered and a wholly unknown civilization was about to come to light.

The Indus Valley civilization

Indus civilization reached its height in about 2000 BC, with over 100 settlements spread across the Indus plain. The spectacular remains at Mohenjo Daro indicate that this was a main centre of the civilization – as many as 40,000 people went about their daily lives in a city with a circumference of over 3 miles (5 km).

This was an ordered place, a city built on a grid pattern similar to many modern cities and probably the first ever to be planned. Along its straight streets stood rows of windowless houses, their blank walls protecting the inhabitants from the blistering summer sun. Within each house were living and dining areas and a bathroom connected to the city's sewage system, all set around a central courtyard.

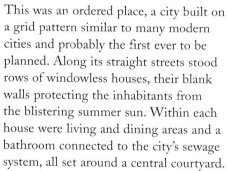

Among the artefacts found at Mohenjo Daro and Harappa are numerous stone seals decorated with animal figures and writing that has yet to be deciphered.

From the things they left behind, we know that these people were farmers and traders. Excavations at Indus Valley sites have uncovered charred seeds and the remains of bones that tell us about the food they ate and the animals they used. They grew barley, wheat, rice, dates and cotton and raised cattle, sheep, buffalo, pigs, dogs, camels and elephants. Metal finds show they had bronze and stone tools and that they made ornaments of gold, silver, ivory and precious stones such as cornelian, much of which must have been brought from great distances. Their trade links seem to have stretched into Afghanistan and across the Indian Ocean as far as Mesopotamia.

TIMELINE

*c.*5000 BC People settle in communities in the Indus Valley

*c.*2000 BC The Indus Valley civilization reaches its height, with over 100 settlements on the plain

*c.*1700 BC The Indus Valley civilization collapses and its cities and script are abandoned

*c.*1826 While travelling in the Punjab, Charles Masson comes across a ruined brick castle at Harappa

1857 Builders of the East Indian Railway demolish much of the site and reuse the bricks as foundations for railway tracks

1873 Alexander Cunningham recovers stone seals covered with ancient writing from Harappa

1921 Daya Ram Sahni carries out further excavations and discovers hundreds of houses from seven or eight distinct archaeological phases. At about the same time R.D. Banerji digs at Mohenjo Daro and finds another ancient city

1924 John Marshall publishes his article 'First Light on a Long-Forgotten Civilization', giving details of the initial finds at Mohenjo Daro and Harappa

1925–31 Under Marshall's direction, extensive excavations are undertaken at Mohenjo Daro, revealing that catastrophic floods in about 1700 BC caused the downfall of the Indus Valley civilization

The public buildings of cities such as Mohenjo Daro remain a mystery, and it has therefore proved almost impossible to conjecture how this society was politically organized. Large buildings identified as public granaries have been found, and at the centre of the city there was a raised citadel where the public baths also stood. This vast structure surrounded by cell-like rooms probably had a religious function but no-one knows what the Indus people actually believed.

Strangely there is no palace in the citadel and no evidence of who – if anyone – ruled this place. There is not even much evidence of wealth disparity among the people, since nearly all the houses are of roughly similar size and have similar facilities. The little booths on the corners of the main boulevards may have been police offices, so someone was regulating the city, but they remain elusive. There is also very little evidence of weaponry. These were a quiet and gentle people.

An elusive language

The language spoken by these people also remains as mysterious as when it was first discovered on stone seals in the 19th century. Since then over 4000 objects bearing the script have been discovered and at least 400 major symbols identified. Yet despite the wealth of material, this language defies translation. No bilingual text has ever been found (such as the Rosetta Stone – see pages 44–7 – which allowed the translation of Egyptian hieroglyphics), nor has the language or even the language group that the script codes for been identified. Attempts at translation are further hampered by the fact that most inscriptions are less than five symbols long and the longest is only 26 symbols, leading some to suggest that this was just a code and not a fully formed written language.

One thing we do know about these people is that they yearned for travel. At the coastal city of Lothal, archaeologists have uncovered a huge dredged canal and docks for sea-going ships; and Indus Valley artefacts, including examples of their mysterious writing, have been found as far afield as Mesopotamia. And whilst we may be unable to read their script, the deciphered cuneiform texts of old Sumeria talk of the people of Meluhha (probably the Indus Valley) who dealt in precious turquoise from India and lapis lazuli from Afghanistan and who traded jade with distant China. Their ships were known at Dilmun (modern Bahrain), where they traded peacocks, monkeys, incense, ivory, precious stones and rare spices with the Sumerians. Perhaps not surprisingly, such compulsive traders also developed probably the earliest accurate system of weights and measures.

What became of the Indus Valley people is the final mystery in their story. Whatever social structures held them together were collapsing by 1700 BC, when most of their cities were abandoned and their script fell out of use. Elements of their culture are found later, suggesting they adapted to the new world they found themselves in, but their civilization's heyday was past and the Indus Valley would never see its like again.

THE DEATH OF A CIVILIZATION

On the plains of the River Indus in what is present-day Pakistan there once flourished one of the greatest, earliest and most enigmatic civilizations of the ancient world. By 5000 BC – nearly 2500 years before the Egyptians built their first pyramid – the Indus people had settled in communities in the valley and they survived there for almost 3500 years.

At the height of their success they were planning cities from scratch – a feat that was not achieved again until the 19th century – and had created the first urban water and sewage system in the world. Then, around 1700 BC, they simply disappeared. Mysterious to the last, they left little in the way of clues – just some artefacts, some evidence of trade with far-off Sumeria and their curious script. We do not even know what they called themselves.

The disappearance of the Indus Valley civilization was swift and savage – it was suddenly simply wiped from the map of the ancient world. What happened has been an enduring mystery, but the clues to its fate lie buried at Mohenjo Daro.

The key to Mohenjo Daro's downfall is the very thing that made it possible – the River Indus. The Indus is what hydrologists call an 'exotic' river, meaning it rises in a well-watered area but then flows through a very dry land. Whilst the River Indus brought life to the dry valley floor, it could also bring death.

A heavy season's rainfall in the distant Himalayas could have a catastrophic effect on cities downstream. Excavations have revealed metres of silt in some areas that must have washed through the streets in minutes, suffocating everything in its path. By 1700 BC these floods were more frequent and were made worse by earthquakes caused by the Indian subcontinent crashing into Asia. It seems that sometime around 1700 BC there were particularly heavy rains. As the billions of tonnes of water hurtled through the Himalayan foothills a series of earthquakes disturbed the course of the River Indus, effectively damming it. The water built up, flooding the valley before crashing through.

For a people who had lived in the valley for over 3000 years, this was the final catastrophe. Their fields were choked and their cities engulfed. Stories of the tragedy may have reached Sumeria, where the legend of Gilgamesh records a terrible flood that destroyed the world. The same myth was later written into the Bible as Noah's flood. For some of the people of the Indus Valley, however, this was no myth. It was the end.

Mohenjo Daro was the largest city of the Indus civilization and probably its capital. Seen here are the ruins of the residential quarter leading to the citadel, which houses the public baths. These are thought to have had religious significance.

THE MEDIEVAL TIME MACHINE

Beneath the Streets of Novgorod, 1929

The name Novgorod means 'new city' in Russian but Velikiy Novgorod ('Great New City') in northwestern Russia is, in fact, the most ancient Slavic city recorded in Russian history. As such, during the formative years of the Soviet state it became a focus for the work of a new breed of Marxist archaeologist. These scientists were hoping to recover from the soil information about the lives of the people of ancient Russia.

Formal excavations began in the city in 1929 under the direction of Artemy Artsikhovsky and almost immediately uncovered a treasure trove. The nature of the Medieval city, confined within its walls and divided by the River Volkhov, had caused the formation of an 8-metre (26-ft) layer of waterlogged clay, in which the lack of oxygen had prevented decay and even the smallest details of everyday life survived.

Novgorod had been an important trading centre from at least the late ninth century, controlling trade routes between the Byzantine empire of the eastern Mediterranean, the Arab caliphate of Baghdad and the Viking and Germanic kingdoms of northern Europe. Its history was relatively well recorded thanks to the large number of Russian chronicles that were written in the city, but the everyday life of the people, who were considered to be largely illiterate peasants, was almost unknown. Now, as Artsikhovsky's excavations expanded to become the largest in Russia, he began uncovering more and more of this 'ordinary' city and found a number of surprises.

A well-planned and well-preserved city

Novgorod was not the modern image of a grimy Medieval city. The dig uncovered rows of houses and workshops, all made of wood which could be accurately dated to the Medieval period by tree-ring analysis. The houses were individually built and well spaced, and had up to three storeys. Each house was set in its own fenced plot, usually measuring 15 by 30 metres (50 x 100 ft), and was entered through a porch and lobby which kept out the bitter winter wind. Light came from candles, oil lamps and whatever daylight penetrated the small windows, which were covered with transparent mica or oiled fish gut. The streets beyond were not muddy quagmires but were carefully constructed from split tree trunks, and in some areas showed evidence that they had been maintained and repaired for hundreds of years.

The first fortress built to defend the city of Novgorod was made of wood and was erected in the early 11th century. It was rebuilt several times and in the late 15th century replaced by the more heavily fortified red-brick Kremlin, traditionally known as the Detinets, which can be seen today. The walls originally ran for 1.5 miles (2.4 km) around the city and had 13 towers.

'Novgorod the Great' was first mentioned in chronicles of 859. This early illustration of the city was made by a traveller named Arnold von Brand (date unknown).

Inside the buildings the remarkable level of preservation meant that even everyday items had survived. Animals seem to have been housed on the ground floor while people resided upstairs, a system that helped to conserve heat in the winter. Fragments of furniture show that tables, benches, sleeping bunks, boxes and sideboards were often elaborately decorated with stylized animal designs. Food was prepared in a clay oven, and rubbish tips showed that the diet included beef, pork, mutton, goat and duck, served in wooden or pottery bowls. Samples of fibres from the excavations also give a hint as to what these people wore. Flax and silk threads have been found together with woollens which must have been imported from western Europe. They also wore leather shoes and boots with fur linings to provide warmth in winter.

In the workshops of the Medieval city the remains of a large number of crafts have come to light, including leather-working, jewellery manufacture, iron tool-making and barrel-making. Finds have included everything from 'strike-a-lights' (for lighting fires) and scissors to padlocks and glass beads. On one street the home of a 13th-century icon painter was discovered, still containing jars of pigment and olive oil, prepared wooden panels and bronze frames.

Games and entertainment

This high level of industry seems to have given at least the wealthier residents time to spend away from work. Numerous gaming pieces for chess, draughts and dice have been found along with the tambourines, bells, pipes and a

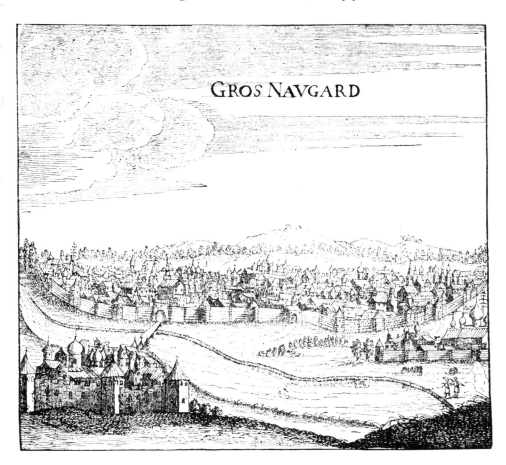

GROS NAVGARD

BIRCH-BARK WRITING

The Medieval boiled birch-bark documents, of which nearly 1000 have been recovered at Novgorod since 1951, have radically altered our view of Medieval city dwellers. Until their discovery, it was assumed that writing was the preserve of the church and the ruling class and that most ordinary people were illiterate. As soon as the first birch-bark documents began to be translated, however, it became clear that they were a record of everyday transactions made by the people of Novgorod.

Most of the documents are ordinary letters of a personal or business nature, written in the local dialect. Mixed in with these are a few in Old Church Slavonic (developed by ninth-century Byzantine missionaries) and even one in Old Norse, the language of the Vikings. They include a request for a neighbour to lend money, love letters, election bulletins, contracts, legal depositions and even a note from a husband asking his wife to send him clean underwear.

Not all the writing is by adults. Letter 210 appears to be a spelling exercise written by a young boy of around seven years old, called Onfim. Onfim seems to have got bored after carefully writing out the first 11 letters of the alphabet and started doodling instead, drawing a picture of himself as a grown-up warrior on a horse, impaling an enemy. To make sure everyone knew who this great warrior was, he wrote his name under it.

Onfim was quite prolific and on other scraps of bark he drew his mother and father, two children playing around a tree, his father dressed as a warrior, some battle scenes and a wild beast. In this last example the animal holds a sign saying 'Greetings from Onfim to Danilo' (probably a school mate) but, possibly unsure that his draughtsmanship had made it entirely clear what this creature was, he wrote '*I am a wild beast*' beneath the picture.

Whilst none of these letters tells us much about the larger history of Novgorod, they are just as important as the major chronicles of the period, since they open a window into daily life in the city and reveal the inhabitants to be far more than anonymous peasants. These are the rarest type of written record – left by ordinary people who never expected, and never received, a place in history. Their notes to each other may seem mundane compared to the thoughts of philosophers and the policies of kings, but they show how a Medieval community really lived, what it hoped for and what it feared. These are the voices of the people who actually made Russia.

stringed instrument known as a *gusli* that must have provided the musical backdrop for such entertainments. Children too enjoyed the benefits of this sophisticated lifestyle – hundreds of toys have been excavated, including wooden hobbyhorses, dolls, carved animals, play swords and bows, leather balls and spinning tops.

Most surprising of all are the wooden rolls that first began to be excavated from the mud on 26 July 1951. They turned out to be pieces of birch bark that had been boiled to remove the outer layers and make the inner pith more flexible. The bark had then been written on using a metal stylus, hundreds of which had already been found but not identified. These scratched impressions in wood proved that the people of Novgorod, far from being illiterate peasants, were members of a literate and often litigious community.

Despite the enormous amount of material recovered from Novgorod in excavations that continue to the present day, only just over 2 percent of the old city has been explored. Novgorod is a Medieval time machine which is only just begining to give up its secrets.

WAR AND PEACE
Restoring the Ara Pacis, 1938

'*When I returned from Spain and Gaul ... after successful operations in those provinces, the senate voted in honour of my return the consecration of an altar to Pax Augusta in the Campus Martius, and on this altar it ordered the magistrates and priests and Vestal Virgins to make annual sacrifice.*'

AUGUSTUS *Res Gestae Divi Augustae* (II. 12)

On 30 January 9 BC the first Roman emperor, Augustus (63 BC–AD 14), and the priests of Rome consecrated a new altar in the city. This was more than a simple act of devotion, more than a political gesture: it was intended to mark the dawn of a new age. Augustus is said to have boasted that he found Rome built of brick and left it clothed in marble. If he had wished to prove his point he need only have directed visitors to the Ara Pacis Augustae – the Altar of Augustan Peace.

This was the finest example of marble carving in Rome – probably the finest in the Roman world – and it stood at the centre of the city as a monument to the new era of peace and prosperity. The senate had issued the decree to begin work on 4 July 13 BC to celebrate the emperor's victories over Gaul and Spain, and no expense had been spared in finding the very best Parian marble and sculptors to create it.

A mirror of the Roman state

The beautifully carved reliefs that decorate the screen around the altar depicted the Roman state as it saw itself. There were personifications of peace and plenty in the form of Tellus (Mother Earth) and images from the mythological foundation of Rome. Here too were the Romans themselves – soldiers, senators and children – and the imperial family led by Augustus in the role of chief priest, walking in solemn procession to make sacrifices. The senate's decree ordered that in the years to come the city's magistrates, priests and Vestal Virgins would take his place here once a year and make sacrifices to the enduring Pax Romana.

Detail from the frieze of carved reliefs on the Ara Pacis, showing the imperial procession. Members of Augustus's family, children included, are depicted at the inaugural sacrificial ceremony.

Originally the monument stood on the west side of the Via Flaminia and formed a symbolic part of a huge public sundial known as the Horologium. However, in the years since the fall of the Roman empire the Horologium and the Ara Pacis had decayed and ultimately been buried under centuries of Medieval buildings. But knowledge of the building and even its location were not forgotten. In 1568, during the construction of the Palazzo Fiano, ten marble fragments had been found; since then small excavations beneath the *palazzo* had revealed more, and by 1902 it was possible to make an attempt

at a reconstruction. For the time being this could be done only on paper, however, because the fragments of relief were by then scattered around museums in Europe.

Glorifying Mussolini's Fascist regime

It was under Mussolini's dictatorship that a plan to fully excavate and rebuild the Ara Pacis first gained momentum. Mussolini (1883–1945) was keen to remind Italians of their Roman past and no less intent on equating himself with Augustus. The Fascists remodelled Rome, clearing ancient sites of later buildings and constructing their own monuments to what they hoped was the beginning of a new Fascist empire. Central to this was the plan to reconstruct the Ara Pacis, and the archaeologist Giuseppe Moretti (1876–1945) was contracted for the job.

Moretti's task was not an easy one. The Renaissance *palazzo* that stood over the buried monument was in a fragile state, and excavations in the soft sand under it might lead to its collapse. So Moretti set about first supporting the building on hydraulic jacks and then casting a concrete bridge beneath it to spread the weight away from the altar. This, he hoped, would leave him with enough space simply to dig out the Ara Pacis from under the bridge. But the plan proved unworkable, for the sand under the palazzo was saturated and as soon as an area was excavated it filled with water. More worryingly, if this water was simply pumped out there was a danger that the foundations of surrounding buildings would be compromised as the sand dried.

Moretti was an engineer as well as an archaeologist, however, and the solution he came up with was unique in the history of excavation. With the considerable resources of the Fascist state behind him, he surrounded the *palazzo* with steel pipes which he filled with refrigerant. By attaching these to an industrial heat exchanger, he turned the whole site into a freezer, creating a solid dam of frozen saturated sand around the site to stop ground water flooding in from under nearby buildings. He then resumed excavations beneath his concrete bridge, and slowly the panels of the Ara Pacis were recovered from the icy sand.

Of course the monument could not be rebuilt in its original location, so Mussolini ordered it to be reconstructed near Augustus's mausoleum – a huge circular brick building, robbed of its original decoration, which had until recently been used as an opera house. Plaster casts were ordered of panels then in other European museums and, on 23 September 1938 – the 2000th anniversary of Augustus's birthday – the Ara Pacis Augustae was opened.

The re-emergence of the Ara Pacis did not mark the beginning of a new Golden Age for Italy, however. Mussolini had chosen a new location for the monument in a plaza named after himself and had restored it largely as a monument to himself. Outside, the world was just months away from war, and the restoration of the Altar of Peace by the Fascists marked the descent of Italy into years of bloodshed. Peace would only be restored with the death of their regime.

THE HOROLOGIUM AUGUSTI

'Augustus used the obelisk in the Campus Martius in a remarkable way, namely to cast a shadow and thus mark the length of days and nights. A paved area was laid out to commensurate with the height of the monolith in such a way that the shadow at noon on the shortest day might extend to the end of the paving. As the shadow gradually grew shorter and longer again, it was measured by bronze rods fixed in the paving.'

PLINY THE ELDER *Natural History* (36.72f)

How Romans measured time has always been a highly disputed subject. We know that they divided the day into 12 equal portions of daylight, thus as the seasons changed the hours grew longer or shorter. But how this was achieved and how a vast empire was run on such an elastic timescale has remained a mystery. Recent excavations and the advent of 3D computer modelling have allowed a new generation of archaeologists to start to answer this question.

We know that there was a great 'sundial' in the centre of Rome which not only told the time but indicated over the course of each year the auspicious dates associated with the imperial family. This device, known as the Horologium Augusti, was constructed on a vast scale. The dial was so huge that no piece of metal could be cast large enough for the vane (gnomon) – instead, an Egyptian red granite obelisk, nearly 22 metres (72 ft) high, had to be brought from Alexandria to serve the purpose.

To mark out midday at the various seasons of the year, a pavement 160 by 75 metres (525 x 246 ft) was constructed into which massive bronze hour markers were set. Recent excavations in Rome have finally uncovered the location of the gnomon and part of the pavement.

An illustration by Giuseppe Vasi shows the excavation in 1748 of the obelisk, which lay buried below building ruins and had been broken into several pieces.

But the Horologium was intended to do more than mark time. The buildings around it, including the Ara Pacis, were arranged so that the shadow of the obelisk would touch them on significant days. On just one day of the year the tip of the shadow passed over the place where deceased members of Augustus's family were ceremonially cremated. On another it touched the very centre of Augustus's mausoleum. And on 23 September, the emperor's birthday, the shadow reached the bottom of the steps of the Ara Pacis itself. This was a device to remind the people of Rome of the gifts, both physical and political, that the emperor had given the city, and to demonstrate that the world and the heavens followed a divine order in which the gods had placed the imperial family above ordinary men and women.

The Horologium itself was not untouched by time, however. Pliny the Elder notes that by his day it was no longer accurate:

'These measurements, however, have not agreed with the calendar for some 30 years. Either the sun itself is out of phase or has been altered by some change in the behaviour of the heavens, or the whole earth has moved slightly off centre. I hear this phenomenon has been observed in other places.'

How this error crept in is not recorded, although it is possible that the gnomon may have moved during an earthquake. It continued to stand until at least the eighth century, but after that time the records fall silent and at some later date the obelisk fell.

It was only rediscovered in 1512, and it was almost another 300 years – 1789 – before it was erected in its present location in Rome's Piazza di Montecitorio, where its previous use was forgotten. Only in recent years has the Horologium started to reveal its secrets.

LIGHT ON A DARK AGE
The Sutton Hoo Ship Burial, 1939

'*I asked which one she would like opened and she pointed to ... the largest barrow of the group, and said "What about this?" and I replied that it would be quite alright for me.*'

BASIL BROWN *Diary of the Excavations at Sutton Hoo* 1938–9

Many stories have been recounted to explain why Edith Pretty (1883–1942) wanted archaeologists to dig in her garden. Edith was a quiet woman who had withdrawn from local affairs after the death of her husband in 1934 left her alone with her four-year-old son in a 15-bedroom house at Sutton Hoo in Suffolk in eastern England. In the lonely years that followed she developed a growing interest in the 'afterlife', and it was perhaps this fascination that drew her to the large grassy mounds in her garden.

From the windows on the south side of the house she could clearly see the huddle of mounds on the sandy heath just below a copse known as Top Hat Wood. They stood in a prominent position on a promontory overlooking the valley of the River Deben, and were assumed to be burial mounds, or 'barrows', probably from the Bronze Age, similar to many others in the vicinity.

A momentous decision

Edith Pretty was determined to excavate the mounds, which, as owner of the 160-hectare (400-acre) estate, she could do at that time without official permission. However, she first sought advice from Ipswich Museum, which put her in touch with an amateur archaeologist, Basil Brown (1888–1977). Brown agreed terms of 30 shillings a week, a room in the chauffeur's cottage, and the help of two estate labourers, and commenced work on 20 June 1938.

Brown's initial investigation of Mound 1, the largest barrow, was frustrated when a pilot trench hit a lump of natural stone. Edith instructed him to try another. Mound 3 was excavated by digging a test hole by the mound to find the ancient ground surface, then driving a trench straight through the middle of the barrow at that level in the hope of uncovering the distinctive rectangular stain in the soil that marked the edges of the burial chamber. This technique, in use since the 19th century, could be disastrously destructive – fortunately, Basil Brown was a more than usually careful archaeologist.

Mound 3 proved something of a disappointment, however. The site had clearly been robbed at some time in the distant past and all that remained in the burial chamber was a small wooden 'tray' that disintegrated on removal, on which lay a few cremated

remains of a human and a horse. Around this lay some broken pottery, a lump of iron (later shown to be an axehead), some bone inlay from a long-decayed box and the lid of a jug that probably came originally from the Mediterranean.

Two more mounds were opened in 1938. They had also been robbed, but at least yielded enough for Brown to deduce that Sutton Hoo was not a Bronze Age burial ground, but Anglo-Saxon, dating from sometime between the end of Roman rule and the advent of Christianity in Britain. It was one of the least understood periods in British history, and despite the paucity of finds Brown and Pretty agreed to another season of work in 1939.

So, on 8 May 1939, Basil Brown found himself once again on Mound 1, which his employer had decided would be the main target of this season. On the fourth day, one of his workmen struck a corroded lump of iron. Brown ordered the shovels put aside and started to explore the sandy soil around the 'lump' which he recognized as the type of rivet that had once held the strakes (planks) of a ship together. Soon another five rivets appeared, and Brown immediately realized that they were in their original position. The wood they had once kept in place had long since dissolved in the highly acidic soil of the heath, but the rivets clearly marked out the shape of the prow of a ship.

Thanks to Brown's painstaking work, by the time a team from the British Museum and Cambridge University arrived, the lines of a large ship, picked out by the flat tops of its rivets, were clearly visible. Brown had also left untouched the unmistakable stain of a

The excavation at Sutton Hoo, clearly showing the lines of the ship burial. The team assembled by Charles Philips included some of the greatest future names in archaeology – Stuart Piggott, later Professor of Archaeology at Edinburgh, Graham Clark, who became Professor at Cambridge, O.G.S. Crawford, founder of the journal Antiquity, *and W.F. Grimes, later Director of the Institute of Archaeology in London.*

burial chamber, carefully preserved amidships. With Britain facing imminent war, the summer of 1939 was not a good time to find experienced excavators for a major project, but a handful of gifted archaeologists were persuaded to take part in the work. Charles Philips (1901–85) of Cambridge University took control, with Brown as his assistant.

Magnificent grave goods

With the danger that the now well-publicized site might be robbed, work began immediately removing the blackened sand from the central hull of the ship. On 21 July, Philips's shout of '*My godfathers!*' gave an inkling of what lay within. A small gold pyramid-shaped stud, inlaid with blood-red garnets, had been unearthed. The next day brought a gold purse frame decorated with strange Anglo-Saxon mythical beasts in the middle of which lay a pile of gold coins. There then emerged gold and garnet buckles and finally a huge gold buckle beautifully worked with a writhing pattern of interlaced animals and with a hinged back. The Keeper of British and Mediaeval Antiquities at the British Museum was summoned and immediately identified the objects, from the style of their decoration, as coming from the early seventh century.

And there was much more still to come. The next few days brought to light a whetstone with a strange stag decoration on one end – perhaps some form of sceptre – plus a shield and a bowl from Coptic Egypt. What looked like another shield turned out to be a huge silver dish, while a heap of purple corrosion drying in the sun fell apart to reveal a stack of ten perfectly preserved silver bowls. Hanging cauldrons and weapons were also appearing, along with more jewellery, including the now famous gold and garnet shoulder clasps. There was a chain-mail coat, gaming pieces, spoons, knives, drinking horns, spears, ladles, combs and even an iron lamp still containing beeswax. Crushed in hundreds of pieces in the corner was also what would prove the most iconic item from the whole site – the famous helmet.

By 31 July the chamber was empty and attention turned to the ship itself. It was a clinker-built vessel almost 27 metres (90 ft) in length, which must have been dragged up from the Deben before being interred, whole, in a vast mound. At the same time, a local inquest was held to decide whether the hoard – which even in 1939 was being referred to as 'the million-pound treasure' – belonged to the Crown or Mrs Pretty. The verdict was not long in coming. Although there was no sign of a body in the mound, the acidic nature of the soil suggested that it had simply dissolved away. The items in the mound had clearly not been buried for later retrieval (in which case, the Crown would have had legal entitlement), but were being taken by their owner to the next world aboard his magnificent ship. As such, the coroner adjudged the entirety of the treasure belonged to Edith Pretty.

By now war was only days away and Mrs Pretty ordered the remains of the excavation covered with dead bracken to protect them. Then in an act of unrivalled generosity, she gave the entire treasure to the British Museum. It is the largest donation ever made to the museum within the lifetime of the donor. In recognition of this she was offered a dameship of the British empire, an honour she modestly declined.

WHO WAS BURIED IN MOUND ONE?

'The belovèd leader laid they down there,
Giver of rings, on the breast of the vessel,
The famed by the mainmast. A many of jewels,
Of fretted embossings, from far-lands brought over,
Was placed near at hand then; and heard I not ever
That a folk ever furnished a float more superbly
With weapons of warfare, weeds for the battle,
Bills and burnies; on his bosom sparkled
Many a jewel that with him must travel
On the flush of the flood afar on the current.'

Beowulf (I – The Life and Death of Scyld)

The question of who was buried in Mound 1 may never be answered unequivocally, as not one of the 263 objects recovered from the site bears the definitive mark of its owner. There are, however, some clues.

The style of decoration on several of the items indicates that they were made around the beginning of the seventh century. The best hope for narrowing down the date of the burial comes from the coins found inside the purse frame. The 37 gold coins found there, along with three blanks, may have been intended as payment for the 40 ghostly oarsmen who would row the ship into the afterlife. The two small gold ingots also discovered may, then, have been for the helmsman and the pilot. The latest of these coins, which all come from Merovingian France, was minted for Theodebert II in around AD 625.

The Sutton Hoo helmet. The lavish grave goods indicated that this must have been the burial of an extremely important Anglo-Saxon, possibly even that of a king.

The sheer range and quality of goods in the grave provide further clues. Many items are made of gold and the craftsmanship is unparalleled; only someone of the highest rank would have had access to the raw materials and the people to work them. The quantity of gold and silver suggests that the dead man belonged to the highest echelon of society – people we know at the time were called kings. Several items also come from a very wide area, implying access to distant trade routes – the great silver dish, for example, was made in Byzantium.

Some of the items in the hoard have a clear symbolic import. Firstly there are objects we might call 'regalia'. The whetstone with its stag finial – surely too ornate to be a functional item – has been interpreted as a sceptre indicating the owner's rank, while an iron stand may be an emblem of Anglo-Saxon kingship. Then there are the religious artefacts. Ship burials with grave goods are pagan – part of the Germanic belief system then prevalent throughout much of southern England and Scandinavia. But two spoons in the grave, one marked 'Saulos' and the other 'Paulos' – Saul and Paul – may be christening spoons. Their owner may have been unaware of their symbolic significance, but it is also possible that he was hedging his bets and taking a few Christian items with him.

So who might fit this description? At this time England was divided into a number of small kingdoms and Sutton Hoo lies in the realm of what was then East Anglia. Between the late 6th and early 7th century, a group of pagan kings ruled this area. More recent excavations have suggested that Sutton Hoo might be their burial site. If so, the owner of Mound 1 was a prominent member of this dynasty.

The historical figure who best fits the bill is a king named Rædwald. According to the Venerable Bede (writing over a hundred years later), Rædwald held the bretwaldaship (a sort of overlordship) over the other kings of Saxon England. We also know that he was a pagan who converted to Christianity before re-embracing paganism.

This may explain the Christening spoons in a pagan burial. Bede further tells us that Rædwald defeated the king of Northumbria in battle. The helmet, sword, shield and other weapons in Mound 1 seem to be those of a great warrior. Yet all this must remain firmly in the realm of speculation; Rædwald is certainly a plausible candidate for the Sutton Hoo burial on a number of counts. But conclusive proof of the owner's identity is tantalizingly lacking.

THE RIDDLE OF THE SANDS
Decoding the Nazca Lines, 1946

The greatest achievement of the Nazca culture of Peru was not the conquest of another people, nor did it lie in the realms of artistic endeavour or architecture. Rather, it was agricultural – the greening of a desert landscape. Between around 300 BC and AD 800, these peoples spread out along the Nazca valley and the southern Peruvian coast, turning vast tracts of dry wilderness into lush farmland.

The Nazca culture built its success on irrigation, particularly the construction of aqueducts, and the wealth that farming brought them enabled them to develop a rich material culture. Nazca pottery includes bold representations of the flora and fauna they encountered – hummingbirds, whales, sharks and cacti – while their dry desert tombs have helped preserve llama and alpaca wool textiles in their original, vibrant colours.

'Paths' in the desert

But the Nazca did not simply decorate pottery and clothes. They decorated the desert itself. In 1926 an American anthropologist, Alfred Kroeber (1876–1960), noted that the Nazca Desert was criss-crossed with unexplained lines, which the Peruvian archaeologist Toribo Mejía Xesspe called 'roads'. It was, however, another American, an archaeologist and historian of science named Paul Kosok (d.1959), who first noticed the sheer extent of the lines from the air and decided to investigate in the 1930s. Following up his aerial photography with a ground survey, he discovered that the lines were in fact artificially constructed 'paths', created simply by moving aside the red desert pebbles to reveal the whiter soil beneath. The Nazca Desert is one of the driest places on earth and forms a remarkably stable environment. The temperature there remains at around 25°C (77°F) all year round, while the absence of wind means that marks that were made centuries – even millennia – before, survive intact.

Kosok noted that these lines must be ancient from the broken pottery associated with them, which bore the distinctive shapes and colours of the Nazcan culture. He also noticed on the summer solstice in 1941 that one of these lines pointed directly to the place on the western horizon where the sun set that day.

But it was the end of the war before Kosok could find an assistant to help him map what he believed must be the astronomical arrangement of these lines. The person he appointed was Maria Reiche (1903–98), a German mathematician who had taken a job

A 'candelabra cactus' geoglyph inscribed into the surface of the Nazca Desert at Paracas, Peru. Many theories have been put forward to explain the significance of the Nazca lines. The fact that most of the animal figures comprise a single line has led to suggestions that they were originally 'walked', perhaps as part of a religious rite.

158

AERIAL PHOTOGRAPHY

Since the invention of the aeroplane in the early years of the 20th century, aerial observation and photography have revolutionized the discovery and interpretation of archaeological sites. From the first manned balloon flights, it was clear that gaining a 'birds-eye' view of the ground gave a new perspective, but it was the military who really brought the profession of aerial photographer to the fore. Many of the early pioneers of photography from the air, such as O.G.S. Crawford (1886–1957), had flown as military observers during the First World War and rapidly realized that an aerial perspective on a landscape gave unique insights.

From the air it was possible to see the full extent of sites and observe their position within the wider landscape. The advent of stereoscopic photography and photogrammetry allowed such information to be taken off photographs and plotted on maps, thus creating the first large-scale plans of whole civilizations. In the case of the Nazca lines, it was only the distant perspective given by flight that allowed the true nature of the features to be identified. Since then, aerial surveys have also been used in this empty desert region to locate Nazca centres, based around vast mud-brick citadels. From the ground, in their heavily weathered state, these appeared to be natural mountain features.

Differences in the colour of soils as seen from the air can also be used to identify sites that are difficult to locate on the ground. Ditches are sometimes filled with a soil of a different colour from that immediately around them, although the difference is often so slight as to show up only in aerial photographs. These are known as soil marks, and can range from the slightest change in tone to the remains of long-demolished structures visible in the scatter of building materials lying in the topsoil.

Aerial archaeology provides more than just a top-down perspective on the world, however. As well as giving context to large features, it can be used to identify buried sites that are entirely invisible from the ground. The growth of crops in fields is affected by what lies in the sub-soil. Cereals growing over a buried wall will send their roots down onto dry mortar and stone and hence grow less vigorously than the plants around them. Equally, plants growing over a buried ditch put their roots into a deeper, richer soil that retains more water, and so grow better than those around them. The varying growth rates among plants over buried features, when seen en masse from the air, form patterns known as crop marks. The visibility of the marks can be accentuated in very dry summers, when only those crops growing over deep, buried trenches survive, and in winter when the greater heat capacity of a buried ditch causes the frost over it to melt before that in surrounding areas. By taking aerial photographs of such sites early in the morning and at dusk, it is also possible to highlight the differences, as the raking light across the site reveals tiny differences in topography.

Since the introduction of this technique to archaeology, hundreds of thousand of sites have been discovered by aerial photographs – ranging from prehistoric hut circles to entire Roman cities. It is ironic that a technology that developed out of military science has given rise to a completely non-destructive way of identifying archaeological remains. It is perhaps the most successful technique available to modern archaeologists.

in Peru as governess to the German consul's children. At the outbreak of war she had refused to return to Germany and now, with hostilities finally over, she began what would prove to be her life's work.

Her first revelation came in 1946, when she began walking the Nazca lines. The first figure she came to was clearly not simply a line but a huge geometric shape carved out in the desert floor. Mapping the line as she went, she realized it was actually in the shape of a spider. Nearby a huge spiral proved to be the tail of a gigantic New World monkey. The Nazca lines were not simply paths across the desert; they also formed pictures on the ground ('geoglyphs'). Soon other figures were discovered, including a hummingbird, a dog and a lizard.

An enduring mystery

Yet the lines are still steeped in mystery. Many of these figures are gigantic – the largest being over 270 metres (885 ft) long – and could never have been properly seen from the desert floor. Indeed, Reiche had to ask the Peruvian airforce to photograph the area from the air to help her plot the hundreds of figures and lines. On the ground she also discovered wooden posts driven into the end marks of some figures, which were dated to between AD 100 and 500, suggesting that these figures had been created at a time long before any form of flight could have aided their makers in drawing them.

Since the publication of Reiche's figures, theories have proliferated about how and why the lines were created. Most notoriously, the Swiss writer Erich von Däniken (b.1935) claimed implausibly that they were landing strips for alien spacecraft. Others have proposed that the Nazcans knew how to build hot-air balloons, indeed a 'replica' of one has even been built, although no evidence for such technology at this early period has ever been found.

A well-preserved example of Nazca textile art, incorporating an animal motif. The Nazcans were one of the first Amerindian cultures to use llama and alpaca wool.

Archaeologists suggest the lines had a number of functions. Reiche noted that some seemed to have astronomical alignment, as her mentor Kosok believed, and thought the animals may represent constellations. However, recent work by archaeo-astronomers, who try to match ancient alignments with the known position of stars and planets at certain dates, has not corroborated this theory. There are even suggestions that the placing of the figures might reflect the presence of groundwater in an area, something we know the Nazcans used to great effect in their irrigation schemes.

Although there is still no definitive answer as to why the lines were created, experimental archaeology has at least ascertained that the technology available to the Nazcans would have enabled them to trace these lines without taking a 'bird's-eye view'. It is testament to their monumental achievement that future generations should need to speculate that they had extra-terrestrial help.

THE WOLF IN THE CAVE
The Dead Sea Scrolls, 1947

The discovery of the Dead Sea Scrolls is an event surrounded by as much mystery as the lives of the people they once belonged to. How much of the story of their original unearthing is truth and how much is myth, elaborately embroidered by antiquities dealers, it is impossible to say. There is no doubt, however, that the find itself is one of the greatest manuscript discoveries of all time.

Towards the end of 1947, news began circulating among academics and collectors that a number of extremely rare manuscripts had come onto the market in Bethlehem. Four of them had been purchased by the Syrian Orthodox archbishop of Jerusalem, while an academic at the Hebrew University had bought three more. The story the buyers were told was that the scrolls had been discovered by a goatherd in the Qumran area around the beginning of that year, perhaps in February. Mohammed Ahmed el-Hamed, known as edh-Dhib ('the wolf') had lost an animal, which he thought must have strayed into one of the many caves that riddle the rock faces of the region. In an attempt to flush the animal out, edh-Dhib had started throwing stones into the mouths of some caves but, to his surprise, in one he heard not the clatter of stone on stone, but the sound of pottery shattering. Clambering into the fissure in the rock he discovered inside a collection of pottery jars which appeared to be very old and which contained manuscript scrolls wrapped in linen. Edh-Dhib grabbed a few of the best-looking examples and then continued his search for the lost goat. The scrolls were then shown by the local Bedouin to the Bethlehem antiquities dealers who, having assured themselves that they were not stolen from a synagogue, began circulating them on the open market.

A treasure trove for biblical scholars
It was early in 1948 before archaeologists first got sight of these scrolls. In February, a Syrian Orthodox monk showed one of his archbishop's scrolls to John Trevor (1916–2006) at the American Schools of Oriental Research in Jerusalem. He and his colleagues quickly confirmed what the Orthodox community already suspected. The scroll was a copy of the biblical Book of Isaiah but, much more than that, it was easily the earliest example of the book known. In fact, it was the oldest Hebrew manuscript ever discovered. The public announcement of the discovery of the scrolls was made by Trevor in May 1948 in the journal *Biblical Archaeologist* and caused an immediate sensation. Along with the Isaiah Scroll, academics had by then also identified: a Genesis Apocryphon; a 'rule book' for the community which it seems had hidden the scrolls; a text on military organization known as the 'War Scroll'; some thanksgiving hymns and

another fragment of Isaiah. The scrolls all dated from the last two centuries BC and the first century AD, up to the time of the First Jewish Revolt against the Romans in AD 66, presumably the date the cache was hidden. The texts all belonged to a community which had preserved the earliest examples of Jewish religious writings – but how would they compare to the later texts that formed the 'official' holy books of the Jewish religion? Christian scholars were also desperate to see the scrolls. Not only did they contain Old Testament texts, they came from around the time a well-known radical Jewish group was operating in Palestine – led by a man named Jesus.

These discoveries were made against a background of increasing violence in the Middle East. In the month the discovery was published, the British mandate over Palestine had ended and the state of Israel had been established, leading to violent clashes between Arabs and Jews. The known scrolls were moved to Beirut for safekeeping, their exact origin remaining a mystery known only to the desert Bedouin and perhaps a few Bethlehem antiquities dealers. What was also becoming clear from the rumours still rife in the region was that these scrolls were just the tip of the iceberg – many more awaited discovery.

A fragment of the 'Community Rule', or 'Manual of Discipline'. This manuscript contains the rules of conduct of a religious sect possibly based at Khirbet Qumran.

Towards the end of 1948, despite the growing violence, the British director of antiquities in Jordan, G.L. Harding (1901–79), began a campaign to search the region and discover the location of the scroll caves. In February of 1949 he struck gold and began excavations in what is now known as Cave 1, the secret resting place of the seven mysterious scrolls. Here his team uncovered another 600 pieces of manuscript, along with fragments of cloth and wood, all miraculously preserved in the still, hot air of the cave. Negotiations with the local Bedouin also produced many more pieces which had been removed before Harding had arrived.

Over the next few years the Qumran hills swarmed with locals and academics searching the thousands of caves for other caches. In 1952 Caves 2, 3, 4, 5 and 6 were uncovered, some by archaeologists, others by local teams working for antiquities dealers. Along with many more biblical texts this produced a unique scroll made of copper which contained a list of the secret hiding places of gold and silver hoards, probably the treasures of the Temple at Jerusalem, hidden during the Jewish Revolt to prevent them falling into Roman hands.

TIMELINE

*c.*21 BC–AD 61 The almost 900 documents known to posterity as the Dead Sea Scrolls are written, including the only known copies of biblical documents made before AD 100

*c.*66 Scrolls are hidden in the caves of Qumran at the time of the First Jewish Revolt

1947 (February) A Bedouin goatherd finds seven scrolls in jars above the Dead Sea at Khirbet Qumran. John Trevor identifies the Isaiah Scroll as the oldest known Hebrew manuscript

1948 G.L. Harding launches a search for the remaining Dead Sea Scrolls

1949 Harding's team, excavating Cave 1, uncover 600 more pieces of manuscript and preserved fragments of cloth and wood

1952 Five further caves are excavated by archaeologists and local antiquities dealers, resulting in the discovery of biblical texts and a copper scroll purporting to reveal the location of hoards of treasure hidden during the First Jewish Revolt

1955 Caves 7–10 are uncovered by archaeologists; modest finds are recorded

1956 Along with other texts and psalms, the Book of Leviticus is found by local Bedouin in Cave 11

To date however none of the sites mentioned has produced any of this treasure. 1955 saw the discovery by archaeologists of caves 7, 8, 9 and 10, one of which held the only Greek language fragments discovered, although the finds were relatively modest. Perhaps not surprisingly, it was the local Bedouin who made the last great discovery, Cave 11, which contained over two dozen texts, including the Book of Leviticus and a book of psalms.

Painstaking conservation

In total, just under 900 documents have been recovered from the Qumran hills to date, including sections of all the books of the Hebrew Bible, with the exception of the Books of Esther and Nehemiah, along with a number that are not in the modern canon such as the Book of Enoch and Book of Jubilees. Alongside these are a number of texts concerning a Jewish religious sect, the Essenes, members of which may have either written or collected and hidden the scrolls. These include the 'Manual of

Ruins of the possible Essene settlement at Khirbet Qumran in Jordan. Members of the semi-monastic Essene sect of Judaism led ascetic lives and saw themselves as the last generation before the coming of the Messiah.

WHO WROTE THE DEAD SEA SCROLLS?

The discovery of the world's largest cache of ancient biblical texts in or around Wadi Qumran near the Dead Sea sparked a heated debate about just how the scrolls came to be hidden there and who wrote and owned them.

At the time of the discovery of the first scrolls, archaeologists thought that the collection had been written and hidden by a Jewish sect known as the Essenes, who are described by the contemporary historian Josephus (AD 37–c100) in his history of the Jewish War, written around AD 75. Excavations of an archaeological site near the caves between 1951 and 1958 unearthed what was claimed to be the home of this group, which included ritual baths, a cistern and assembly room and a scriptorium in which the scrolls could have been written. The site had been occupied from sometime around 150 BC until its destruction by the Romans in AD 68.

As more of the scrolls have been conserved and translated, however, this idea has begun to be questioned. The huge corpus of writing is not always consistent in terms of the beliefs described and some texts go against what we know from other sources of Essene theology. A similar argument that the scrolls were the work of an Essene-like group – the Sadducees – suffers from the same problem of a lack of complete agreement among the scrolls themselves and differences between them and known Sadducee beliefs.

Even the archaeological site at Qumran has been recently reinterpreted, not as a religious centre but as either a trading post, a private villa or a pottery factory. In this last view, the 'ritual baths' so definitively described in the 1950s excavation might actually be water tanks used in ceramic production. Such are the dangers of excavating a site with preconceived ideas of what will be found.

More recently it has been suggested that the scrolls are in fact the remains of various Jerusalem libraries, smuggled out of the city and hidden during the Roman siege of AD 68–70. This might explain the eclectic nature of the texts, as well as the presence of the copper scroll which, it is argued, contains a list of treasure so vast it could only have come from the temple there. It would also explain why only copies of literary texts have been found without any of the local correspondence or administrative accounts we might expect if the cache was the product of a local sect. It has even been suggested that the Dead Sea Scrolls are the library from the Great Temple itself, although the lack of agreement among them perhaps makes a source from several different libraries more likely. Either way, if these are the holy books taken from one or many libraries in Jerusalem during the Jewish Revolt, they make the find even more important, since they reflect not simply the beliefs of one sect but the intellectual life of the people of Judea in the first century AD.

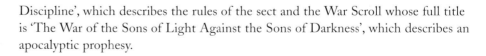

Discipline', which describes the rules of the sect and the War Scroll whose full title is 'The War of the Sons of Light Against the Sons of Darkness', which describes an apocalyptic prophesy.

Most of the scrolls were written on either leather or papyrus, with the exception of the copper scroll and one fragment written on a broken piece of pottery known as an ostracon. Their extreme fragility and the priceless information they contain have made their preservation a cause of much debate. It has taken many years' painstaking work just to piece together the fragmentary texts, of which 15 percent still remain unidentified. For many years, however, the restored texts were made available only to a handful of academics and only on condition that they did not publish their results, which has inevitably led to a host of conspiracy theories. Now the texts are widely available and archaeologists and historians can begin investigating the lives of a people living at a crucial moment in the development of the Jewish and Christian religions.

SHIP OF A MILLION YEARS

Kamal el-Mallakh and Khufu's Boat, 1950

Located on the outskirts of Cairo, the Giza plateau is a complex of ancient Egyptian monuments. Seen here in the background is the second-largest pyramid at Giza, which houses the tomb of the fourth-dynasty pharaoh Khafre (Chephren).

It was said that Kamal el-Mallakh (1918–87) resembled a pharaoh, tall and upright as he was, with a high forehead and receding hair. He was born on 26 October 1918 into a devout Coptic Christian family in the city of Assiut in Upper Egypt, and initially trained as an architect before studying to become an Egyptologist at the School of Archaeology in the University of Cairo.

He began a career that would have been a source of pride to any pharaoh – travelling the country using his architectural skills to recover and restore the monuments of the past – and it was this that brought him into the employment of the Antiquities Department on the Giza plateau in 1936, under the shadow of the Great Pyramid. El-Mallakh worked on the site for 14 years, trying to decipher the complex arrangements of pyramids and temples. Then, in April 1950, he began monitoring the construction of a new road around the site designed to improve tourist access.

An archaeologically rich country

The Giza plateau is studded with pharaonic monuments and every step of the construction had to be carefully supervised to ensure that important finds were not bulldozed in the process. It was during this work that el-Mallakh first noticed a layer of limestone powder across an area of the site, with a layer of pink mortar beneath. On investigation, it appeared to run right round the edge of two pits, the largest measuring 32.5 metres (107 ft) long. Each pit was covered with over 40 huge limestone slabs weighing between 17 and 20 tons each, and marked with the cartouche of Djedefre, the successor to the builder of the Great Pyramid – Khufu.

In another country such a find might have brought all other work to a stop, but in a country as archaeologically rich as Egypt the general opinion was that these were simply foundations around the pyramid and therefore of little interest.

El-Mallakh did not agree, however. He had noticed that next to some of the more minor pyramids, boat-shaped pits had been dug in antiquity. Nothing had ever been found in any of these cavities, but what if the slabs he had uncovered were not simply foundation blocks but capping stones over another unopened pit, one associated with

the Great Pyramid itself? It took four years of cajoling before he could persuade his superiors to allow him to excavate the pits, but in 1954 he finally received permission and began work.

Clearing all the sand from the area, el-Mallakh's team identified two slabs set slightly further apart than the others and on 26 May 1954, he began to dig away the material between them. El-Mallakh continued to scrape away the mortar, going ever deeper until he was so deep that he had to be held upside down and lowered into the cavity he had excavated, pressing his body against the stone on one side to allow a little light from above to fall on the area he was working on.

The sweet smell of success

Then, quite suddenly, his hand disappeared below him into a void. He closed his eyes to try to accustom them to the dark before peering into the hole and, as he did, a strange smell drifted up around him — sweet and dusty. For a moment he feared it was just the smell of decay, the only remnant of what had once lain in the pit below him. In fact, it was the air from 4500 years earlier, pungent with the unmistakable scent of cedar wood.

Shouting to his team above him, el-Mallakh asked for a small shaving mirror to be lowered down. Then, as he hung with his head down in the gap between the stones, he

A carved relief found in Queen Hatshepsut's Red Chapel at Karnak temple near Luxor shows an Egyptian funerary procession, complete with funeral boat borne aloft by footmen.

THE PHARAOH KHUFU

The pharaoh Khufu, also known as Cheops, ruled in Egypt's first dynastic era, known as the 'Old Kingdom', between about 2589 and 2566 BC.

He is remembered today as the builder of the only Wonder of the Ancient World that is still standing, the Great Pyramid at Giza, which remained the tallest man-made building in the world until well into the 19th century. Yet despite this monumental epitaph, little can be said with certainty about his life. Faint inscriptions in Sinai and at Aswan record the presence of his people in these areas – troops securing the border of the former, and workmen quarrying red granite for his sarcophagus and valley temple at the latter – but little else exists.

Later traditions state that he was a cruel and ruthless ruler, a reputation that came down to the Greeks. On visiting the Giza plateau, the Greek historian Herodotus (c.484–425 BC) was told that one of the small pyramids was built by a daughter of Khufu whom he forced into prostitution to help pay for his tomb. The story relates that as well as asking for money from her clients she asked each

for a block of stone, and it is from these that her pyramid is built. Such stories certainly got the attention of ancient writers but there can be little doubt that they are later inventions.

One of the problems with understanding Khufu's reign is that almost nothing (other than his boat and pyramid) can definitely be identified with him, and those items which might have been his rarely contain an inscription to prove it. The only statue we can positively say is of the man who built Egypt's largest monument is a diminutive ivory, just 7.5 centimetres (3 in) tall, which bears his name.

Even his pyramid is something of a mystery, as no items have ever been found inside it that can be identified with Khufu. The great sarcophagus in the King's Chamber, deep inside the pyramid, is empty and may never have been used. As for the pharaoh's body and the magnificent grave goods we might expect to find in such a lavish tomb, nothing has ever been recovered. If any of his funerary goods have survived the ravages of time and tomb raiders, they still await discovery.

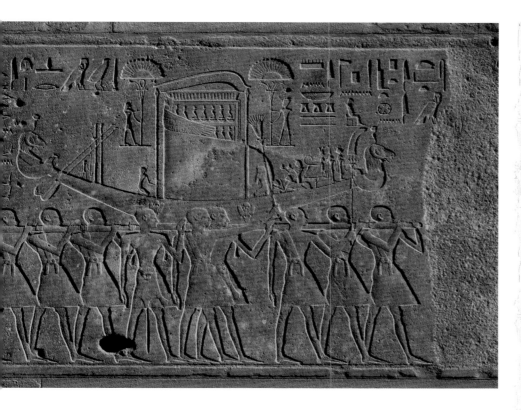

TIMELINE

*c.*2589 BC Khufu becomes pharaoh of Egypt

*c.*2566 BC Khufu dies and is probably buried in the Great Pyramid at Giza

*c.*400 BC The Greek historian Herodotus visits the pyramids and hears stories of Khufu

AD 1936 Employed by the Antiquities Department of Egypt, Kamal el-Mallakh begins working at the Giza plateau

1950 While supervising construction of an access road near the Great Pyramid, el-Mallakh discovers two deep pits covered with massive limestone slabs

1954 After four years of campaigning, el-Mallakh is granted permission to begin excavation of one of the pits. On 26 May he discovers the carefully dismantled pieces of Khufu's boat

1987 A non-invasive exploration of the second pit is undertaken. Photographs reveal pieces of another dismantled boat, which has yet to be excavated

twisted and turned the mirror, trying to catch a shaft of sunlight and direct it down into the void. Forcing his head and body ever harder against the stone, he eventually caught a glint of light which shot through the darkness and landed on a smooth surface. As he squinted into the darkness he saw that it was the blade of an oar, apparently one of many, and cried out:

'It's the boat! It's the boat!'

A perfectly preserved boat

El-Mallakh's hunch had been right. The boat-shaped cavities around the Giza site had once contained real ships, which had been dismantled and sealed deep inside pits in order to accompany the pharaoh into the next life. Most of them had been plundered or had rotted away in antiquity but this one, one of Khufu's own boats, had survived, sealed in from the air and the outside world and forgotten for four and a half millennia. Here, carefully deconstructed, was a ship in its entirety – deck, cabin, reed matting, hull, oars, flint tools, even the ropes, all miraculously preserved and arranged as if just waiting to be reassembled.

An honourable scar

When el-Mallakh was eventually hauled back to the surface, his team was shocked by his appearance. His head was streaming with blood from a gash caused by hitting it against the stone as he twisted and turned in the gap between the slabs. But he was too overjoyed to care and simply dabbed off the blood with a handkerchief as he told of the treasures that lay below. In later years that wound was still visible on his forehead in the form of a white mark, which he called his 'honourable scar'.

*The boat discovered in pieces by Kamal el-Mallakh in 1954
has been assembled and is housed today in a purpose-built
museum just a few metres from the site where it originally
lay buried for over 4000 years.*

KHUFU'S BOAT

The boat that Kamal el-Mallakh discovered at Giza in 1954 did not remain entombed for long. Once exposed to the air, there was a danger that the wood, reed and rope which made up the boat would begin to decay, so the capping stones were removed from the pit and the finds photographed before being removed. Now all that remained was to reconstruct the ship.

As found, the ship consisted of 1224 dismantled pieces, but each piece had been placed in the pit in such a way as to give an idea of where it belonged on the reconstructed vessel, in a series of 13 carefully arranged layers. On the top level lay reed mats and the ropes that held the ship together (most of the wooden parts of the ship were connected by rope rather than wooden dowels or nails). Under this lay 58 poles from which the structures of the deck were formed, along with five doors and 12 oars. Beneath this was the deck and then the planks of the hull. At the western end stood the prow, a long wooden column in the form of a papyrus stalk, connected by two long wooden strips that ran the length of the vessel to the stern post, also in papyrus form.

When reassembled – a job that took over ten years to complete – the ship proved to be over 43 metres (140 ft) long, displacing 45 tons, and constructed almost entirely of cedar wood, at that time a fabulously rare commodity which would have been imported from distant Lebanon. On the aft deck stood a cabin (or possibly a shrine) made from wooden poles and reed matting, while further up the deck another cabin may have been for the captain. There was neither mast nor sails, and the ship was propelled solely by her ten oars and controlled by two large steering oars at the stern.

There is still a great deal of speculation as to the exact purpose of this boat. It is clearly a river vessel designed for use on the Nile rather than a seagoing craft, but there is no sign of water staining on the hull from regular use. Furthermore, it was found in one of five boat pits associated with the Great Pyramid at Giza. It has been suggested that four of these pits once contained ritual ships intended to take the pharaoh's soul to the netherworld (via each compass point), while the last was a vessel actually used in Khufu's funeral.

We know that items involved in royal funerals were considered to have become 'dangerous', imbued as they were with the magic and mystery of the king's final journey into the next world. As such, Khufu's boat may have sailed down the Nile bearing his body before being ritually 'buried' next to him. Another suggestion is that the ship is a 'solar barque' designed to carry the pharaoh's soul across the heavenly ocean, following the sun god Re in his 'ship of a million years'.

Whatever its original use, Khufu's ship is a unique discovery – one of the oldest and certainly the largest complete boats to have come down to us from the past. Even if it never sailed on the Nile it undoubtedly was capable of doing so and there can be little doubt that when pharaohs travelled their kingdoms 2500 years before the Roman empire was even born, it was in vessels such as these.

We may still gain further insights into these extraordinary craft. This ship is, in fact, not quite unique. Kamal el-Mallakh uncovered two boat pits next to each other in 1954 but only explored one of them. In 1987 permission was finally given for a non-invasive exploration of the other pit, and a small hole was drilled through the mortar to enable a tiny camera probe to be inserted into the chamber beneath. Photographs from within reveal that another dismantled boat lies inside, waiting to tell its secrets. For the time being the pit has been resealed to ensure its long-term survival. One day it too may be recovered and rebuilt, and another chapter in the life of the pharaohs can be written.

THE FIRST TOWN
The Strange World of Çatalhöyük, 1958

English archaeologist James Mellaart (b.1925) spent much of the 1950s surveying Turkey's Konya plain. He was looking for sites from the Neolithic – the New Stone Age – when people first began to move away from hunting and gathering food in the wild and turn towards agriculture. Although Turkey was studded with archaeological sites, little was known about this early period in the region – indeed most of the important developments in the Neolithic were thought to have taken place in distant Mesopotamia.

In November 1958 Mellaart and two colleagues found two mounds on the plain at a place called Çatalhöyük. The mounds were clearly artificial, the product of centuries of building and rebuilding on a single site. The team therefore decided to search for artefacts at the top and bottom of the mound to get an idea of when this site began and ended. Usually in this region they might have expected to find that the site was occupied from prehistory up to periods of Greek or Roman settlement, but this place was different. Mellaart, at the bottom of the mound, found some sherds of pottery and called up to his friends, *'I've got Neolithic, what have you found?'* To his astonishment they called back, *'We've got Neolithic, too'*. The whole mound, which was 15 metres (50 ft) in height, appeared to be a settlement from the period Mellaart had been looking for – a permanent settlement from a time when the idea of settlement itself was new.

Between 1961 and 1965 Mellaart and his team excavated Çatalhöyük, uncovering more than 160 buildings, and from September 1993 onwards excavations have continued at the site under the direction of Ian Hodder (b.1948) from Cambridge University (and now Stanford). They have uncovered one of the oldest permanent settlements anywhere in the world, a thriving village that flourished between 9400 and 8000 years ago.

Compared to the Sumerian cities of the Tigris–Euphrates plain Çatalhöyük is not spectacular nor is it filled with impressive public buildings or elaborately furnished burials, but it is as important as any of these and its survival opens a window on a crucial period in human history. What Mellaart and Hodder uncovered is a small town (or perhaps a large village) inhabited at various times by between 3000 and 8000 people. These people were among the first farmers, growing cereal crops and rearing domestic animals. Although they still collected wild plants and hunted game, including wild pigs, horses and bulls, their crops and herds required that they stay in one place, unlike

previous hunter-gatherers who had continually moved across the countryside. A new way of life was needed, one in which people built permanent houses and lived together in large groups.

A close-knit community

The settlement at Çatalhöyük consists of hundreds of individual family houses, packed tightly together with no roads or alleys between them. Instead, the houses were entered from a hatch in the flat roof, and much of the outside life of this community must have taken place across this roofscape. Inside, the houses generally follow a similar plan, with one main windowless room that contained an oven, the staircase to the roof and various platforms, including one mat-covered area beneath which the dead were buried. Off this room, small doorways led to side rooms used for storage or for domestic chores.

But the buildings the archaeologists have uncovered were not sterile boxes. Many of the houses were richly decorated with paintings, plaster sculpture and figures which hint at the complex beliefs of these people. Away from the area around the oven – which also seems to have been where stone tools were manufactured and other 'dirty' processes such as extracting grease from bones took place – the walls of the room were smoothly plastered and often painted. Sometimes they were decorated with geometric designs that have echoes in modern Turkish carpet-making, sometimes with animated scenes of hunting and, in one case, even a depiction of a settlement, possibly Çatalhöyük itself, with a volcano erupting in the distance. There are also scenes that are clearly symbolic and whose meaning we can only guess at, including images of vultures flying over headless human bodies. The discovery of human skeletons without skulls and of skulls

Çatalhöyük is the first farming community known to date. The site ruins have revealed about 300 houses of mud brick and plaster, grouped together with no paths or alleys separating them. Access to the individual units would have been through the roof.

TIMELINE

c.9400–8000 YEARS AGO Çatalhöyük becomes one of the earliest permanent settlements anywhere in the world

19TH CENTURY AD Archaeologists used the 'cultural history' philosophy to assign similar objects to specific places and periods of history

1958 James Mellaart and colleagues discover two artificial mounds at Çatalhöyük on the Konya plain in Turkey

1950S–60S The theory of processualism (New Archaeology), comes to the fore, in which hypotheses are formed (and later tested) about the original purpose of artefacts. Processualists believe that archaeology should ask and answer questions about humans and the way they lived

1961–5 Mellaart's team excavates the larger mound, uncovering more than 160 buildings

1980S Post-processualists argue that archaeological interpretation is subject to bias. At Çatalhöyük their views result in a shift away from a single interpretation of finds to acceptance of numerous narratives

1993–PRESENT Ongoing excavations at the site continue to provide valuable information about the lives of the early settlers at Çatalhöyük

that had been plastered to recreate their owners' appearance in life, sometimes placed in other graves, suggests that the head of a deceased family member was considered to have particular power.

The belief system of the people of Çatalhöyük is almost impossible to know given that this settlement dates from long before written records were made. Areas in some houses which Mellaart identified as shrines incorporated wild bull horns, set in plaster 'heads' mounted on the walls. Small fat female figurines have also been found all over the site and may have been votive offerings placed in grain bins and new buildings to ensure prosperity.

Social equality and family units

Although one such figurine shows a woman 'enthroned' between two leopards, no evidence of social hierarchy has been found at Çatalhöyük. If this community had a ruling élite, they did not live very differently from everyone else. No public spaces or buildings have been found and none of the houses is much larger or better decorated than the others. Instead, the social structure of the settlement seems to be based around individual households. While there are no paths between buildings, the houses are not 'terraced' – each one is self-contained within its own four walls and is separated from its neighbour by just a small gap. This suggests that each house was its own unit, its own focus, and that its owners had full control over it. The permanent family home was something of a novelty at this date, and this appears to have been the main building block of society at Çatalhöyük.

Its residents were even particular about how they demolished and rebuilt their homes and it is largely thanks to their scrupulousness that so much archaeology has been found at the site. Before demolition the house was cleaned and its walls scoured. The roof was then removed and the walls pulled down to a height of about 1 metre (3.3 ft). The remaining space was filled with building materials, often enveloping existing structures such as the ovens. This platform formed the foundations for the new house, and so the mound of Çatalhöyük slowly grew.

To date the ongoing excavations have uncovered only about 5 percent of Çatalhöyük, and the smaller of the two mounds (which seems to take up the story where the sequence in the main mound ends) has barely been touched. The life of these early villagers is only just beginning to be revealed but it is already one of the most important stories in archaeology – how people first came to call a place 'home'.

Many artefacts have been uncovered at Çatalhöyük, including this stone figurine of a woman seated between two leopards. The symbolic significance of the figure is not known.

THEORETICAL ARCHAEOLOGY

Archaeology is not simply a matter of digging up the past, indeed excavation is just one part of a far larger subject. During the 20th and early 21st centuries archaeology has come to concern itself with exactly what we can say about the things we uncover and to what degree our conclusions are influenced by who we are today and the questions we ask.

During the 19th century the philosophy behind much of archaeology was what we now call 'cultural history': archaeologists looked at assemblages of objects and structures from sites and noted similarities between them, which they attributed to certain 'cultures'. When they saw elements of one assemblage appearing in another area they inferred that it had arrived there by diffusion – either through invasion from the 'parent' culture or by trade, social links or migration. Hence archaeologists came to view human development as a single strand, with each phase beginning in one place and dispersing from there.

In the late 1950s and early 1960s a new wave of archaeologists began to question this view. These proponents of the so-called New Archaeology (or 'processualism') were interested in asking questions about human society and the ways in which it had functioned, questions that required them to understand what the material recovered from excavations actually meant to its owners. Previously it had been thought that once an object entered the archaeological record all such information was lost, and while it might be possible to hypothesize, all an archaeologist could really do was document, record and create a timeline of events. Processualists, on the other hand, believed that changes in society were driven by evolutionary processes that were predictable and capable of being understood; by framing hypotheses and testing them (as scientists do), they could learn something about the people who had once used the objects they had excavated.

This view itself was questioned in the 1980s by another group of theoretical archaeologists, who called themselves 'post-processualists', led by Ian Hodder. Post-processualists felt that the New Archaeology was wrong to assume that cultural changes in the past were predictable and that a 'scientific' method of hypothesis and experiment could be applied to them. They believed that because there were no right or wrong answers in archaeology everything required a human interpretation; hence all archaeological interpretation was subject to bias. Archaeologists, they claimed, could not frame a question without falling prey to this bias and, as a result, tended to find hypotheses that led them directly to the answers they wanted.

This may sound rather academic but it has had a direct effect on how sites, including Çatalhöyük, have been excavated. Under Mellaart large numbers of houses were uncovered and attempts were made to create a scientific method of working in which every excavator used the same processes in the hope of piecing together a single story preserved in the remains. Under Ian Hodder's direction, although many of the scientific techniques of recovering information have been retained, individual excavators are encouraged to make their own interpretations of the area in which they are working and of the site as a whole, and their ideas are considered as valid as any other interpretation.

As a result, the work at Çatalhöyük is no longer directed towards uncovering one 'true' story of the site but aims to create many narratives, each influenced by the unique experiences of individual excavators. Together the narratives will provide a 21st-century view of people's lives 9000 years ago.

Arguments about the theory behind archaeology are not over, however; indeed archaeologists should never stop questioning the assumptions they make in their work. In the future there will no doubt be new interpretations and new philosophies which will make our current ideas seem antiquated. The first concern for an excavator therefore is to record every site dug to the highest possible standard in order to provide later generations with raw data to which they can apply their theories.

THE DUNGHILL OF THE UNIVERSE

The Sunken City of Port Royal, 1966

Port Royal near Kingston, Jamaica, has a grand name for a small fishing village of some 2000 people. But it was not always a fishing village, and the unique combination of its vivid history and the single moment in time that lies preserved in its harbour makes it one of the most important archaeological sites in the Caribbean.

Port Royal was founded as an afterthought. The British force that landed there in 1655 had been sent to seize the island of Hispañola from the Spanish, but disease and bad leadership had forced a shambolic withdrawal. In search of a consolation prize, the men landed on the sparsely inhabited island of Jamaica and claimed it for Cromwell's British Commonwealth. Within weeks the first British settlement, Point Cagway, was under construction on the 18-mile- (29-km-) long sand spit known as the Palisadoes which arced out into Kingston harbour, providing a safe haven for up to 500 ships. With the restoration of the monarchy back in Britain in 1660, Jamaica became a royal colony and the little city of Point Cagway on the sand bar was renamed Port Royal.

The port offered shelter for large fleets, with deep water close to shore where privateers could clean and refit their ships. Lying on the Spanish trade routes between Panama and Spain, it quickly attracted some of the most notorious pirates in the Caribbean and the British authorities were in no hurry to remove them. With insufficient resources to prosecute their wars or protect the town, they welcomed buccaneers who were willing to attack Spanish and French shipping. As the profits from this lucrative and violent piracy flowed into the port the city quickly gained a reputation for wild living and lawlessness.

'Wine and women drained their wealth to such a degree that ... some of them became reduced to beggary. They have been known to spend 2000 or 3000 pieces of eight in one night; and one gave a strumpet 500 to see her naked. They used to buy a pipe of wine, place it in the street, and oblige everyone that passed to drink.'

CHARLES LESLIE *A New History of Jamaica from the Earliest Accounts to the Taking of Porto Bello by Vice-Admiral Vernon* (1740)

Polite commentators called it the 'richest and wickedest city on earth'; the less polite 'the Sodom of the Indies' or 'the dunghill of the universe'. The inhabitants didn't seem to care about reputations, however, and the cramped town, laid out on just 21 hectares

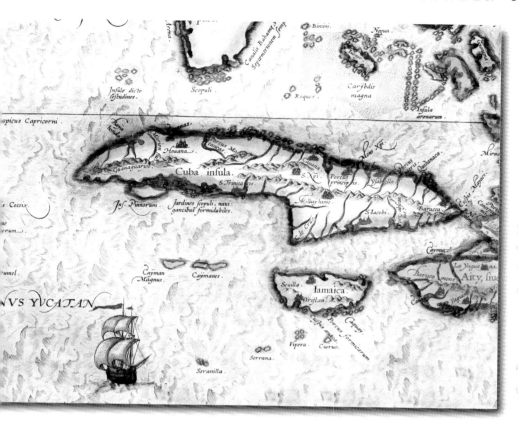

This map of the West Indies was made in 1570 in Antwerp, Belgium. It shows the islands and seas of the region, with Cuba at the centre and Jamaica below.

(52 acres) of land, rapidly grew to become the most important city in the New World after Boston, its streets as densely populated as those of 17th-century London.

Catastrophe strikes

Yet many felt the town would one day suffer a terrible judgement and on 7 June 1692 disaster struck. Shortly before midday the ground started to rock. As the shaking intensified, the sand spit on which the city was built began to liquefy and, in a matter of minutes, two-thirds of Port Royal sank beneath the waves. After the earthquakes came a tsunami which scoured the remaining buildings, killing many of those who survived the initial shocks. The city was mortally wounded. The part left on dry land would be rebuilt, but fire and hurricane would destroy it again. As the merchants and seamen lost heart and moved to safer ground in the new town of Kingston, Port Royal faded to become the small fishing village it is today. But beneath the waves lie the remains of what was once the richest city in the West Indies.

Since 1966 five separate archaeological investigations have been carried out at the sunken city, which lies under some 15 metres (50 ft) of water. Other towns survive from this date but they have all been built on and changed many times. What makes Port Royal unique is that – destroyed as it was in a matter of minutes – it preserves a moment in time. Nowhere else is there an entire set of buildings and streets still filled with the goods of its 17th-century inhabitants.

TIMELINE

1655 British forces land on Jamaica after withdrawing from their attack on the island of Hispañola; shortly after, the first British settlement is constructed at Point Cagway

1660 Following the restoration of the British monarchy under King Charles II in the aftermath of the English Civil War, Jamaica becomes a royal colony. Point Cagway is renamed Port Royal

C.1660s In the early years Port Royal is a haven for pirates and buccaneers, giving it the reputation of the richest and wickedest city on earth

1670s–80s With the expansion of Jamaica's sugar plantations piracy is no longer condoned. Port Royal flourishes as a major trade centre in the Caribbean, exporting sugar and slaves to Europe and the New World and importing exotic goods from China and Europe

1692 (7 June) Three earthquakes followed by a tsunami hit Port Royal; two-thirds of the city is submerged, and up to 5000 lives are lost directly or indirectly

1966 Diving teams begin exploring the sunken portion of the city

1981–90 The Institute of Nautical Archaeology, the Nautical Archaeology Program at Texas A&M University and the Jamaica National Heritage Trust begin full excavations of the sunken city

Underwater archaeologists at the site have had to deal with an entirely new type of work. Usually marine archaeologists investigate shipwrecks, whereas here lie whole streets lined with buildings, and over two million artefacts have been recovered to date. Investigations have revealed the truth behind Port Royal's reputation and its success. In the most recent work a whole row of buildings along Lime Street (the town took its street names from famous London streets) has been excavated, revealing the organized chaos of the city and the dramatic nature of its collapse. This was a working town, not a beautiful town, and many buildings are simply wooden frames rammed into the earth. But it was also a wealthy town (during its brief life possibly the wealthiest in the New World), and other houses are carefully constructed brick complexes with glazed windows. Many seem to have been places of business: pipe shops, cobblers, warehouses and taverns have all been identified. Indeed the city had one tavern for every ten residents. These were the places where privateers and pirates such as Captain Morgan, Roche Brasiliano and John David once drank.

The notorious Dutch buccaneer Roche Brasiliano arrived in Jamaica in the 1670s, having left Brazil after the Dutch colonies there were seized by the Portuguese.

Evidence of trade in goods and slaves

The artefacts recovered speak of Port Royal's importance as a trade centre and include not just the tin-glazed English pottery and pewter cutlery of the day but exotic and expensive imports such as Chinese porcelain, European gold jewellery and Delft plates. Evidence has also come to light of the city's less romantic side. As sugar plantations expanded on Jamaica, tolerance of piracy waned – two of the most notorious pirates, Calico Jack and Charles Vane, would later be hanged at Gallows Point near the town. Their Spanish gold was supplanted by an even more valuable commodity – slavery – and the slave shackles known as 'bilboes' found in the town point to the growth of this trade.

The underwater ruins have also preserved evidence of the moment when disaster struck. Three earthquakes hit the city in quick succession, the last being the most damaging. Built on sandy fountains, many of the buildings quickly disintegrated. Outside buildings 4 and 5 on Lime Street a collapsed wall was excavated and revealed the remains of a young child beneath; the bodies of two more children were found inside the houses. Other bodies were found trapped between buildings or buried in the sand. This tallies with a contemporary account of the scene:

> *'Immediately we ran out of the house, where we saw all people with lifted up hands begging God's assistance. We continued running up the street whilst on either side of us we saw the houses, some swallowed up, others thrown on heaps; the sand in the streets rise like the waves of the sea, lifting up all persons that stood upon it and immediately dropping down into pits; and at the same instant a flood of water breaking in and rolling those poor souls over and over; some catching hold of beams and rafters of houses, others were found in the sand that appeared when the water was drained away, with their legs and arms out.'*

Building 4 on Lime Street may also provide corroboration for another contemporary story. Archaeologists found the remains of a ship lying across the front wall and floor of the building; it had clearly been washed up into the sinking town and landed on the house. Historical records suggest that the fifth-rate warship HMS *Swan* was in the town's careening dock having her hull scraped at the time, and was lifted up and dropped on 'Lord Pike's House'.

CONSERVATION

Many of the artefacts recovered from archaeological sites, particularly marine sites, require conservation to preserve them. Early archaeologists tell of many wonderful objects being uncovered which then crumbled to dust in the excavator's hands. Today archaeological conservation is a science in itself.

Some items survive burial in archaeological sites well, notably stone implements, some ceramics and non-tarnishing metals such as gold. In these cases archaeological conservation focuses on restoring items and recovering their original form rather than preventing decay. But many other materials deteriorate rapidly when removed from the archaeological site in which they were preserved.

Some archaeological conditions, such as waterlogging, preservation in humic acid (in peat bogs, for instance) and burial in silt, can preserve artefacts. This occurs naturally either by excluding oxygen, thus preventing oxidation, or by creating an environment in which microbes that would otherwise destroy the objects are prevented from thriving. However, when these artefacts are removed from such conditions they become vulnerable and the process of decay can begin again. The key to their conservation is to stabilize them and prevent them from decaying further.

On marine sites where oxygen levels are low organic materials such as wood and leather, which rarely survive in dry sites, can often be recovered. But these are particularly fragile, usually becoming waterlogged and soft over time. The archaeologist's first job is to keep the item in conditions resembling as closely as possible those in which it was found – wet items are kept wet and dry objects are kept dry. Conservation scientists must then consider the best method of preserving the object in the long term.

For small organic items the technique of freeze-drying is often used to remove the water: the item is frozen in a low-pressure chamber and the frozen water allowed to sublime directly from a solid to a gas before being removed. This prevents bacteria, which need moisture to survive, from attacking the material. If the item is then sealed using a synthetic wax, it can be displayed at room temperature. For larger items a more complex method is needed. In the case of ships' timbers the wood is usually sprayed, often for years, with fresh water to remove the salt that might otherwise crystallize and damage the structure of the wood, before being treated with increasingly strong solutions of synthetic wax to replace the water in the cells.

With metal objects corrosion caused by oxidization is the usual problem. This can damage and obscure the surface of the object and even lead to its total destruction. Corroded items must be carefully dried and the corrosion removed. In the case of coins, drying is often achieved using a bath of acetone which bonds strongly with water, after which the corrosion can be removed using ultrasound. Because metal items from archaeological sites are often very heavily corroded, it is often advisable to x-ray the item first to discover how much, if any, of the metal survives beneath.

Despite advances in conservation, there is no room for complacency. New techniques may appear to protect artefacts but we have little information on how preserved objects will fare over long periods of time and whether the conservation techniques themselves may have side effects. Conservation science is a continual battle against the elements and all archaeologists can do is to try to use the best possible practices of the day. It will be for future generations to tackle any mistakes made now.

Archaeologists have also been able to determine the exact time the earthquakes struck, as a pocket watch dating from around 1686, made by the French maker Paul Blondel, was found in the ruins near Fort James. Its hands were stopped forever at 11.43.

In total some 5000 people died in the disaster and the aftershocks, floodings and epidemics that followed, and many of their remains still lie in the waters of Kingston harbour. After 40 years of excavation, only a small proportion of the sunken city has been properly explored and the ruins have become one of the most valuable resources for post-medieval archaeologists – a 17th-century city trapped forever in a moment of time.

THE FLOWER OF ALL SHIPS
Finding the Mary Rose, 1967

'*Your good ship, the flower, I trow, of all ships that ever sailed.*'

SIR EDWARD HOWARD *Letter to Henry VIII from Onboard the* Mary Rose (1513)

On 19 July 1545, there was a flat calm in the waters of the Solent which lie between the Isle of Wight and the south coast of England. It was not what the English fleet then at anchor off Portsmouth wanted, for the enemy was now very much at the gates.

The French fleet had landed raiding parties on the Isle of Wight and the coast of southeast England and was preparing to destroy English naval power, such as it was. The French had the advantage of galleys that could be rowed into position regardless of the wind, but given a breath of wind the English had an ace up their sleeve. The *Mary Rose* was a purpose-built warship, one of the first that could fire a broadside − a devastating fusillade from its 91 guns, which could reduce an enemy ship to splinters. As a breeze finally gathered in the late afternoon, the 700-ton *Mary Rose* hoisted her sails and prepared to engage the French. Moments later she keeled over and sank. Only about 30 of the 500 crew survived.

The loss of the *Mary Rose* was a disaster for Henry VIII (1491–1547), although in the end the French were unable to capitalize on it. The king had lost one of his finest ships along with nearly all its crew and a fortune in guns and equipment. Attempts were made immediately to raise the wreck and salvage what they could from her but, despite the proximity to the shore, she had already sunk into thick, oozing clay.

The first visitors to the wreck
And so the *Mary Rose* vanished from history into the sea bed outside Portsmouth harbour until 16 June 1836 when a fisherman snagged his nets on something. By chance a diver was already at work on the nearby wreck of the *Royal George* and, in return for a half-share in whatever they found, he agreed to dive on the site. There he found a bronze gun and ship's timbers, like a row of ribs, jutting up through the mud.

The technology available in 1836 did not allow for a very thorough salvage of the wreck: the water was deep and visibility was often reduced to a few feet in the Solent's silty waters. After a few dives the wreck was abandoned and its location forgotten until 1965. In that year Alexander McKee (1918−92) initiated a project with the local sub-aqua club to locate Solent wrecks, and in particular the wreck of the *Mary Rose*. McKee had a great advantage over his predecessors in that he could search for ships from the surface using newly developed side-scan radar which plotted anomalies in the sea bed.

180

Even so, it was 1967 before a particular anomaly caught McKee's attention. He wrote to Professor Harold Edgerton (1903–90), who had developed the technology:

> '... the feature appears to form some sort of discontinuity or "break" in the geological strata, and as this cannot be the results of an earthquake the hypothesis that it results from the insertion into the sea bed of 700 tons of battleship seems likely, particularly when we consider that the findings ... are consistent entirely with the wreck of the Mary Rose.'

Between 1968 and 1971 several seasons of diving were arranged on the site, still almost entirely unfunded and relying on the goodwill of local sponsors and divers. Various fragments of wood were recovered and, by probing the mud with poles, it became clear that something large was lying under it. On 5 May 1971 one of the divers went down to the site after a severe spring gale. Large amounts of sediment had been moved around

A 20th-century painting of the Mary Rose by William Bishop. The most powerful of Henry VIII's warships and his pride and joy, the vessel was probably named after his sister, Mary, and the symbol of the Tudors, the rose.

181

by the churning waters and now something new emerged from the gloom – not broken fragments but a row of ship's timbers. The *Mary Rose* had reappeared.

A perfect cross-section

The excavation of the *Mary Rose* was one of the most important in the history of marine archaeology. The ship sank so quickly that almost everything and everyone on board went straight down with it, sinking into the soft mud of the sea bed and preserving a moment in Tudor history. The ship lay on her starboard side at an angle of about 60 degrees. Everything that had rested above the level of the sediment had been worn and eaten away, but what remained was a near perfect cross-section of Henry VIII's warship with all its contents in place.

Objects recovered from the Mary Rose *include instruments for navigation such as this pair of dividers (bottom), a pocket sundial (centre) and a slate compass rose (top).*

Interest in the find mounted and funding eventually became easier. By 1979 the newly formed Mary Rose Trust could afford to place a proper salvage vessel, the *Sleipner*, over the wreck and hire a team of divers, surveyors, archaeologists and conservators to record and excavate it. The site was first divided into grid squares using yellow gas piping and each cell was then carefully excavated, often in zero visibility, using trowels. Each item found was drawn and photographed *in situ* (where possible) before being lifted to the surface for conservation and study.

By now it had been decided to attempt to raise the entire wreck itself so every item and every timber from each companionway and cabin first had to be found, plotted and removed. In total 27, 831 dives were made and 20,571 artefacts recovered – the greatest Tudor treasure trove ever discovered.

Life on board

The cabin of the barber-surgeon responsible for the physical wellbeing of the sailors was found almost intact. It contained a walnut medical chest filled with instruments and corked bottles of medicines. There were bleeding bowls, razors and even a velvet hat. The carpenter's cabin, too, still held the tools of his trade, while across the ship lay the remains of the crew, their clothing and shoes, coins from their pockets, the plates they ate off, their tankards and even animal bones and a basket full of fruit stones from their last meals.

A huge amount of military material was also recovered, from the bronze and iron cannons to boxes full of bows, quivers of arrows and even the wooden linstocks – poles which held the fuses to ignite the cannons. Away from battle, life on board could be dull and there was evidence of how sailors

RAISING THE MARY ROSE

Once the finds were logged and removed and much of the internal structure dismantled, the Mary Rose Trust undertook one of the most ambitious excavations in the history of archaeology – the removal and recovery of the hull itself.

Removing the remains of a wooden warship that had rested on the sea bed for over 450 years presented enormous challenges. While the timbers of nearly half the ship were intact and still connected, most of the metal bolts that held key elements together had corroded away. The wood was preserved by the silt, but much of it was softened from years of waterlogging. Then there was the problem of suction – how to lift the delicate hull out of thick, cloying mud without tearing the structure apart.

The enormity of the problem can be gauged by looking at the ship's size. By the time the *Mary Rose* sank she had been refitted twice and weighed 700 tons. Her total length was 45 metres (148 ft) and she was 11.7 metres (38 ft) in the beam. But since the sinking, one side of the ship had been totally lost, dramatically reducing the rigidity of the hull. If she were to be raised by the usual method of placing strops under the timbers and lifting her in a sling, there was a danger that the remaining hull would simply collapse under its own weight.

The method devised to solve these problems was a triumph for the engineers, naval architects, salvors and archaeologists involved. Initially a metal frame was suspended over the hull on hydraulic jacks sunk into the sea bed. Steel wires were then connected between bolts drilled into key strong points on the hull and the frame. Each bolt had to be drilled through the wooden hull and secured to a spreader plate on the underside. This required divers to dig tunnels into the clay beneath the ship, crawl under, find the bolt by touch and then attach the plate, a process repeated 67 times. As each bolt was attached to its wire, the tunnels could be excavated further to the next strong point without the risk of the hull collapsing on the diver below.

With all the wires in position the 12 hydraulic jacks began, very slowly, to lift the hull a few centimetres off the sea bed in order to overcome the suction of the mud. When the hull was clear a crane barge was used to lift the hull and frame, still underwater, away from the excavation and into a specially constructed steel cradle cushioned on a series of air bags. The lifting frame and cradle were then bolted together to form the lifting cage, and the divers set to work strengthening the hull for the final lift to the surface. This meant adding a further 103 bolts to protect the weaker joints in the woodwork, which would come under severe stress when the hull moved from the relatively weightless underwater environment out into the air.

Finally the crane began the slow process of lifting the hull in its cage from the water and onto a barge. On 11 October 1982 the *Mary Rose* sailed back into Portsmouth harbour aboard its barge, 437 years after she had left that port. Ahead lay years of conservation and reconstruction but Henry VIII's warship was finally home, no longer a fighting ship but a window onto a lost world.

passed their time. A shawm (a predecessor of the modern oboe) would have provided music, and backgammon sets and dice helped while away the hours. There were even some wooden pocket sundials to tell the crew just how much time had passed.

The contents of the *Mary Rose* are unique in two ways. Firstly, the sediment of the sea bed preserved some of the rarest finds in archaeology: organic objects made of wood, bone and leather which normally rot quickly. Secondly, they provide a snapshot of a side of Tudor life that is usually poorly recorded. This is not the Tudor England we see at Hampton Court Palace or in the paintings of Hans Holbein but a rarer treasure: the ordinary things from everyday life aboard ship.

THE PEOPLE OF LAKE MUNGO
The First Australians, 1968

The so-called Walls of China are a dramatic feature of the landscape of Lake Mungo National Park. Carved into fantastic shapes by the occasional rain which falls in the area, this crescent-shaped dune lies along the eastern shore of the dried-up lake.

The early history of human occupation in Australia is a key chapter in the story of how people spread around the world. Australia has not been joined to any other continent at any time since mankind first emerged, so even during eras of very low sea level the first Australians would still have had to cross at least 31 miles (50 km) of water. This implies the existence of a technologically and culturally sophisticated people, yet well into the 20th century the origins of the aboriginal people of Australia were largely ignored by archaeology. European settlers in the country had traditionally considered it 'virgin' territory despite the presence of indigenous peoples, and their history and culture were largely written off as 'primitive' and irrelevant. This view would only finally be overturned in the 1960s.

The Willendra Lakes region of New South Wales in Australia is itself a fossil from a distant age. Today there is no water there, indeed all 17 lakes in this World Heritage Site have been dry for thousands of years. During the last ice age, however, this desert landscape was 6 to 10°C (11 to 18°F) colder. A rich system of waterways and lakes fed by the rainwater of the Great Dividing Range supported dense vegetation and exotic animals. Here at various times roamed 3-metre- (10-ft-) tall short-faced kangaroos, marsupial lions and half-ton flightless birds. And here too walked something else.

The oldest human remains
In 1968 Jim Bowler, a geomorphologist studying the climate of prehistoric Australia, noticed something unusual eroding out of the crescent-shaped sand ridges that run for 16 miles (26 km) down the eastern shore of what was once Lake Mungo. Bound up in a block of mineral deposits were blackened pieces of bone. Finding bones of this date in the area was not uncommon but the blackening was. Cutting around the bones, Bowler lifted the block and had it transported to the Australian National University, where a Ph.D student named Alan Thorne spent a year excavating the bone from the block and reconstructing the pieces. The results would revolutionize Australian archaeology.

TIMELINE

*c.*50,000 YEARS AGO The first settlers migrate to Australia, possibly from Asia

*c.*40,000 YEARS AGO Mungo Man lives in the Willendra Lakes region of New South Wales, Australia

*c.*40,000–25,000 YEARS AGO Mungo Lady lives in the Willendra Lakes region

1968 Jim Bowler uncovers the remains of Mungo Lady; Alan Thorne estimates them to be between 25,000 and 40,000 years old and establishes that they represent the earliest known cremation

1974 The discovery of the remains of Mungo Man confirm Bowler's earlier findings; the remains are dated to 40,000 years old and are the world's first known human ritual burial – further evidence of the sophistication of the humans who inhabited Australia in the distant past

1991 The remains of Mungo Lady are returned to the aboriginal community at Lake Mungo National Park

The bones Thorne removed belonged to a woman who had died between 25,000 and 40,000 years ago, making her one of Australia's earliest known human inhabitants. This date in itself was extraordinary enough, pushing back massively the origins of humans on the continent, but it was the blackening of her bones that proved most exciting. Mungo Lady, as she became known, clearly belonged to a sophisticated society. After her death her remains had been cremated then smashed into small pieces and cremated again before being buried in a small depression. That makes her body not just the earliest cremation known in Australia, but very possibly the earliest known anywhere in he world. And Lake Mungo held still more secrets.

Bowler struck gold again in February of 1974. After prolonged rains the previous year, he noticed a human skull eroding from the dunes just 500 metres (550 yds) from where he had found Mungo Lady. These remains were even more complete and, rather than being cremated, they had been deliberately buried. Mungo Man, as he was christened, had died 40,000 years ago and after his death had been carefully placed on his back in a grave with his hands over his groin. The body had then been sprinkled with red ochre before the grave was filled in. These early Australians were clearly among the most culturally advanced people on earth at the time.

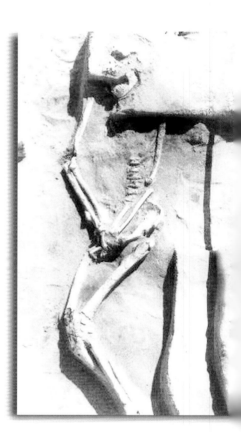

The remains of Mungo Man, discovered in 1974, had been covered in red ochre during a deliberate burial ritual. The hands were interlocked and positioned over the groin.

A rich and varied diet

Around the lake there was also evidence of the lives these first Australians had lived. Scatterings of stone tools, the remains of hearths and the bones of the animals they caught were also coming to light. The people who lived in this once lush environment were hunters, catching wallabies, kangaroos and even Tasmanian tigers. These animals were butchered with stone tools and cooked on camp fires around the lake edge. The lake itself also provided food and the large numbers of golden perch bones recovered, all relatively large, suggest that the Mungo people caught them in fishing nets. Mussels, crayfish and frogs added to the varied diet.

Since the discovery of Mungo Lady and Mungo Man, arguments over the exact date of the bodies have continued; but even taking the latest possible estimates they are still some of the earliest examples of sophisticated human culture: these people were descended from the voyagers who first crossed the open sea from Asia and settled a new continent, and they buried their dead with ritual and care. Mungo Lady and Mungo Man have also restored their

THE ARCHAEOLOGY OF ANIMALS

The remains of animals found at archaeological sites can provide a valuable insight into how our ancestors lived and they often hold much more information than first appearances suggest. When trying to reconstruct such distant past lives as those of Mungo Lady and Mungo Man, animal remains are among the few clues available to archaeologists.

Buried or fossilized animal remains tell us a number of things. Firstly, it is usually possible to identify the species and, by collecting samples over a large area, an idea of the range of animals that lived there can be gauged. From these distribution patterns it is often possible to learn something of the climate and even the local landscape. The presence of lions, for instance, suggests a warm, open environment, the presence of hippos or crocodiles indicates water nearby, while monkey remains imply some forest cover. Different types of animals in separate archaeological layers can therefore be used to show how climate and environment have changed in an area over time.

The bones themselves also hold important clues as to how they were used by early human populations. Under the microscope it is often possible to see small scratches on bones, known as butchery marks, where tools were used to remove the flesh. These can indicate the types of tools in use and the techniques employed in butchery. Breaks to long bones also show where bone marrow was extracted.

The spread of bones also holds information which can be analyzed by specialist 'faunal taphonomists' who study what happens to bones and their distribution after death. The presence of only one type of bone may indicate that an animal was not killed at the site but butchered there and then the 'cuts' of meat taken away. In addition, the arrangements of bones can show how an animal died. Completely articulated skeletons suggest that the creature died naturally and was quickly buried without being found by carnivores, which would scatter the bones as they tore the carcass apart. Tooth marks made by animals such as hyenas on bones found at human habitation sites imply that the humans may also have been scavengers – if they had killed the animal themselves they would certainly have tried to keep other scavengers away from their prize.

Animal remains can even provide information on human activity. In the case of the people of Lake Mungo, the presence of fish bones all of a certain size or above suggests they were caught in nets, since smaller fish would have escaped through the holes. Burning and cracking on bones can demonstrate that meat was cooked. Where a large number of bones are found it is also possible to build up a profile of the age and sex of the animals, which can tell us whether they were being hunted in the wild or had been domesticated. In domesticated herds, for example, females often greatly outnumber males as they are needed to bear the next generation and fewer males are required. Likewise, herders are unlikely to kill very young animals that are still growing but equally are unwilling to keep very old animals that are no longer productive.

Finally, the totality of animal remains on a site provides clues to the human diet, showing the proportions that came from wild species and (at times when animals were kept) domesticated species, as well as the quantity of meat consumed. Together all this information gives us a snapshot of life at places like Lake Mungo, constructed simply from objects discarded by those Australian pioneers.

descendants, the modern aboriginal people, to their rightful place as the real discoverers of Australia. It is perhaps fitting therefore that the remains of Mungo Lady have been returned to the care of aboriginal communities at the Lake Mungo National Park. In return, these groups have lifted a 20-year moratorium on excavation in the region (their permission was never sought in 1968 or 1974), and now archaeologists and native peoples can work together to uncover the incredible story of the first Australians.

LETTERS FROM THE WALL
The Vindolanda Tablets, 1973

One day in about AD 105, Flavius Cerialis ordered a bonfire to be lit. He was the commanding officer of a Roman auxiliary unit raised originally in the Netherlands and posted to the fort of Vindolanda in Britain, just south of the line that would soon be marked by Hadrian's Wall. His men – the ninth cohort of Batavians – had been there since around AD 92 but they had received their marching orders. They were to return from this corner of the Roman empire and prepare to fight in another – Dacia, modern-day Romania.

It appears that Flavius Cerialis was doing some housekeeping. There was a great deal of material dealing with the running of the fort that he could not take with him but that he did not want to leave behind. In particular, there was his extensive correspondence, written in black soot ink on postcard-sized pieces of alder and birch wood, no more than a millimetre thick. These notes concerned every aspect of the life of the fort, and Cerialis wanted the information destroyed – hence the bonfire. But instead of consigning his private thoughts to the fire, he was unknowingly bequeathing them to posterity.

Signs of burning

1870 years later Cerialis's thoughts finally reached the modern world. The site of Vindolanda fort had been the scene of archaeological investigations since before the Second World War. At that time

the British archaeologist Eric Birley (1906–95) had bought the site and begun excavating it, joined later in this work by his sons Robin and Anthony. Robin Birley was supervising the excavations in the 1970s when evidence of an area of burning came to light on what had been the road outside the commanding officer's house. Amid all the charcoal and soot, pieces of wood soon began to emerge – hundreds of thin slivers of birch and alder which, though charred, had miraculously survived the fire.

After the fire had gone out, nearly 2000 years earlier, the area had been abandoned. When the Romans returned, they capped the whole of Flavius Cerialis's site with clay and turf before building a new fort on top. This capping layer had a very particular and unexpected effect. It sealed in whatever remained of the earlier fort in a damp, oxygen-free level.

Running for some 73 miles (117 km) across northern England from Wallsend-on-Tyne in the east to Bowness in the west, Hadrian's Wall was built in c.122–30 to separate the Romans from the northern 'barbarians'.

One of the great problems of archaeology is that normally only imperishable items survive. We can uncover bricks and tools, pottery and metal, but what we find is only a part of the particular period of history, for it is a world without wood and cloth, bone and leather, and without food and drink. But exceptionally, at sites like Vindolanda, the oxygen-free conditions prevent insects and soil bacteria from breaking down these organic compounds, meaning that they survive. And that includes the remains of Flavius Cerialis's bonfire.

Mysterious letters

When the Birleys broke through the capping layer to reveal the early fort beneath, they opened a time capsule. The wooden tablets that emerged from under this level were initially a mystery. Many of them appeared to come in pairs, as though a single piece of wood had been scored down the middle and folded over like a letter – which is exactly what they turned out to be. When the two sides were prised apart, their inner faces were found to be covered in strange spidery writing unlike anything else that had been found on inscriptions at the site. It was also incredibly fragile and, within minutes of being exposed to the air and light, the words on the 'pages' began to fade and disappear.

Fortunately it was discovered that the writing still showed up in infrared photography, so the tablets were photographed and the mystery writing sent to Roman handwriting experts. The news that came back to Vindolanda was astonishing. The writing was indeed Latin, but in a cursive handwriting script – the sort of script used for dashing off letters and notes. It could also be translated, and what these letters contained opened up a new era in Romano-British history. Before Vindolanda our knowledge of everyday Roman life in Britannia came from Roman histories, formal inscriptions and the archaeological material recovered from the earth. But just as the normal imperishable finds of archaeology only tell half a story, the formal writings of the Roman period do not give a complete picture.

Everyday life in Roman Britain

What the Vindolanda letters contained was the day-to-day correspondence of Roman Britons. These were not histories or diaries designed with an eye for posterity, but letters and notes, invitations and lists, which would have been used for a moment and then consigned to the bin. Over 1900 such tablets have now been recovered from the site and their contents – ranging from official correspondence, duty rosters and accounts of financial transactions to personal letters and greetings cards – are opening a window onto a side of Roman life we guessed must have existed but believed we would never actually know – the everyday trivia of the lives of ordinary people.

For this reason, the Vindolanda tablets are perhaps the greatest treasure ever uncovered from Roman Britain, allowing us as they do to hear the Romans speak for themselves about their lives and concerns. It is a treasure made up of soggy wood and soot as opposed to the gold and silver of more famous Roman hoards, but it is rarer and more valuable to archaeology than any object however costly and well made.

WHAT THE TABLETS SAY

The Vindolanda tablets were the day-to-day disposable records of the people who lived at the fort and those who corresponded with them, and therefore cover a vast range of themes. At one end of the spectrum are the letters that Flavius Cerialis wanted burnt – the official correspondence of a Roman commander. This included letters of introduction from important Romans and distribution lists ensuring the men were fed and supplied – on the back of one is a draft of another formal letter, this time an appeal for clemency.

Then there are the accounts, such as the 'Octavius Letter', which is concerned with finding suitable supplies for an influx of legionaries to the area. In it he make arrangements for the purchase of corn, ox hides and sinew and he takes the opportunity to complain about local tradesmen who are exploiting shortages brought about by the new arrivals to push up their prices.

Other official documents give an insight into the manning of the fort. A report of around AD 90 states that out of a supposed complement of 751 men, 470 were currently absent, some in London, some off collecting pay and some at another fort. Of those remaining at Vindolanda, 30 were reported as unfit for service. Along with duty rosters, requests for leave and accounts there are also intelligence reports that give us an insight into the soldiers' view of the native peoples they ruled:

'The Britons are unprotected by armour ... The cavalry do not use swords nor do the wretched Britons take up fixed positions in order to throw javelins.'

Whether this refers to Britons outside the fort or perhaps even new recruits into the army we do not know, but it does tell us one thing – the nickname the Roman soldiers had for the British people was *Brittunculi* – 'wretched' or 'little' Britons.

The postcard-sized Vindolanda letters were made of local birch or alder wood and written on with a pen using ink made from carbon, water and gum.

In contrast there are some intensely personal letters that speak of the hopes and concerns of people, many of whom found themselves a long way from home. The first letter found, in 1973, was to an ordinary soldier and says, *'I have sent you ... socks from Sattua, two pairs of sandals and two sets of underpants ...'.* This is the first mention we have of the use of socks or underpants in the northern provinces and suggests that the recipient was finding his posting a little chilly.

Another reminds us of the role of slaves in the Roman world. It is from one slave to another, asking for his Saturnalia present (a Roman festival). Not only were slaves present at Vindolanda, they were clearly literate. Evidence of how young Romans became literate has also been found. On one sheet a piece from Virgil's *Aeneid* has been copied out. Like schoolchildren across the ages, the writer's mind has wandered from the painfully formed letters of his text and he has left off the ending of the passage. Below this someone – probably a teacher – has written 'seg', short for *segnis* – sloppy!

Finally, a number of greetings and invitations survive. One letter to Cerialis begins 'Happy New Year' while one from Claudia Severa is unique:

'Claudia Severa to her Lepidina, greetings. I send you a warm invitation to come to us on 11 September for my birthday celebrations, to make the day more enjoyable ... Give my greetings to your Cerialis. My Aelius greets you and your sons. I will expect you, sister. Farewell, sister, my dearest soul, as I hope to prosper, and greetings.'

This letter would be valuable just for being Britain's first party invitation but, while most of the letter was written by a scribe, the final farewell is in Claudia Severa's own wobbly script. Dating from AD 100, it is the earliest known handwriting in Latin by a woman.

A GIRL CALLED LUCY
The Origin of the Species? 1974

'*We are an unprecedented and totally unanticipated species, and hopefully an awareness of the deep biological roots we share with one another and the rest of nature will point us in the direction of our best dreams rather than our worst nightmares.*'

DONALD JOHANSON

Donald Johanson (b.1943) woke at dawn on 30 November, 1974, knowing it was going to be a special day. How he knew he could not say – there was nothing to suggest this was any different from another day, no intelligence from the previous day that hinted at something unusual. He just knew. The place in which he awoke was a strange one. He emerged from his old army tent onto the banks of a small, muddy river, the Awash, about 100 miles (160 km) north of Addis Ababa in Ethiopia, in an area known as Hadar. A desert landscape greeted him, a wasteland of rock, gravel and sand, bleached by the sun and scoured by the occasional torrential rainstorm. But that is why Hadar was so important.

In search of early humans

Johanson was here to lead an expedition to discover what this area had been like in the very distant past and, most importantly, who and what had lived here. The Afar desert, in which Hadar lies, was once an ancient lake, long since evaporated and filled with the ash and sand and debris of years of geological history. When storms hit the region the driving rain swirled around in gullies which carved deep incisions into this layer cake of history, revealing cross sections of millions of years of Hadar's past and washing out the fossilized remains of the creatures and plants that once lived here. This was what Johanson's team had come for.

But today did not seem like a day for fossil hunting. Even at dawn the temperature was already creeping above 27°C (80°F) in the shade of the finds tent, and the opportunity to catch up on cataloguing and mapping the huge number of animal remains already found seemed tempting. It was at that point that Tom Gray, an American graduate student, came in. He was in Hadar to study the fossilized animals and plants of the region and was busy marking their find sites on a large map. Johanson cast a glance across the map and asked casually:

'*When are you going to mark in Locality 162?*'

Gray replied that he was not even sure where 162 was and at that moment Johanson made his decision not to stay in camp that day but to go out into the field with Gray

Situated in northeastern Africa, Ethiopia is a country of spectacular landscapes. Most of the country consists of an enormous plateau, divided from north to south by an earthquake fault line known as the Great Rift Valley.

WHO WAS LUCY?

The origin of modern humankind is a subject that is still surrounded in controversy. The simple fact is that finds of early fossils of what may or may not be human ancestors are relatively infrequent and usually only fragmentary. Without firm dating, extensive examples and possibly DNA analysis, the human family tree remains open to a large amount of interpretation.

Finds as complete as Lucy's skeleton, however, do allow us to say something about our common past. From her pelvis, hip and knee joints we know that she stood upright, like we do, and that makes her a hominid which, simply defined at least, is a primate that habitually walks upright. But while modern humans are hominids, Lucy was certainly not a human.

Lucy was small, standing just over 1 metre (3.3 ft) tall. She was fully grown, however, as shown by the existence of wisdom teeth and the amount of wear on them. Her teeth are unlike those of modern apes, being more the size and shape of human teeth, despite her diminutive stature. Her brain was much smaller than ours – somewhere between 375 and 500 cubic centimetres (23 and 30 cu. in) compared to a modern average of around 1600 cubic centimetres (98 cu. in). The shape of her pelvis confirms that Lucy was female and evidence from her spine also suggests that she was beginning to suffer from arthritis.

Finding so complete a skeleton also tells us something of her death. Lucy died quietly. There were no tooth marks or breakages on her bones to suggest she had been attacked by one of the sabre-toothed cats or lions that roamed the open woodlands where she lived. Her remains were found together, which precludes her body having been torn apart by scavengers. Rather, it seems that Lucy lay down one day

by the edge of a lake or stream and died unnoticed. Her body was quickly covered by sediment and, as the layers built up and compressed, that sediment turned to rock and her bones became fossilized within it. Millions of years later that process began running in reverse as the flash floods of what is now the Afar desert scoured away the rock, bringing Lucy's remains to the surface again.

So is Lucy our ancestor? It is a question to which the answer is that there is no conclusive proof as yet. As we have seen, she is certainly not a human: while we are taxonomically described as *Homo sapiens*, she is usually assigned to both a different genus and species, *Australopithecus afarensis*. But her skeleton shows signs which are strangely human – her teeth and her upright posture, for example – and which are unknown among the other modern primates.

It may be that she is a distant cousin of ours – that her family tree leads to some as yet undiscovered dead end long ago. Even if that is the case, it seems that she probably shared a common ancestor with us in the ages before Hadar. Just as likely, however, is that she is, in fact, our ancestor, perhaps one we share with chimpanzees – not yet human but another step on the evolutionary path that leads to *Homo sapiens*. Some of Lucy's blood may run in all our veins.

A sculpture reconstruction of what Lucy may have looked like. Scientists believe that she lived roughly 3.2 million years ago; her discovery has been one of the most significant developments in our understanding of human evolution.

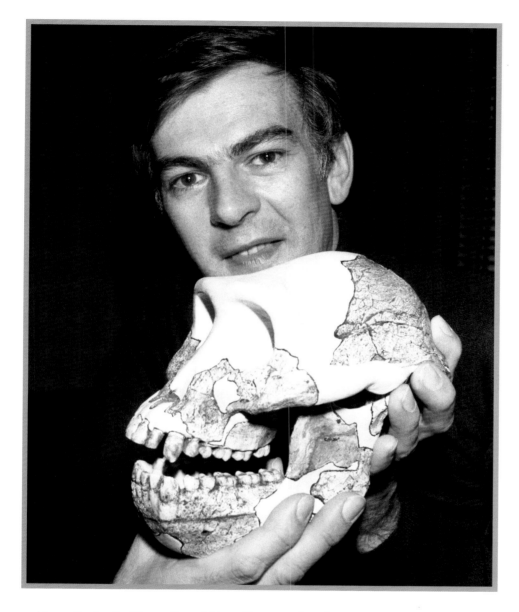

The American palaeoanthropologist Donald Johanson displays a plaster cast of Lucy's skull. Johanson has dedicated most of his career to the search for the origin of the human species.

and hunt for fossils. He swallowed his coffee, turned to Gray and said:

'Then I guess I'll have to show you.'

Before they headed off in the expedition's old Land Rover, Johanson just had time to scrawl in his diary: 'Nov 30, 1974 To Locality 162 with Gray in A. M. Feel good.' 'Feeling good' might not be the most scientific of descriptions, but finding fossils in Hadar requires not only skill but a great deal of luck. Experienced staff could walk a gully a dozen times and find nothing, but with just a slight change of light, a whole raft of fossils might be found. Johanson was a good fossil hunter, although not as good as some of the Afar tribesmen and women he employed. More importantly, he was lucky.

Arriving at locality 162, Johanson and Gray set about the search as the temperature in the desert rose ever higher. After a couple of hours the thermometer was topping 43°C (109°F) and all the searchers had to show for their efforts were a few teeth from an extinct species of horse, part of a skull from an extinct pig, some antelope teeth and a piece of monkey jaw.

Gray suggested heading back and Johanson agreed, but in order that the morning should not be completely wasted he decided to return through a small gully, known as Locality 288, and search there en route. It was a gully that had been searched before, several times in fact, but Johanson felt lucky. Almost immediately, as he walked down the slope he noticed something on the ground.

'That's a bit of a hominid arm', he exclaimed.

But Gray wasn't convinced:

'Can't be. It's too small. Has to be a monkey of some kind.'

They both crouched down to look at the find. It was tiny. Much too small. Gray was still sceptical:

'What makes you so sure?'

Johanson gestured:

'That piece right next to your hand. That's hominid too.'

Gray turned and looked: *'Jesus Christ!'*.

As their eyes scanned the slope, more and more pieces of bone came into view – a femur, a rib, some vertebrae. Could they all be part of a single skeleton? The thought seemed impossible. Previous finds of human ancestors, at least those earlier than Neanderthalers, had never consisted of more than fragments – an odd tooth, a piece of skull – yet here was nearly half of an early hominid skeleton, a creature from our own family tree that lived in Hadar over 3 million years before.

The couple raced back to the Land Rover and tore across the rugged terrain back to camp. Johanson tried to keep a lid on his mounting excitement – what if they were wrong? But they both knew they weren't and as the car skidded into the camp Gray hit the horn, bringing the other team members running from their tents. More than three weeks of intensive collecting still lay ahead and after that many years of wrangling over exactly who and what this little creature was, but that evening it was time to celebrate.

Lucy gets her name

No-one could sleep, and throughout the night the team drank beer and listened to one of the few tapes they had with them. At full volume one track echoed out again and again into the dark desert – 'Lucy in the Sky with Diamonds' by the Beatles. And so that night the greatest early hominid find of all time gained a new name to replace her official designation as AL 288-1. That night she became Lucy.

TIMELINE

3.75 MILLION YEARS AGO A volcano in east Africa, at Laetoli in modern Tanzania, erupts, covering the surrounding ground in a layer of ash. Rain turns the ash to cement, which is baked by the sun; impressions of animal footprints are preserved in the cement after another layer of ash falls

3.2 MILLION YEARS AGO The *Australopithecus afarensis* now known as 'Lucy' lives in the Afar region of present-day Ethiopia

1974 (30 November) Donald Johanson and Tom Gray find female hominid remains at Locality 288 at Hadar in Ethiopia; later that day the remains, are given the name Lucy

1976 A member of Mary Leakey's team based at Laetoli discovers footprints in a dry stream bed

1977 Following the discovery of apparently human footprints, Leakey is eventually persuaded to begin excavations on the site. She discovers over 50 footprints, made by three upright creatures

1978 After four years of studying the remains of Lucy, Johanson announces that she belongs to an as yet undescribed species which he names *Australopithecus afarensis*; the footprints and remains found by Leakey at Laetoli are thought to be of the same species

MARY LEAKEY AT LAETOLI

Lucy was the find of a lifetime, but yet more remarkable evidence of her kind was brought to light two years later. Long before modern humans walked the earth, a volcano erupted in east Africa, in an area now known as Laetoli in Tanzania. The culprit – Sandiman – was not about to cover the region in lava but was just coughing clouds of ash into the air at random intervals. The material ejected by the volcano drifted down over the surrounding area, leaving a 1-centimetre- (0.4-in-) thick layer of fine grey ash on the ground. It began to rain. As the water soaked the ash, it turned from a fine powder into a sort of wet cement, across which walked animals of that distant era, leaving footprints behind them. The sun baked the cement hard. Then Sandiman coughed again, filling the footprints with another layer of fine ash and sealing the impressions in. Eventually about 20 centimetres (8 in) of ash fell before the volcano returned to its long sleep and the events at Laetoli were forgotten.

Laetoli returned to the spotlight when the eminent anthropologist Mary Leakey (1913–96) began excavations there in search of fossils of early humans. There is precious little in the way of entertainment at the isolated Laetoli site, and one hot afternoon in 1976 some of Leakey's team were throwing dried elephant dung at each other. During this distinctly African 'snowball fight' a young anthropologist found himself ducking dung in a dry stream bed; as he searched around for some ammunition he noticed what looked like animal footprints in the rock beneath him.

The footprints were recorded and the next year the team uncovered more, this time including the unmistakable tracks of an elephant alongside what looked like human footprints. Arguments raged over what type of creature had made these rather indistinct tracks, and Mary Leakey was becoming increasingly exasperated with the bickering. When a young

Mary Leakey holds a cast of a 3.75-million-year-old footprint. As well as footprints, she excavated skeletal remains of Australopithecus afarensis *at Laetoli.*

scientist on her team, Paul Abell, produced a new, much clearer print from another area of the site, it was initially identified as that of a hoofed animal, and Mary forbade excavation there. After much pleading and cajoling she eventually agreed that someone with nothing better to do on the site could take a quick look. The job fell to the team's maintenance man, Ndibo.

Ndibo quickly proved that he was more than just a maintenance man, and when he returned from the area the next day he announced that he had discovered two footprints, one about 25 centimetres (10 in) long. Mary relented and full excavations began.

What the dung fight and later finds had uncovered was the layer of ash blown out by Sandiman all those aeons ago. Now part of the overlying strata had weathered away, revealing the cement-like layer in which the ancient creatures of Laetoli had once walked. But what type of creatures were they?

As each fragile impression was uncovered it had to be consolidated with a chemical hardener before the next piece of topsoil could be removed. It was painfully slow work but eventually over 50 footprints emerged, covering a distance of more than 23 metres (25 yds). They had been made that day 3.75 million years ago by three creatures, all of which walked upright – one large set of prints down the middle of the excavated area, a smaller set to the left and a third walking in the footprints of the larger one. Whether they walked together we cannot say, but analysis of the footfalls shows they were unbothered by Sandiman's blustering and strolled slowly across the wet surface. Here were the footprints of some of the first hominids to walk upright – the first creatures to stand on their back legs and look out across the African plains, creatures like Lucy, taking the first steps on the long road that leads to modern humans.

GUARDIANS OF ETERNITY
The Terracotta Army, 1974

In the early 1920s, in the foothills of the Qinling mountains in Shaanxi province, China, a farmer began digging a well to irrigate his fields. As he dug, to his great satisfaction the bottom of the well slowly began to fill with water, until his progress was suddenly halted as he hit upon something hard. Imagining it to be a stone, he thrust his spade down hard, only to hear the object crack. At that moment the water in the well drained away as if by magic, and the broken head of a man appeared in the bottom of the hole. The farmer wasted no time. This part of Shaanxi, near the city of Xian, was well known for stories of ancestors appearing in the soil. This was clearly some malign spirit that had drunk the water out of his well. He hastily buried it again and went to dig elsewhere.

And so rural life around the ancient city of Xian continued, planting crops, digging irrigation wells, and telling stories of the buried ancestors. Until 1974. This was a hard year in Shaanxi. There was a prolonged drought and farmers were forced to dig ever deeper wells in their fields to reach the rapidly sinking water table. So hard had it become that groups of farmers had taken to digging wells together, using their combined labour to reach the deep water sources before they drained away. So it was that Yang Zhifa and his neighbours came to be digging in a field some 40 miles (64 km) from Xian and just over 1200 metres (1300 yds) from the peculiar artificial mound known as Mount Lishan, which tradition said was the last resting place of the First Emperor of China, Shi Huangdi (*c.*259–210 BC).

Buried treasure?

The faces of the terracotta soldiers, each one different from the next, are thought to have been modelled on real soldiers. The life-size figures have a solid lower half and a hollow upper part and were originally painted in bright colours.

They had dug down over 4 metres (13 ft) without finding water when Yang's shovel hit something hard, leaving a red clay streak in the soil. Puzzled, he knelt down and began clearing away the earth from around the obstruction. As he dug, more and more of the strange object appeared and it began to dawn on him that this had the look of pottery rather than stone. But why would anyone bury a pot 4 metres (13 ft) down in a field in rural China? Hoping that they had stumbled upon some great treasure, the three men began widening the hole to get a better look at their find. They were astonished to discover that what stared back at them was not a pot but a human head, and not just a

A Mausoleum Fit for an Emperor

The terracotta army originally formed only a small part of the wonders of the mausoleum of the First Emperor at Shaanxi. Today the site of the burial itself lies hidden under a huge man-made mound which has yet to be excavated by archaeologists, and our only knowledge of what may lie inside comes from the descriptions provided by the Grand Historian Sima Qian (c.145–90 BC).

The *Shiji* (known in the West as 'The Records of the Grand Historian') recount the history of China from the days of the legendary Yellow Emperor until Sima Qian's own time under the Han, who eventually restored dynastic control to China after the collapse of the First Emperor's dynasty. Sima Qian recorded in his history some of the few details we have of the First Emperor's death and his subsequent entombment near Xian and included in this record a description of the mausoleum itself. He tells us that:

'As soon as the First Emperor became king of Qin, excavations and building had been started at Mount Li, while after he won the empire, more than 700,000 conscripts from all parts of the country worked there. They dug through three subterranean streams and poured molten copper for the outer coffin, and the tomb was filled with models of palaces, pavilions and offices as well as fine vessels, precious stones and rarities ... All the country's streams, the Yellow River and the Yangtze were reproduced in quicksilver and by some mechanical means made to flow into a miniature ocean. The heavenly constellations were above and the regions of the earth below. The candles were made of whale oil to insure their burning for the longest possible time.'

The emperor's tomb was therefore meant to be a jewelled model of the entire empire, set in a sea of flowing mercury (which the emperor believed could instil immortality) under a heavenly vault picked out in gemstone stars.

Such a tomb would obviously be a lure for any thieves who might dare to brave the atmosphere, filled with choking mercury vapour as it must have been, so the emperor took precautions to protect his treasure. Shortly before the tomb was sealed, the architects, engineers and builders of the complex were invited into its inner sanctum. The doors were then shut and bolted from the outside. All those who had a knowledge of the layout and contents of the tomb would accompany into the next world the hundreds of the emperor's concubines who also cowered in the tomb. No living soul who knew the secret was allowed to survive.

According to the *Shiji,* the emperor also took practical measures to ensure that his mausoleum was not rifled by later tomb-raiders. It records that:

'Artisans were ordered to fix up crossbows so that any thief breaking in would be shot.'

If this is true it represents perhaps the earliest automatic anti-theft device in history.

Just how effective the emperor's attempts to preserve his tomb and treasure have been is unknown because the Chinese authorities have never excavated the interior and have no immediate plans to do so. Ongoing archaeological work around the site has unearthed over 180 other pits around the tomb, containing everything from terracotta dancers, acrobats and musicians (presumably placed there to entertain the emperor in the next life) to over 200 sets of stone armour (which may have been placed there to placate the angry spirits of the soldiers who died in the emperor's army).

The mound itself has only been disturbed by some limited sampling and non-invasive radar and resistivity studies. The results of these are tantalizing, however. Remote sensing has shown that the entire mound is the weathered remains of a collapsed pyramid – in its day larger than the Great Pyramid at Giza – into which is set a tomb which appears to contain large numbers of coins. Soil samples also show an unusually high level of mercury residue in the soil above the tomb. Could this be evidence of the astonishing mausoleum described by Sima Qian, with its rivers and seas of mercury? Until archaeologists have the techniques to properly excavate and preserve this unique site, the First Emperor will hold onto his last great secret.

head – the neck continued down, in fact the figure went down as far as the farmers could dig. Here, in their field, was buried a life-size terracotta model of a soldier, but a soldier from long before their time – a visitor from China's distant past.

Yang Zhifa was not as superstitious as those farmers who had stumbled upon such things before. He did not bury his find and run off to dig his well elsewhere. Instead, he reported the discovery to officials in Xian and soon the whole area was swarming with archaeologists. Although Yang was unaware of the fact, the archaeologists knew the strange man-made mountain near his farm was indeed the last resting place of the First Emperor, but no survey had ever fully uncovered the extent of the site. Was this soldier a one-off – an outlying spirit guarding the approaches to the tomb – or was the whole site far larger than had ever been realized?

Bodyguard for the afterlife

Extensive excavations of the whole area seemed to be the only way to resolve the issue and over 30 years later this ongoing work is still revealing what has become one of the wonders of the world. Yang's soldier was not performing a lonely vigil, he stood amongst thousands of his comrades – 8099 such figures have been excavated to date. Here, buried around the emperor's tomb, was an entire army, a terracotta army, each man unique, slightly larger than life size, moulded by hand in clay, then baked hard, brightly painted and buried in rank after rank.

Pit 1, containing the emperor's main army, held 6000 horses and warriors. Of these infantrymen equipped with light packs, 204 formed the vanguard of the army, followed by 30 lines of chariots alternating with more infantry. To the right and left of this formation were two lines of infantrymen facing outwards, guarding the detachment. Pit 2 appears to have been modelled on the imperial bodyguard and contained 1400 archers, infantrymen and chariots, while Pit 3 apparently held the 68 high-ranking commanders of the army arranged around a spectacular war chariot, drawn by four

Ranks of footsoldiers and cavalry arranged in battle formation guard the tomb of the First Emperor. Models of chariots, horses and crossbowmen were also included.

THE FIRST EMPEROR

The First Emperor was one of the most extraordinary rulers in Chinese, indeed world history. Born into the ruling family of the state of Qin during the era of Chinese history known as the Warring States Period, he was given the personal name Zheng, after the name of the month in which he was born.

Zheng ascended to the throne of Qin at the age of 12 and was placed under a regent. It was a period of intense warfare both between the rival states that would one day form China and between the major families within each state as they vied for power. Zheng was 21 by the time he managed to seize personal power from his regent in a palace coup and he immediately turned his attention to ending the incessant fighting by an audacious series of military campaigns that would subdue the neighbouring Chinese states and bring them all under the command of a single man, Zheng himself.

In 221 BC the 800-year-old state of Qi became the last to fall in the face of Zheng's huge and ruthless army. China was now his and in that same year, now aged 38, Zheng announced that he would be known as Shi Huangdi – the First Emperor. His successor would be known as the Second Emperor and so on for, as he put it, 10,000 generations.

Unifying the warring states of China was a herculean task but one which the emperor and his prime minister, Li Si, set about with extraordinary audacity and confidence. Abolishing centuries of feudalism, they divided the empire into regions, each commanded by a civilian governor and a subordinate military commander, both appointed (and dismissed) on the whim of the emperor.

Separating civilian and military control effectively prevented too much power from falling into the hands of any one imperial servant, while the appointment of independent Inspectors in each region ensured that the emperor heard exactly how his nominees were behaving. To further prevent his governors becoming over-mighty, each command was rotated, ensuring that no individual had enough time to build up a power base in any one area.

The emperor also set about unifying his new country, initiating an extensive programme of road and canal building which both improved trade and provided his army with the ability to rapidly suppress trouble in any quarter. To further integrate his government, he ordered the Chinese script as well as all Chinese weights and measures to be standardized, and he set in place a single codified legal system. To protect China's borders he also ordered the construction of the prototype of the Great Wall of China.

The emperor's rule was revolutionary but highly autocratic and differences of opinion were not allowed. Books, including many of the earliest Chinese writings, were systematically burnt and scholars who disagreed with his methods were executed. As the emperor grew older he also appears to have become more paranoid, developing an obsessive fear of death and spending his last years searching for the legendary 'Island of the Immortals' which was said to lie off China's eastern coast and to hold the secret of eternal life. During this time historians record that the emperor also began taking mercury pills in the belief that they would prolong his life indefinitely, and the poisonous effects of these may have further damaged his deteriorating mental state.

Zheng died in September 210 BC in a provincial palace, and the journey back to his capital would take two months. Fearing a rebellion, Li Si hid his death, entering the imperial wagon each day during the journey home, allegedly to speak with the emperor. To prevent his entourage from becoming suspicious he ordered fish wagons to travel in front of and behind the emperor's carriage to mask the smell of the rapidly decaying body.

Li Si's fears were well founded. Zheng's empire was held together by his own extraordinary personality and within four years his son, the Second Emperor, was dead and chaos returned to China. The First Emperor's dream of immortality in an eternal empire was at an end, and he would have to content himself with the immortality given him by historians and the extraordinary treasure buried secretly in his mausoleum.

horses. All the figures had patiently stood guard there for the greater part of Chinese history (over 2000 years), hidden from the world and not mentioned in any records – a secret army that had last seen the light of day in 210 BC.

Just what this army's purpose was is still a matter of debate, although it seems most likely that they were a spirit army designed to protect the highly superstitious emperor in the afterlife. Certainly he had invested a great deal of time and resources in preparing it, apparently in secret, since no records from the period even make mention of it. The soldiers seem to have been prepared on a production line, individual pieces being moulded and fired before being joined together to create each figure.

Meticulous detail

A contemporary portrait of Shi Huangdi, the ruler who united the warring clans of ancient China and became their First Emperor.

Great care was taken to ensure that no two soldiers were identical, and each was moulded with the precise insignia and hairstyle appropriate to his rank. The finished figures were then lacquered and painted (although only traces of the paint survive) to further increase their realism. They were armed with a selection of real weapons, some dating back to 228 BC, which may actually have been used in the emperor's wars to unify China. The army was then arranged in battle order in three huge trenches and buried, never to be seen again (as far as the emperor intended). Chinese archaeologists have estimated that the work would have taken some 700,000 craftsmen and labourers 38 years to complete.

The emperor's necropolis itself survived intact for a mere five years after his death before being sacked by the warlord Xiang Yu. According to the near-contemporary records of the Grand Historian Sima Qian, Xiang Yu's army looted and burnt the site but may in the process have unwittingly saved the First Emperor's greatest legacy. The wrecked necropolis, no longer a wonder in itself, soon disappeared from public attention, its precincts being returned to fields and nothing remaining above ground save for the strange man-made hill. And so the terracotta army was allowed to sleep for 2000 years.

TIMELINE

259 BC Zheng is born into the ruling Qin family of China

247 BC At the age of 12, Zheng succeeds to the throne, which is in the hands of a regent

221 BC Zheng seizes power in a palace coup and embarks on a series of wars to take control of the whole nation; he declares himself Shi Huangdi (First Emperor) of China and orders the construction of an elaborate mausoleum at Mount Li

210 BC The emperor dies and his body is carried back to his capital in secret; according to historian Sima Qian, he is interred within the mausoleum and all those who knew the details of the construction, together with hundreds of imperial concubines, are buried with him. A huge terracotta army guards the inner tomb

1920S AD A farmer finds the broken head of a man in a well in Shaanxi province; believing it to be an evil spirit, he buries it again

1974 Digging for water during a drought, Yang Zhifa strikes a piece of pottery which reveals itself to be the life-size figure of a soldier; he reports it to the authorities, and excavations begin at the location near the place where the First Emperor is said to lie buried

BLOOD RITES

Uncovering the Aztec Templo Mayor, 1978

MEXICO

• Tenochtitlán

GUATAMALA

HONDURAS

Aztec empire

PACIFIC OCEAN

In 1978 a team from the local electricity board was excavating power cables in the centre of Mexico City, close to the Metropolitan Cathedral, when they hit upon a stone. As the workmen cleared away the earth and debris, it soon became clear that this was no ordinary piece of building rubble but a circular relief 3 metres (10 ft) across, and depicted on it was an image from another time, from another city that had once stood on this site.

The ancient city that lay beneath Mexico City was by no means unknown. It had been described by the Spanish conquistadors as a wonder of the world and one of the largest cities on earth – Tenochtitlán. The city had originally been built on an island in Lake Texcoco and since its founding in 1325 had spread over the marshy waters of the lake.

At its height the city had covered between 3 and 5 square miles (8 and 13 sq km) and was connected to the mainland by causeways to the north, south and west, across which lay sections of bridge that could be raised in times of attack. The city was divided into four quarters, each consisting of 20 districts separated by canals, and each district had its own speciality craft and its own market. At the centre of the city lay the public buildings including temples, ball courts and schools together with the ruler's palace which, under the Aztec emperor Moctezuma, had 100 rooms, each with its own bath. Two terracotta aqueducts brought fresh water to the city, for the lake was brackish. Some conquistadors who visited claimed it was as large as any in Europe, and its population at this time probably exceeded 200,000.

The Spanish invaders

But those same visitors who marvelled at its size and complexity were also about to destroy it. On 13 August, 1521, after a long siege, Hernán Cortés and his allies stormed the city and set about demolishing it, covering the site with a new capital. Now, in 1978, next to the place where those Spanish conquerors had chosen to build a cathedral to their Christian god, the central temple of that previous civilization was about to be uncovered.

Excavating in the centre of modern, living cities is usually a constricted affair but the Mexican government, keen to rediscover their pre-Columbian history, determined on a

massive excavation, removing whole blocks of buildings around the find to reveal the remains of one of the most startling and important edifices in the New World.

What the electricity workers had stumbled on was the Templo Mayor – the main temple of Tenochtitlán. This central structure was as important to the Aztec rulers of Mexico as the great cathedral was to their Spanish conquerors. It was more than just a religious site, it was a statement of Aztec power and belief. The excavations revealed a building strikingly similar to the early Spanish descriptions of the centre of Tenochtitlán. The temple had twin sanctuaries on a stepped pyramidal platform – one dedicated to the war god Huitzilopochtli and the other to the rain and agriculture god Tlaloc. This vast complex had been built shortly after the foundation of the city and rebuilt and enlarged at least five times since. Although little other than foundations

The Aztec capital Tenochtitlán, built on an island and reclaimed marsh land in Lake Texcoco, was once one of the largest cities in the world. At its heart was a huge temple complex and royal palace, and numerous canals crisscrossed the metropolis.

remained of the last temple, which had been systematically razed by the conquistadors, earlier buried remains were still alive with life-size ceramic sculptures, painted stone wall reliefs and buried caches of exotic imports and luxury goods sent as tribute from the areas conquered by the Aztecs.

A site for human sacrifices

But it was the find made by those electricity workers that gave the first clue to why this amazing structure had been so thoroughly demolished and forgotten. The circular stone plaque, found at the bottom of a staircase, depicted a nude female figure lying on the ground, dismembered and bleeding. She represented the moon goddess Coyolxauhqui who, in Aztec mythology, was killed by the war god Huitzilopochtli.

This myth formed a cornerstone of Aztec rule. Huitzilopochtli was the patron of the Aztecs, a conqueror who required constant sacrifices to placate him and ensure the success of the Aztec state. In front of his shrine a wedge-shaped stone was uncovered over which human sacrificial victims had been stretched. Their bodies would then have been cut open with knives and their beating hearts removed before they were decapitated and quartered, just as the goddess Coyolxauhqui's had been. The body parts were then cast down the steps, perhaps to lie on the circular relief of Coyolxauhqui itself. Elsewhere on the site there was further evidence of human sacrifice in the form of a *tzompantli* – a vertical rack decorated with stucco skulls where the real heads of sacrificed captives (usually warriors) had once been displayed.

Human sacrifice was a central part of Aztec culture – a ritualized and public way of expressing the martial values of the civilization's élite who gained their power and prestige through conquest. It appalled many of the conquistadors and this may have been the reason for the thoroughness with which the latest versions of the temple had been destroyed. However, the conquistadors were themselves members of a martial culture whose wealth and prestige derived from conquest, and many were not averse to the large-scale slaughter of the native population. The removal of the Templo Mayor may have been dressed up as a pious act on the part of the conquerors but in fact it marked the conquest and suppression of the Aztecs themselves and the replacement of the central ideological structure in their world with a new Spanish equivalent. This was built next to the *templo* – a Christian cathedral dedicated (no doubt to the bafflement of many Aztecs) to a god who sacrificed his own son.

The 'Wall of Skulls', or tzompantli, *found at the Templo Mayor, is a stark display of the skulls of human sacrificial victims.*

THE AZTECS

The Aztecs, who referred to themselves as 'Mexicas', were the main pre-Columbian civilization of central Mexico first encountered by the Spanish in the early 16th century. Their origins are unclear but the Aubin Codex (a pictorial history of and by the Atzecs) claims they were originally one of a group of seven tribes from Aztlán, a place allegedly north of the valley of Mexico.

A golden mask found at Tenochtitlán. Aztec rituals often involved the use of masks to harness the power of deities or ancient ancestors.

system of tribute from conquered states. This tribute could be brought to Tenochtitlán on one of the Aztecs' greatest achievements, a series of new roads, lined with rest houses and latrines every 6 to 9 miles (10 to 15 km). This tightly controlled network kept the rulers in Tenochtitlán in touch with their vassal states and provided an extensive trade system along which both everyday necessities such as food and firewood and more exotic luxuries travelled (all by foot, since wheeled vehicles were unknown here at this time).

Wherever they originated, the Atzecs arrived in the valley of Mexico in the mid-13th century to find it already studded with sophisticated city-states, and their early history is one of alliances and expulsions as they tried to establish themselves in the region. According to their own mythology, they were to found their future capital at a place where they saw an eagle perched on a cactus, grasping a snake in its talons. Such a sight was witnessed on Lake Texcoco, and in 1325 they built their city of Tenochtitlán there.

But the Atzecs were still not the dominant culture in the region, and it was only by forming a triple alliance involving themselves, the exiled rulers of Texcoco and the city-state of Tlacopán that they slowly grew to prominence. By the mid-15th century their power extended from the Pacific shore to the Gulf of Mexico through a series of tribute-paying states, and they had eclipsed their allies. Around this time the leader, Tlacaelel, began reforming the state and its religion, rewriting the early history of the Aztecs to promote the belief that they had always been a powerful and conquering people. This mythologizing included the creation of the 'Flower Wars' – a long-running series of conflicts with neighbours that provided training for Aztec warriors and a constant supply of captives for the human sacrifices that their religion now required in order to keep the sun moving in the sky.

The Aztec empire did not provide central government over the whole area it controlled but survived on a

The centralized ideology of the Aztec state was reinforced through a system of compulsory schooling for both sexes – one of the first such systems anywhere on earth. Children were educated at home (under the supervision of their local district) until 14 and then at 15 went to a school either to learn practical and military skills or theology, astronomy and statesmanship. The advanced level of schooling is reflected in the sophistication of the Aztec calendar, which came about through intensive astronomical study, and the rich mythology elaborated in their writings. Even warriors were expected to be skilled in the arts, and poetry was considered a suitable pastime for soldiers when there were no wars to fight.

The collapse of Aztec civilization came at the hands of Europeans and their own native enemies who wished to be free of their domination. The Spanish conquistadors sacked Tenochtitlán in 1521 with the active help of some indigenous states, but it was the outbreak of European diseases, notably smallpox and typhus, that brought the city to its knees. The empire's population just before the Spanish arrival has been estimated at 15 million. By 1581 it was less than 2 million. With no immunity to new diseases and little ability left to fight their attackers, Aztecs and their native enemies could no longer resist Spanish rule and a new era in the history of central America, an era of European domination, was born.

WATER WORLD
The Bronze Age Rituals of Flag Fen, 1982

In 1982 a mechanical digger was clearing a drainage ditch on the flat fenland to the southeast of the city of Peterborough in central England. As the machine scraped along the side of the ditch, a number of wooden posts were dragged out of the peaty soil and cast onto the spoil heap. In this area of intensive farming the discovery of a few old fence posts hardly constituted a great archaeological find, but a local archaeologist, Francis Pryor (b.1945), who was monitoring the work, had a chance to examine them and noticed something odd. The posts were clearly man-made but had not been cut with mechanical saws; in fact they had not been cut with saws at all. Instead, each post had been shaped by hand with an axe-like tool known as an adze, a technique that had not been used for centuries. Pryor suggested sending samples of the timbers for radiocarbon dating and when the results came back they bore a date of 1000 BC.

The hunt was now on to find exactly where these posts had come from and discover what they belonged to. Walking the drainage ditches on foot, cutting away their edges with just a trowel, Pryor eventually found the site. Looking to the opposite bank, he discovered more posts disappearing under the peat. Flag Fen, as the area was known (because of the profusion of flag irises that grew there) was no ordinary farming field. Someone, 3000 years ago, had put a great deal of time and effort into building a structure across what was then open fen, but what was it? The answer would come after almost of a quarter of a century of large-scale excavations in the dark, wet peat which revealed not only the largest prehistoric wooden structure known in Britain, but brought to light a treasure trove of artefacts from the Bronze Age.

A bridge across the fen
Three thousand years ago the sea, which is today miles away to the north at the Wash, was much closer, and Flag Fen stood on a marshy inlet with land to the south and west and open sea to the north. To the east stood more open fen, edged with reed, rush and flag iris. Behind this rose another piece of land – Northey Island, standing a few feet, but no more, above the water. But this was not an uninhabited area. Wherever there was

dry land there were farms and between them lay a vast and elaborate system of field boundaries. Across the open fen over on Northey Island stood a few round houses scattered across the landscape, each separated from its neighbour by a cattle droveway and surrounded by its own system of fields.

On Northey Island, however, stood something special. There, connecting the land with the island more than half a mile (1 km) away, via a strange artificial island, stood one of the greatest engineering achievements of British prehistory – a long causeway of 60,000 wooden posts, driven into the silt of the marsh and bridging the gulf of open fen.

Were it not for the fact that this landscape, like the moors, was later covered in a protective layer of peat, we would know nothing of this wooden wonder. The monuments of earlier ages built in stone have survived much better than these organic remains, yet sites like this may well have been the successors to the circles and standing stones of earlier times, and Britain may once have been home to many thousands of them. The survival of this monument and its remarkable rediscovery give us a glimpse into a new and strange world.

The vast display area at Flag Fen, known as the Preservation Hall, houses an area of excavated posts 10 metres (33 ft) long, representing just 1 percent of the length of the Bronze Age causeway. Most of the timber posts date from 1350 to 950 BC and have been left in the positions in which they were found.

*c.*1350 BC A Bronze Age community inhabiting fenland in present-day Northamptonshire in central England constructs a giant wooden causeway linking Northey Island to the mainland

*c.*950 BC The wooden causeway stops being regularly repaired and begins to fall out of use, possibly because of rising water levels. The site retains its ritual significance well into the Iron Age

AD 1982 A mechanical digger working on drainage clearance at Flag Fen drags a number of wooden posts from the peaty soil; they are sent for radiocarbon dating and found to be 3000 years old

1986 Further excavations reveal a causeway of wooden posts reaching across the fen. Hundreds of man-made objects, all deliberately discarded by their owners, are found to the landward side of the causeway

1989 Excavations at Peterborough power station reveal another section of causeway. It is estimated that the entire structure contains 60,000 to 80,000 posts and perhaps 4 million other timbers. Ongoing research and excavation continue to bring new insights into life in Bronze Age England

To call this structure simply a bridge, however, would be to underestimate it. This long line of posts, over 7 metres (23 ft) wide in places, was covered with white sand which dusted the slippery surface of the track to prevent skidding; but what was next to the causeway was more surprising. In what were once shallow waters archaeologists found hundreds of man-made objects – some of the rarest commodities of the day. There were bronze rapiers and daggers, black shale bracelets, flesh hooks for pulling meat from boiling cauldrons, a set of bronze shears still in their wooden case and even a wooden wheel (the first we know of in Britain).

These were not simply items lost whilst crossing the fen. In a world in which bronze was rare and valuable, someone losing a dagger would stop to retrieve it from the waters. Nor were all these items randomly scattered beneath the posts. Most lay on the landward side of the alignment, making random loss unlikely. The swords were also strangely damaged. One blade had been repeatedly hit against a hard corner, ruining the edge. Other blades had clearly been bent or even snapped, but not because they were old tools being discarded; in fact, some seem to have hardly been used before being broken.

Deliberately discarded

The people who came to the Flag Fen causeway were deliberately disposing of perfectly good, high-value items in what must have been some form of ritual. Before being deposited, these objects had been 'killed' – deliberately turned from useful items into unusable ones. Francis Pryor has suggested that this may be the closest insight we have to the religion of the people of the fen. In this theory the post alignment was not simply a bridge between places, but a bridge between worlds – between land and water (the air that gives breath and the water that denies it), between life and death, and between heaven and hell.

It is perhaps too much to ask what such rituals may have meant. We know from the archaeological work at Flag Fen that high-value items were being deliberately placed in the water as some form of offering, but the exact reasons for this must remain as mysterious as the ancient language spoken over such rites. What we do know is that the things they consigned to the waters had cost them a lot to obtain – rare objects often transported over long distances and certainly commanding a high 'price', however that was paid. These people were not throwing pennies in a fountain but casting away the equivalent of diamond rings and sports cars.

Among the remarkable finds at Flag Fen are these bronze shears, complete with the original carved wooden case – evidence that livestock, including sheep, may have been farmed in the area.

SECRETS OF THE SOIL

Modern archaeology is not simply concerned with finding things in the soil – the soil itself can hold clues to the past. In the case of sites that were very different at the time of their occupation from the way they appear now, such as Flag Fen, finding these clues can be as important as recovering artefacts and structures.

Soil is a complex mix of organic materials and minerals, and the various layers of soil in an archaeological site and the things they contain reflect the world in which they were created. Soils often contain seeds and fragments of plants, which can be removed by immersing a sample in water. As the soil breaks up, the seeds usually float to the surface, where they can be collected and sieved. By looking at the range of seeds from a number of samples across the site, it is often possible to determine whether or not the area was used for growing crops in the past and to identify the specific plants. The presence of cereal grains can sometimes indicate individual areas of a site, such as storage pits (which may contain a large number of 'raw' seeds) or cooking areas (where the seeds are more likely to be carbonized).

Under the microscope, soil samples can also reveal smaller clues. Pollen survives well in the archaeological record and, by taking sample columns of soils from a site, it is often possible to reconstruct the environment at different times in history. The presence of large quantities of domesticated species might indicate farmland, whereas lots of tree pollen would suggest woodland. Equally, many species of plants have a limited range, preferring conditions that are either dry or wet, salty or fresh, warm or cold; by comparing the proportions of these the nature of the local flora and hence the local landscape can be established.

Of course pollen is light and can be blown a long way, but other things in the soil can help to narrow the margin of error. In particular, soils often contain the remains of large numbers of mollusc shells and many of these species are equally sensitive to their environment. Because snails are far less likely to be blown on the wind than pollen, they can help to pin down the exact conditions that prevailed at the time.

Finally, there is the structure of the soil itself, which contains evidence as to how it was laid down. By analyzing this, specialists known as soil micromorphologists can tell archaeologists whether a soil came from a ploughed field, a roadway regularly trampled underfoot, or even whether it came from a ditch that was filled in centuries or millennia before.

It is through such studies that it has been possible to show that in the Bronze Age Flag Fen was not the flat, arable field miles from the sea that it is today – we have evidence that it stood on the banks of a marshy inlet with the sea directly to the north and a low, farmed island to the east, bordered with reeds and the flag irises that gave the site its name.

A wooden 'Canute'?

Perhaps the offerings and even the causeway itself were an attempt to ritually control the rising waters that were threatening the local farmland more with each passing year. Perhaps the bridge marked out the boundaries of ownership in an increasingly 'pressed' society; a Bronze Age wooden 'Canute' holding back both the watery tide and the tide of people the rising seas were slowly displacing.

The causeway may have served more prosaic social functions as well, being the largest landmark for miles around, and possibly a place where the disparate communities of the Bronze Age fen could meet up to find husbands and wives and exchange the livestock that was so essential to keep the bloodlines of both humans and animals healthy. Perhaps far less practical considerations ruled here. Either way, at Flag Fen we begin to see a type of worship that was replacing the old monumental world of the stone circles and henges of the Neolithic period, marking the dawn of a new age.

THE BODIES IN THE BOG
The Burials of Lindow Moss, 1983

On 13 May, 1983 the police were called to a commercial peat-cutting site at Lindow Moss near Wilmslow in Cheshire, in the northwest of England. During the morning's work the peat-cutting machine had dug up something unexpected, something which at first glance looked like an old football but which on closer examination proved to be a human head. The supervisor suspected foul play – the head still had hair, some skin and even one eye attached so could not have been buried there long – and the police agreed.

In fact the discovery was not very much of a surprise for the police. They had been expecting a find like this to come to light one day, and an initial forensic examination confirmed their suspicions. The head was that of a woman, aged between 30 and 50, and had been buried in the bog for at least five but no more than 50 years. All that remained was to confront her murderer with the evidence.

Police had for a long time suspected that a local man, Peter Reyn-Bardt, had murdered his wife some years previously. The couple's marriage had been short and turbulent, indeed it was over almost before it began. Reyn-Bardt, it was later said, had only married Malika to provide a gloss of respectability at work, where he feared his homosexuality would be discovered.

They argued from the start and separated in 1959 but she had subsequently disappeared in June 1961 and never been seen again. One of her last known journeys was to the area where Reyn-Bardt lived in a house overlooking Lindow Moss. He had never admitted to seeing her, however, and not a single piece of evidence to suggest her whereabouts had emerged in the 22 years that had passed since.

But now the case seemed close to being solved. Here were the recently buried remains of a woman of the right age in the right area, and whilst the severed head was sent to Oxford University Research Laboratory for Archaeology to provide final confirmation of the victim's age, the police went to see Reyn-Bardt.

An unexpected confession
But if the police had expected a long struggle to get information out of the usually reticent Reyn-Bardt they were in for a surprise. When presented with the evidence,

The remains of Lindow Man are on display in the British Museum in London. His official name is Lindow II, and he is sometimes also known as 'Pete Marsh', a reference to the peaty bog in which he was found.

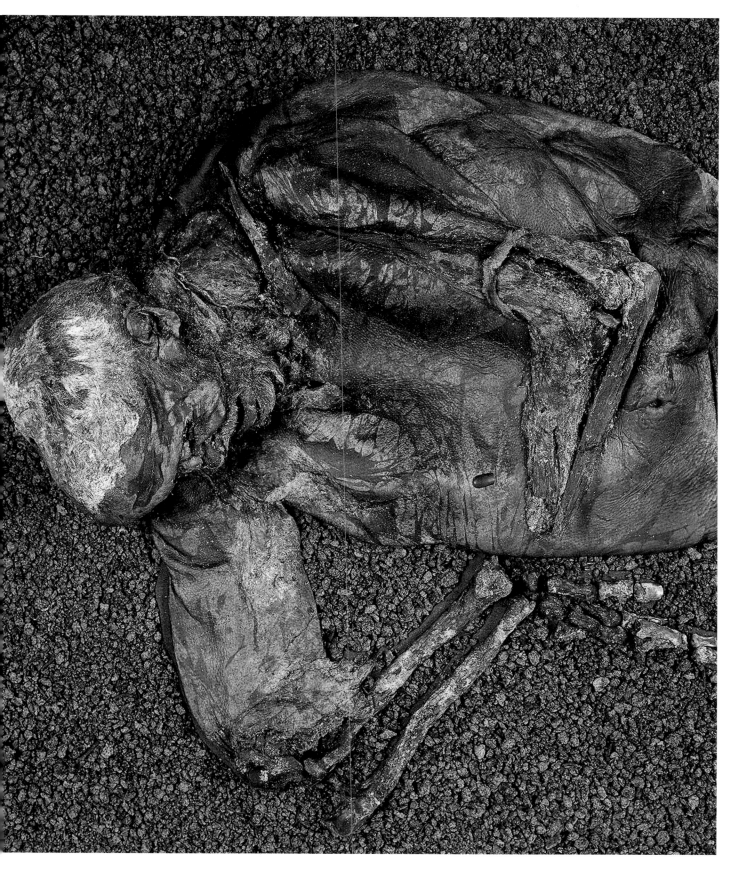

THE STRANGE DEATH OF LINDOW MAN

Lindow Man is the only prehistoric Briton we are still able to look in the eye, but they are the blue-grey eyes of a man whose last view of the world was terrible and violent.

From his beautifully preserved body we know that he was a perfectly ordinary man, someone who would go unnoticed in the modern world if dressed in suitable clothes. He was about 1.67 metres (5 ft 6 in) tall, well built and tanned. He was also apparently careful about his appearance – his nails were finely clipped, his hair cut quite short and his beard and moustache were neatly trimmed. He was, however, only 25 years old when he died, not old even in the first century AD, and the evidence we have of his last moments is that they were anything but ordinary.

He was possibly a relatively important man, judging from his manicured appearance, not the sort of person used to manual labour. The even development of the muscles on both sides of his upper body reinforce this theory. He had recently eaten a light meal of unleavened bread made from wheat and barley and cooked on a heather fire on the edge of the bog. This food was washed down with a drink that curiously contained mistletoe pollen and moss. He then walked out onto the bog and, although we have no way of knowing who was with him, we know that he was not alone. Two thousand years ago Lindow Moss was still a peat bog, a watery and dangerous place where one false step could prove fatal, but this man did not stumble to his death.

Here he stood, on the site that would become his grave, naked save for a fox-fur armband, and awaited his fate. What happened next we know about from the marks those subsequent events left on his body. Firstly one of the people with him suddenly dealt two savage blows to the back of his head with a blunt instrument. His knees crumpled and he fell to the floor, but his attackers had not finished with him yet. A thin cord was then placed around his neck and tightened, garrotting him and, with the cord still held tight, a knife was plunged into his throat, severing his jugular vein, before his bleeding body was lowered face down into a pool of water.

We do not know if Lindow Man was a priest or aristocrat chosen for sacrifice or even a prisoner sentenced to death. The elaborate sequence of events involved in his death probably precludes this being a straightforward execution – no-one is executed three times – but his silent lips cannot give us clues as to whether he went quietly and willingly to his death or if his screams echoed across Lindow Moss that day.

Using a replica of the skull and evidence of its remaining tissue, facial features were modelled in wax to produce a likeness of Lindow Man. Hair and eyes were added to match those found on the original.

Nor can we be sure of the reason for his death – was it in response to a specific event or was it a usual, if macabre, part of the prehistoric ritual calendar. What we do know is that the people of the Iron Age believed watery areas such as marshes and bogs to be charged with a religious significance. They were perhaps viewed as liminal places where this world and whatever 'other' world they believed in met. As such it is not unusual to find objects 'sacrificed' here, including perfectly good and highly valuable weapons such as swords and spears deliberately broken and cast into the water along with other tools and offerings. We also know that sometimes the gods of these times required a greater sacrifice – the ultimate sacrifice that a society could give – one of its own. And this was a demand that the people of prehistoric Britain were quite prepared to fulfil.

he quietly confirmed that the remains were indeed those of his wife and that he had murdered her. He claimed that the estranged Malika had come to visit him and threatened to expose his homosexuality if he did not pay her. In a rage, he had then strangled her, cut her body into pieces and buried it close to his cottage on Lindow Moss.

On the basis of this damning confession Reyn-Bardt was committed to trial for murder at Chester Crown Court in December 1983, but just before the trial began strange news arrived from Oxford. Carbon-14 dating showed that the head had not lain in the bog for 21 years. It had been there closer to 1800 years and was not that of Malika Reyn-Bardt but belonged to an unidentified female occupant of Roman Britain.

If Reyn-Bardt celebrated this unexpected news, he celebrated too soon. English law does not require that a body be found in a murder case, and his confession stood. The trial went ahead and he was convicted.

More body parts
Yet while the discovery of Lindow Woman (as she became known) closed one case, it opened up many more. The following year, on 1 August, parts of another body appeared in the peat cuttings at Lindow Moss, this time that of a man. Although the peat-cutting equipment had damaged the body it was still exceptionally well preserved and nearly complete. The remains were carefully lifted out of the bog and sent to the mortuary of a nearby hospital, pending scientific investigations.

This time no modern murder enquiry was launched. The body was soon dated to a similar time, around the first or early second century AD. The question now on everyone's lips was, what were these people doing buried in a bog? In September 1984 a detailed autopsy was carried out on the second body, which revealed it to be that of a 25-year-old male. But the most startling fact to emerge was that he had met with an extremely brutal death. His skull had been fractured in two places, his throat had been slit, severing the jugular vein, and he had been garrotted by a leather thong, snapping his neck.

The preservative qualities of peat
Normally human remains from the past consist of little more than bones or ash. Soft tissues buried in the ground quickly decay as insects and bacteria get to work breaking them down, but conditions in peat bogs are different. Wet peat acts as a preservative, leaching humic acid into the water which effectively pickles anything organic lying in it.

This aggressively acidic environment is also very poor in dissolved oxygen, preventing the usual aerobic bacteria that decompose organic matter from thriving. Lindow Man was therefore preserved as well as if he had been put in a bottle of vinegar. Not only did his skin and hair survive, so did his fingernails, his internal organs and even the contents of his stomach. In his gut were found traces of the parasites he had suffered from in life, including whipworm eggs, and even the residue of his last meal.

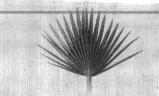

TIMELINE

43 The Romans invade Britain and record the use of human sacrifice amongst the Iron Age inhabitants of the land

c. FIRST CENTURY Lindow Man and Lindow Woman are killed in a Cheshire peat bog; their bodies are preserved in the oxygen-free environment

1959 Peter Reyn-Bardt and his wife separate after a brief and turbulent 'marriage of convenience'

1961 In June Malika Reyn-Bardt disappears after travelling to her husband's house near Lindow Moss

1983 (13 May) Peat cutters at Lindow Moss dig up a human skull; the police are called and interview Reyn-Bardt, who confesses to the murder of his wife 22 years earlier; he is committed to trial. Shortly before the trial begins, scientists state that 'Lindow Woman' is 1800 years old. The trial goes ahead, and Reyn-Bardt is convicted of murder

1984 (1 August) The same workmen in the peat-cutting site find more body parts, which are well preserved and found to be from the first or second century AD. The victim is named Lindow Man; it is established that he suffered a violent death through head trauma, garrotting and knife wounds, but the reason for his death in the peat bog remains contentious

BOG BODIES

Lindow Man and Woman are by no means the only bog bodies to have been recovered in Europe, indeed the remains of over 1000 individuals have been found in areas where peat bogs provide the necessary chemistry to preserve soft tissues.

The bodies range in date from that of Kolbjerg Woman who probably simply drowned in a bog by accident around 10,000 years ago to a 16th-century Irish woman who may have been placed in a bog following her suicide (which precluded her burial in consecrated ground). The vast majority of remains however come from the Iron Age in the centuries immediately before and after the Roman conquest of much of Europe.

Most of these bodies, where enough remains to make an assessment, seem to have met violent ends. Tollund Man, perhaps the most famous body after Lindow Man, was found in a Danish bog, naked except for a belt and a leather cap; a rope around his neck had apparently been used to hang him. The Yde Girl from the Netherlands, who was around 16 years old when she died, had been hanged and stabbed above the collarbone. Old Croghan Man, discovered in County Offaly in Ireland in 2003 had a yet more horrific death. He had been tortured, as evidenced by the deep cuts under each of his nipples, before being stabbed in the chest, decapitated and finally cut in half. Like Lindow Man, he was found naked save for an armband. Other bodies frequently show evidence of severe head trauma, knife wounds and neck ligatures.

It is hard to say exactly why these people were killed. Some of the 'wounds' to the bodies may have been caused after death, particularly during the cutting of the peat that so often reveals them, although this is hotly disputed in the case of Lindow Man. Even when the evidence of deliberate death is overwhelming it is hard at a distance of some 2000 years to say if the victim was murdered, executed for a crime or sacrificed to the gods. In the case of Old Croghan Man, a wound to his arm suggests he tried to defend himself from his attackers but in other cases there appears to have been no sign of a struggle. It has been suggested that the Yde Girl was drugged before she died to prevent a struggle and

that the last meal of Tollund Man included a substantial quantity of the hallucinogenic ergot fungus, which may have been used to put him in a mental state in which he would not fight his fate.

What is certain is that many of these deaths were 'special', and the careful preparation of the victims, their unusual dress and position, and the amount of 'overkill' involved in many of their deaths suggest that they were intended to send a message, either to the gods or to their fellow men and women. Through the unique properties of the places in which they were buried, it is a message that they can now begin to give to the people of the present.

To find such a body – a time traveller from the distant past – is to find one of the rarest treasures in archaeology. Most of the archaeological record is made up of hard, durable things such as stone, metal and pottery, and yet for much of our own lives today, and considerably more of the lives of our ancestors, we are and were surrounded by organic, perishable things which simply rot away. Rarest of all is possibly that most fragile of our possessions – the human body.

Finding human remains from the Iron Age is close to impossible. Whatever funeral rite they used, they do not generally appear to have buried or cremated their dead in a way that we can recognize today in the archaeological record. We have their sturdier possessions but almost none of their physical remains – not even bones.

Here in Lindow Moss were whole people from the past, whose faces we could see, whose lives we could reconstruct forensically and whose deaths would open up yet more controversy. For although the discovery of Lindow Man did not result in a modern murder investigation, it did open an ancient one.

The closed eyes and peaceful look on the face of the amazingly well-preserved Tollund Man are in stark contrast to what we know was his fate: autopsy reports reveal that this 30- to 40-year-old man was hanged before being dumped in a Danish peat bog some 2500 years ago.

A SOLDIER'S TALE

The Archaeology of Custer's Last Stand, 1984

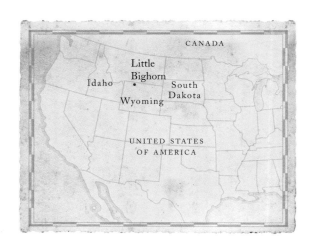

Archaeology has no cut-off date and its techniques are applied today to many recent sites that would once have been considered the preserve of historians alone. Even at apparently well-documented locations archaeology is able to provide new insights into the events that took place there and, in particular, the lives and times of those people who were not considered significant enough to find a place in the historical record.

The summer of 1983 was hot and dry in the southeast of Dakota, and the grassy plains of the state were becoming a tinderbox. Then, on 11 August an unidentified driver on Highway 212 threw a lighted cigarette out of his car window, setting the surrounding hillsides alight. The ensuing fire was a disaster for local wildlife but, when the flames were finally extinguished, the barren landscape revealed a hidden secret. For this was no ordinary hillside, it was the location of one of the most iconic battles in American history – Custer's 'Last Stand' – and with the grass and vegetation gone, ghosts from that battle could be seen littered across the ground. Those ghosts came in the form of spent cartridges and bullets, uniform buckles and arrowheads; and their subsequent archaeological analysis has caused the history books to be rewritten.

Military action against native dissent

The reason for Custer's Last Stand at the Battle of the Little Bighorn can be traced back to 1868 when the Second Treaty of Fort Laramie granted the Black Hills area of Dakota to the native American peoples who lived there. It was a treaty made at a time when the Black Hills were of relatively little value to the white settlers in the region, but in the following decade the discovery of gold there would change everything. Prospectors began flooding into the area whilst the government attempted to confine the native Americans to reservations. The Sioux and Northern Cheyenne peoples were not happy to be simply pushed aside, however, and reports that they were breaking out of their allotted areas brought a military response from the government.

In the spring of 1876 the US Seventh Cavalry was charged with shepherding them back into their reservation. On 25 June Lieutenant-Colonel George Armstrong Custer (1839–76) received word from his native Crow scouts that there was a large native encampment on the banks of the Little Bighorn river and decided to attack.

Until archaeological evidence retold events at the Battle of the Little Bighorn, Custer was immortalized in American history as a romantic hero. This 1876 painting shows him bravely holding off the enemy as his soldiers are killed around him.

Custer split his men into three columns to create a pincer movement, but as his own detachment of five companies moved along the ridge it began to dawn on him that he had made a terrible mistake. The encampment was huge, perhaps 7000 strong, and he had divided his troops into small, vulnerable units. He scribbled a note to Frederick Benteen (1834–98), commander of the first unit, which read:

> 'Benteen, come on. Big village, be quick, bring packs.'

The note was handed to bugler John Martin who, as he turned to leave, became the last man to see Custer and his 210 men alive. What happened after that was a matter of speculation and myth, until 1984, when archaeological investigations of the battlefield first began.

Uncovering the true story

The fire at the site of the Battle of the Little Bighorn gave archaeologists an opportunity to re-evaluate what had actually happened on Sunday 25 June 1876. There were 'historical' accounts, often taken from native Americans at the battle and of course a great deal of myth-making. The official story was that Custer was a hero who had valiantly fought against overwhelming odds, gathering his men around him in the famous Last Stand in which he and all his men lost their lives.

But these histories carried political baggage. Custer's widow was desperate to paint her husband as a hero, the white settlers were keen to portray the native Americans as savages with no right to their lands and even the native Americans themselves played up the heroism of their enemy, perhaps to flatter them in later sensitive treaty negotiations or to emphasize their own bravery.

Last Stand Hill has become a national monument, with gravestones marking the burial sites of the US soldiers who died. The headstone in the foreground marks the grave that held Custer's remains before his body was reinterred at West Point Cemetery in 1877.

Since none of Custer's men survived the battle only archaeology could help to explain what really happened. The archaeological plan at the Little Bighorn was to treat the site like a crime scene and use forensic techniques to uncover the true story.

The entire site was first gridded and swept with metal detectors, each signal that resulted being marked with a small flag. Walking immediately behind the metal detectors came excavators who uncovered each metal item. These were then photographed, plotted on a map and their depth and orientation in the soil recorded before being removed. The majority of finds were bullets and cartridge cases, both of which we know from crime investigations can hold unique information. Bullets, for example, bear scratch marks caused by the rifling grooves in the barrel of the gun, which can be used to identify the type of firearm and even the individual weapon that fired them. Cartridges similarly have 'pin marks' (where the firing pin hit the percussion cap) that are unique to each weapon.

Outnumbered and outgunned

By recording these microscopic details it proved possible to determine which weapons had been fired at which location and to plot how each weapon (and hence its owner) had moved around the battlefield. Results showed that at least 47 different gun types had been used by native Americans in the battle, along with the traditional bow and arrow (as attested by a metal arrowhead).

The different marks on bullets and cartridges indicated that they carried at least 415 guns in total – including Colt revolvers and Springfield carbines that must have been taken from the US army in previous battles – as well as more ancient muzzle-loading weapons. It was also observed that the native Americans preferred repeating rifles such

Custer's first detachment to attack at the Little Bighorn was led by Major Marcus Reno. Realizing they were outnumbered, Reno ordered a retreat, during which several of his men were killed. Reno's retreat is depicted in this illustration by Amos Bad Heart Buffalo.

221

as the .44 calibre 1866 Winchester, whereas the US cavalry had only their single-shot Springfield rifles. Whilst the latter had greater accuracy, in the thick of battle the repeating weapons gave the Sioux and the Cheyenne a distinct advantage.

As well as metal detector surveys, the archaeologists undertook excavations of 252 marble markers on the battlefield, placed there to mark the spot where each of Custer's men fell. These had been set up 14 years after the battle, however, and over nine years after the bodies has been disinterred and taken to a mass grave on Last Stand Hill. There are also more markers than there are US soldiers known to have died in the battle.

The excavation work led to the identification of most of the false markers and the discovery of the partial remains of at least 44 individuals, usually represented by the smaller hand and foot bones that earlier burial parties had missed. Distinctive fractures in skull pieces found beneath some of the markers also indicated that reports from a native American witness that wounded cavalrymen were finished off with clubs and hatchets were true. Likewise crush marks on skulls suggest that the Sioux custom of smashing the heads of fallen enemies was followed in the hours after the battle.

The hard life of a soldier

Forensic tests on the bones also revealed something of the lives of these US soldiers. Unlike their romantic portrayal in movies, these men lived hard lives, their skeletons showing signs of frequent fractures and serious back problems, probably side effects of a life in the saddle. Dental hygiene was poor and most had bad teeth, but the presence of high-quality tin and gold fillings in one jaw shows that dental treatment was available for those prepared to pay for it. Nearly all the men's teeth were stained from the frequent use of coffee and tobacco.

More controversially, the plotting of the bullet and cartridge finds on the site, together with the analysis of the locations where cavalrymen fell, have been used to reconstruct the actual movements of men during the battle. The legend of Custer's Last Stand is still iconic but the actual firing patterns of individuals on the battlefield suggests that the popular image of Custer and his men resolutely facing an overwhelming enemy and dying gun in hand is a myth.

Custer's command breaks down

Archaeology implies that Custer's men resisted at first, but, outnumbered three to one, their fight soon turned into a rout. Custer had expected an easy victory and in the face of a well-organized enemy his command disintegrated and chaos ensued. Later native American reports of the cavalry stampeding like buffalo and firing wildly into the air like drunken men now look closer to the truth than the more famous image of Custer's loyal soldiers standing by him to the last. Historians and archaeologists continue to argue just how much of a 'last stand' Custer put up, but the Little Bighorn battlefield has certainly proved that archaeology can bring new insights even into events that were already considered historically 'known'.

FORENSIC ARCHAEOLOGY

The development of forensic science has had a direct impact on the way in which archaeologists interpret the human remains they uncover, and in return archaeology has begun to influence modern forensic work. While forensic analysis of the Little Bighorn battlefield has helped to recover a narrative for events that occurred there, today forensic archaeologists are taking those skills back into the modern world of crime investigation.

Forensic archaeology is the application of archaeological methods to crime scenes. Today archaeologists may be called in to help police investigators in the search for human remains or objects associated with a crime, and a full range of archaeological tools, both traditional and technically advanced, is deployed in the work.

At an Argentine cemetery in 1984 a forensic anthropologist digs out bodies – victims of the so-called Dirty War (1976–83) in which an estimated 30,000 people 'disappeared' at the hands of the military.

Bullet markings can be used to discover the weapon from which they were fired, blood samples can be sequenced to compare with DNA from people involved in the crime and footprints can be cast in plaster to identify shoes worn at the scene. Samples of soil can also be taken and analyzed for pollen, seeds and other microscopic materials which might help identify where a body has previously been and even the time of year when it was buried.

Years of excavating ancient burial sites have also given archaeologists valuable experience in reconstructing the appearance of individuals, even from partial human remains. This has led to the development of forensic anthropology, in which skeletal and dental material is analyzed to provide information on the age, sex and height of an individual, as well as information on their health in life and how they met their death. This can be of particular use at crime scenes where the body is no longer easily identifiable.

Initially archaeologists may be asked simply to locate a crime scene by using the techniques of geophysical survey, such as ground-penetrating radar and resistivity, to find buried objects. When a location has been identified it can then be treated as an archaeological site in the hope of recovering more evidence than just the object or body that might have been found previously.

In the case of human burials, archaeologists can infer a great deal about the circumstances of a death from what lies around the body. Items in the grave will be excavated and then drawn and plotted onto a map to try to isolate the order of events.

Forensic archaeology takes the story of archaeology into the present day, showing how its techniques can be applied to recovering information from any given period. As recently as 50 years ago archaeology was considered to be a subject that looked only at the distant past, but today's archaeologists can be found working on all manner of cases from robbery investigations to war crimes trials for the United Nations, providing investigative teams with vital evidence with which to bring criminals to justice.

MISSING IN ACTION

Finding the Site of the Battle of the Teutoburg Forest, 1989

Metal-detector users do not always have a good name among professional archaeologists, who are only too aware of the damage illegal 'treasure hunting' can do to sensitive archaeological sites. The vast majority of metal detector enthusiasts, however, are highly motivated amateur archaeologists and historians themselves, and their work can lead to discoveries of international significance.

Major Tony Clunn (b.1946) is just such an enthusiast. As a British army officer he was posted to the Royal Army Medical Corps's barracks at Osnabrück, Germany, in 1987 and took the opportunity to investigate the local archaeology. His military background gave him a particular interest in one episode in Germany's history, known in detail from historical accounts but the location of which had been lost – the devastating defeat of the Roman legions by German tribes in AD 9 at the Battle of the Teutoburg Forest.

Clunn began his investigations by visiting the local professional archaeologist Wolfgang Schlüter to ask his permission to search the surrounding area for evidence. Schlüter was a little taken aback, in the first place at being asked permission and secondly because, as he pointed out to Clunn, in his 13 years of working in the region he had not discovered a single Roman artefact. Despite this unpromising start, he agreed to help and told Clunn of an old military road running to the north of the city, through a region called Kalkriese. In the 19th century a German historian, Theodore Mommsen (1817–1903), had noted that local farmers often found Roman coins here (in an area well outside the borders of the Roman empire), all of which were from the time of the emperor Augustus (63 BC–AD 14). So many coins had come from a single field outside the town of Bramsche that the locals called it the *Goldacker* (field of gold). Mommsen had suggested that such a find of Roman coins of a similar date outside the empire's boundaries might imply that this was the site of the famous battle. But as no Roman military equipment had ever been recovered from the area, his theory was largely ignored.

Tony Clunn determined to re-explore the region. Armed with Mommsen's records, he began locating the sites where coins had been found and plotting them onto modern maps. After four months of working in his spare time he isolated one area by the old road, in the region where coins had been found, which his military training told him

The Roman invasion of Germany and its governors' attempts to subdue the local people were often brutal. This illustration depicts Varus torturing German tribespeople.

would have made a suitable observation point for either a Roman army intent on conquering Germany or German scouts intent on stopping it. Laying a grid over the area, he started to use his metal detector.

Artefacts and ammunition

That first day he discovered a Roman silver coin from the first century AD, which pre-dated the battle. The following weekend he returned and found another 105 Roman coins. It was the largest, indeed the only, find of Roman material in the region in modern times. But if it proved that there was Roman activity here, it certainly did not prove that a battle had taken place. Huge numbers of Roman coins were in circulation both inside and outside the empire, and large numbers are often found along trade routes. What increased

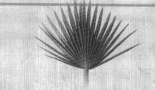

TIMELINE

7 Varus becomes governor of the Roman province of Germania and makes a gift of coins to his troops

9 Lured by false reports of a rebellion among subject German tribes (fabricated by the Roman-educated German leader Arminius), Varus leads a force of 24,000 men to quell the revolt; Arminius and allies ambush the troops and their large entourage. Almost all the Romans are massacred, and the battle ultimately redefines the boundaries of the Roman empire

15 A Roman expedition to the region discovers the bodies of the slaughtered troops and civilians and buries them in large pits

19TH CENTURY Theodore Mommsen interprets the discovery by farmers of large numbers of first-century Roman coins in the 'field of gold' as signs that the Battle of Teutoburg Forest took place here; his theory is ignored

1987 Tony Clunn arrives in Germany and approaches Wolfgang Schlüter, seeking permission to search for the site of the battle; his initial explorations reveal Roman coins and lead slingshots

1989 Under the direction of the Osnabrück Museum, excavations begin, uncovering numerous artefacts and human remains, finally confirming the site of the Battle of the Teutoburg Forest

the likelihood of this being a battle site was the discovery of something apparently worthless that farmers had probably ignored – three lead slingshots. This was the ammunition used by lightly armed Roman auxiliary troops, the military material that Mommsen had been unable to find.

The pattern of the finds also led in one direction, to a narrow pass in the hills to the south of the area known as the Kalkrieseberg. The site seemed to Clunn to be ideal for just the sort of ambush Roman sources describe: a narrow defile between a hill and an area of marshland. So, in 1989, that was where excavations began under the auspices of the Osnabrück Museum authorities.

The result of those excavations was a flood of artefacts, all Roman, all dating from AD 9 or earlier. In addition to the numerous coins there were military items including a spectacular silver mask once worn by a Roman cavalryman and even the imprint of a soldier's sandal in the hardened mud. The discovery of items stamped with the mark of the 'First Cohort' (although we do not know which legion this cohort was from) also attests to the presence of Roman heavy infantry along with the cavalry and auxiliary slingers. Further excavations have since uncovered Roman swords and daggers, the tips of javelins, arrowheads, fragments of plate and chain-mail armour and more slingshots.

Signs of slaughter

Other finds speak of a large expedition meeting a terrible fate here. There are spoons and cauldrons, hairpins and brooches (women also travelled with the Roman expedition), hammers and pickaxes, razors, locks, surgical instruments and writing equipment. This suggests that whatever happened here was more than a skirmish involving a few Roman scouts – these are the remnants of a large group that included doctors, cooks, scribes, craftsmen and engineers. There were also the remains of the people themselves. Five pits contained human bones, many bearing the signs of violent attack. Analysis of the bones has shown that they were exposed for some time above the ground before being buried, which ties in with Roman reports that an expedition sent six years after the disaster found the bodies still decaying where they had fallen, and buried them. As well as the finds there was also evidence of construction. To the south someone had built a turf wall, 1.5 metres (5 ft) tall and over 700 metres (765 yds) long along the slope of the hill with a wooden palisade running along the top – the ideal base from which to spring a trap.

Among the items discovered at Kalkriese was a mask that would have been worn by a Roman cavalryman, similar to the replica above, which is shown here with an elaborate helmet.

Perhaps the final piece of evidence that this was the site of the Battle of the Teutoburg Forest came from the very things that had first interested Clunn in the site – the coins. Not only were these all dated to before the battle, but at the battle site itself some bore the stamp VAR, probably an abbreviation for Varus, the governor of Germania who had led his troops to their deaths. These coins were probably part of a gift Varus made to his men in the summer of AD 9 when he was appointed governor and set out to crush the local tribes over whom he was to impose Roman rule. Later that year those same men died with the coins still in their pockets, in a land that would now never be Roman.

THE BATTLE OF THE TEUTOBURG FOREST

'... they saw that he (Augustus) was so greatly affected that for several months in succession he cut neither his beard nor his hair, and sometimes he would dash his head against a door, crying, "Quinctilius Varus, give me back my legions!" And he observed the day of the disaster each year as one of sorrow and mourning.'

SUETONIUS *The Lives of the Twelve Caesars*
(AUGUSTUS 23.4)

In AD 7 Publius Quinctilius Varus was named governor of the Roman province of Germania. The Roman empire, under the leadership of Augustus, already stretched from France and Spain to Greece, the coastal regions of the Near East, Egypt and North Africa. But, as Julius Caesar (100–44 BC) had warned, the tribes of Germany were an ever-present danger and, while they were free of Roman control, they were always a threat to the empire.

The Roman plan for dealing with Germania had been a combination of threat and promise. One of the main German leaders, Arminius, had grown up as a hostage in Rome and received a Roman military education there. Now thoroughly 'Romanized', he was expected to ally his people to the empire as it looked to expand its territory across the Rhine towards the Elbe.

Varus's style of government was highly unpopular in the region, however, not least with Arminius, and as the governor planned his subjugation of German territory, so Arminius was secretly allying himself with other Germanic tribes in a plan to rid themselves of Roman dominion forever.

In September of AD 9, as Varus was moving from his summer campaign camp back to his winter headquarters on the Rhine, he received news that a revolt had broken out among some subject tribes. Impetuously, Varus decided to quell the rebellion immediately and set out across territory unknown to the Romans, with a force of three legions, three cavalry squadrons and six auxiliary cohorts – about 24,000 men in total. Varus was unaware that the expedition had been engineered by the supposedly loyal Arminius who now rode at his side. There was no revolt and Arminius was leading the legions into an ambush in an alien land.

Shortly before the huge expedition reached a natural 'pinch point' in the terrain, Arminius excused himself, claiming he was going to contact local Roman allies. Instead he met up with his own troops and, with three other tribes, prepared to attack the legions. By now the Roman force had given up its usual tight formation and was strung out along miles of track as it tried to pick is way through the forests and marshes. It could not have been more vulnerable, and at this moment Arminius struck.

Just how long the battle lasted is a matter of dispute. Classical sources say the Germanic tribes attacked over two or three days, although some modern historians have suggested it might all have been over in a matter of hours. Either way, it was an utter slaughter. Arminius had been trained in military tactics by the Romans and he knew exactly how to turn them against his former masters. The Roman force was massacred almost to a man. Varus and many of his commanders, seeing all was lost, fell on their swords. The bodies of the dead were, according to the Roman historian Tacitus (*Annals* 1.61), left where they fell or nailed to trees by the victorious Germans. He describes how a Roman expedition found them six years later :

'In the centre of the field were the whitening bones of men, as they had fled or stood their ground, strewn everywhere or piled in heaps. Near, lay fragments of weapons and limbs of horses, and also human heads, prominently nailed to trunks of trees. In the adjacent groves were the barbarous altars, on which they had immolated tribunes and first-rank centurions ... And so the Roman army now on the spot, six years after the disaster, in grief and anger, began to bury the bones of the three legions, not a soldier knowing whether he was interring the relics of a relative or a stranger, but looking on all as kinsfolk and of their own blood, while their wrath rose higher than ever against the foe.'

The defeat of the formerly all-conquering Roman army was a shattering blow to Augustus and the people of Rome. It was an event that the emperor never forgot and, although other expeditions were sent against the Germanic tribes, it proved impossible to break their alliance and Rome had to settle for a boundary on the Rhine.

227

THE LOST SQUADRON

The Ice-bound Aircraft of Greenland, 1990

Greenland

BW-8 air base
Crash site
Iceland
BW-1 air base
Goose Bay
CANADA
ATLANTIC OCEAN

Operation Bolero was conceived in 1942 as a method of getting badly needed US aircraft to Europe for the fight against Nazi Germany. But carrying planes on ships was slow and involved running the gauntlet of German U-boats, so a daring plan was hatched to fly Lockheed P-38 Lightnings and Boeing B-17 Flying Fortress bombers from Canada to Greenland, then on to Iceland and finally across to England. It was a dangerous journey and not every flight arrived.

Early on 15 July 1942, two P-38 squadrons, each escorting a B-17, took off from the west coast of Greenland on the second leg of Operation Bolero, bound for Iceland. As the planes climbed above the icecap, however, the weather began to deteriorate and the flight became enveloped in dense cloud. Unable to navigate safely, the commander ordered them to return to base (BW-8, in western Greenland) but in such atrocious conditions the entire flight became disorientated. When they next glimpsed the mountains of Greenland they found to their horror that they were not back on the west coast but two hours away from the base on the other side of the country. Without enough fuel to cross the icecap again, the only option was to land on the glacial terrain and hope for rescue. Fortunately for the crews that day, rescue came after several bleak nights spent on the ice. But the eight planes themselves were beyond rescue, far out on a glacier, way beyond the reach of recovery crews. And so they would remain for 50 years.

Although the planes were lost, the memory of them was not. As technology improved, recovering the aircraft became at least a theoretical possibility and from 1977 onwards 12 privately funded teams scrambled to find them. By this time the P-38, once the most common US fighter plane in the sky, was a rarity with only 20 full or partial examples remaining and just a handful still flying. Here, so it appeared, was a collection of six more – along with two even more rare bombers – just waiting to be picked up.

Advanced recovery technology

After almost four decades on the Greenland icecap, however, the planes were nowhere to be seen and the teams were forced to admit that they might now be buried under an unknown depth of ice. Enlisting the help of the archaeological techniques of geophysical survey seemed the only way to discover where the planes were. Various

The inhospitable terrain of Greenland, almost 95 percent of which is covered by an icecap. Even in good visibility, navigating over such a landscape is hazardous, with few landmarks to aid orientation.

228

TIMELINE

1942 (16 July) As part of Operation Bolero six P-38s and two B-17s take off from the BW-8 air base on the west coast of Greenland bound for Iceland and, ultimately, Europe. Bad weather forces the planes to land on the icecap. Several days later the crew members are rescued, but the planes remain on the glacier

1977–92 Twelve different teams attempt to find the abandoned planes

1983 Sub-surface radar registers metal anomalies 80 metres (260 ft) beneath the ice

1990 A hole is melted down through 70 metres (230 ft) of ice, revealing broken remnants of a B-17

1992 Thermal drilling equipment is used to search for a complete plane; once located, the recovery team use steam hoses deep inside the drill shaft to melt the ice. A well-preserved P-38 is uncovered and dismantled before being brought to the surface in pieces

2002 (26 October) After being restored and reassembled in Kentucky, 'Glacier Girl' flies again

GEOPHYSICAL SURVEY

As the need to locate and study archaeological sites without damaging them grows, geophysical surveys are increasingly being used. Geophysical surveying is a broad term for a series of methods employed to locate buried features that are not visible on the surface. Three techniques are most commonly used in archaeology: magnetometry, resistivity and ground-penetrating radar.

In magnetometry, an instrument is used to measure minute variations in the direction and strength of the earth's magnetic field. Readings from a hand-held magnetometer carried over a gridded site can be plotted to produce a map of magnetic variations, which can indicate the presence of buried objects, particularly metals with magnetic properties, such as iron.

Resistivity operates by measuring differences in the electrical resistance of the soil. To do this, two metal spikes are placed in the ground a set distance apart and a current is passed between them to gauge the resistance. This is repeated at regular intervals over a gridded site to produce a map of local variations in resistance, which can indicate buried structures such as ditches and walls.

Ground-penetrating radar surveys involve the use of a radar transmitter and detector, usually carried on a sledge or remote vehicle. The device travels over the site emitting pulses of electromagnetic radiation in the microwave band into the ground and recording the reflected signal as it bounces back off buried structures. These 'echoes' can then be plotted as cross sections through the ground over which the device is travelling.

Geophysical surveying is not simply a tool that can help archaeologists to discover sites for excavation, however. For a long time, archaeologists have been aware that every excavation is an unrepeatable experiment. Any information held within a layer of soil which is not identified and recorded during that dig is lost forever when that layer is removed in order to uncover the one beneath it. For this reason, in areas that are not directly under threat of disturbance, geophysical surveys are often used now in order to identify and protect sites where no archaeological investigation is currently planned. In that way our still unexcavated archaeological heritage can be preserved for future – and hopefully more skilful – generations of archaeologists to uncover.

attempts were made using magnetometers (which map discontinuities in the magnetic field left by metal objects) and small airborne radar systems to 'look' through the ice. They had no success until, in 1983, a radar system specifically tuned to see through ice found two metal anomalies and then, two days later, six more. The planes had been found, but there was a problem – they were buried under nearly 80 metres (260 ft) of solid glacier.

Members of the first expedition to actually see one of the planes were disappointed. In 1990 a team managed to melt a hole down through 70 metres (230 ft) of ice to one of the B-17s, only to find that it had been torn apart by the slow, grinding movement of the glacier that had engulfed it. Two years later, however, the team struck gold.

Patience is rewarded

Having moved on to the site of a P-38 Lightning, the team set a tailor-made piece of thermal drilling equipment, known as the gopher, to work. Suspended over the site on chains and tackles, the gopher began melting a vertical hole just over 1 metre (3 ft) wide at a rate of 0.5 metres (1.6 ft) an hour. After a month of continuous work and by now at a depth of over 80 metres (260 ft), the gopher finally hit something metal and was winched up. Humans now had to take over the difficult and dangerous task of

excavating whatever the gopher had found. Each day a team member made the 25-minute descent to the bottom of the deep, narrow ice hole to excavate a cavern around the find using steam hoses. Slowly a plane emerged: here on the ice surface of 1942 lay an almost perfectly preserved P-38.

Removing a plane through a 1-metre- (3-ft-) wide hole was obviously impossible, so the aircraft was dismantled in its underground cavern and brought up to the surface in pieces to begin the long process of restoration. Back in a hanger in Kentucky the plane was completely disassembled and each part scrutinized to see whether it could be repaired and reused or whether it needed replacing before the airframe could be completely restored. It was a process that would take ten years and on Saturday 26 October 2002, in front of 20,000 spectators, the P-38 Lightning, serial number 417630 – now renamed 'Glacier Girl' – took to the skies once more in its first flight since that fateful journey over Greenland 60 years earlier.

Top: A restored P-38 Lightning flying at an air show.

Inset: A P-38 on the glacier in Greenland, with a B-17 in the background.

THE ICE MAN COMETH
An Alpine Traveller from the Copper Age, 1993

In September 1991 two German hill walkers, Erika and Helmut Simon, were hiking in the Ötztaler Alps near the borders between Italy and Austria when they made a gruesome discovery. There, 3200 metres (10,500 ft) up in the mountains on the Similaun glacier, lay the well-preserved, frozen body of a half-naked man lying face down, partly encased in ice.

Fatalities among climbers are commonplace in mountain regions and the Simons assumed this was the body of a man who had died up here a few years earlier and been buried under the snow. Taking a photograph of the scene, they headed back down the mountain to alert a recovery team. When the mountain recovery team arrived they were less certain that this was just an unfortunate climber. The corpse had a large wound to the head, and parts of the body were covered with unusual marks that looked like branding. Could this be a murder scene? But it was the objects lying scattered around the body, the former possessions of this poor soul, that were really confusing. There were no climbing boots, no nylon ropes and no synthetic jackets; instead the area was strewn with pieces of straw and fur. Then there were the man's tools, still carefully hafted into their wooden handles. But the blades were not stainless steel, they were flint and copper – the tools of another age.

Ötzi, the ancient ice man

Unsure whether they had a murder, an accident or a greater mystery on their hands, the recovery team gathered up everything they could find from the site and sent it to the Institute of Forensic Medicine in Innsbruck, Austria, where a professor at the Institute of Early History, Konrad Spindler (1939–2005), was called in to make an examination. Spindler realized immediately that this was no modern body. Tools like these had been found across Europe – never still bound to their wooden handles – but identical nonetheless. And they came not from the recent past but from the end of the Stone Age. Spindler suggested taking carbon-14 dates from the body and when the results came back his theory was confirmed. The man in the ice, who had been given the nickname 'Ötzi' after the region he had been found in, had died there some 5300 years before. His was the earliest frozen body ever discovered anywhere in the world, a visitor from the very dawn of the age of metalwork, an ancient European come back from the glacial ice to meet his descendants.

The realization that Ötzi's corpse had survived for so long caused an immediate storm in scientific circles and the media. The man and his tools were almost perfectly preserved save for damage caused in removing them from the ice, and scientists from across the world clamoured to gain access to them in an attempt to uncover Ötzi's story. Research is ongoing but already the results are remarkable.

When Ötzi was discovered he was face down and appeared to be naked but in fact the clothing on his back had simply been torn and blown away. Beneath and around him much of the outfit he had worn – our only real knowledge of clothing from this period – had survived. He had gone into the mountains well prepared. He wore thick shoes with bearskin soles, deerskin insteps and chamois uppers, laced up and stuffed with shredded tree bark for extra insulation. On his body he wore leggings, a loincloth and a poncho all made of goatskin, and a cap of bear fur was strapped to his head. The remnants of a woven grass mat may have formed a rain cloak, similar to those worn by local shepherds well into the 19th century.

The Ice Man was equipped with an impressive collection of tools and weapons. His hunting kit included a beautifully preserved yew bow and a chamois hide quiver still containing 14 arrows, of which two had been finished. Each complete arrow was fitted with a flint arrowhead and fletched with an arrangement of three feathers that ensured it spun in flight, increasing its accuracy – a remarkable and previously unimagined level of sophistication for this date. He also carried a copper axe, hafted into a yew handle. This is the only complete prehistoric axe ever found, as usually the wooden handle and sinew or cord bindings rot away. As well as confirming how prehistoric axes were hafted, it speaks of a key moment in European history.

Heralding the age of metal

Ötzi was a man of the Stone Age: most of his tools are flint and in his world stone was the major material for tool-making. But his axe is made of something new – it is 99.7 percent pure copper – and represents an early stage in the transition from Stone Age to a new age, that of metal. More traditionally he had a flint knife – its blade set into a short ash handle which he kept in a sheath woven from fibres of birch bark – and a retouching tool made of wood and fire-hardened deer antler which could be used to prepare and recut the edges of his flint blades.

The reason why he took with him some of the other items found is less certain. He carried a white marble bead on a leather cord, two birch-bark cylinders which may have held a fire-lighting kit, some ibex bones

A model of Ötzi in the South Tyrol Museum of Archaeology in Bolzano, northern Italy. The Ice Man was well prepared for his mountain trek, with warm clothing and plenty of tools and weapons.

and a wood and hide structure that has been interpreted as either a backpack or snowshoes. More mysteriously, he also carried two pieces of birch fungus attached to a leather strip. It is known that this type of birch fungus has antibiotic properties so this may have been his medical kit. These fungi also make good tinder when dried, so they may have been brought along simply to light fires.

If Ötzi's tools and clothes were exceptional finds, the survival of his body made him unique. Preserved in the ice for 5300 years, here was the near complete body of a Stone Age man, with the remnants of his last meals still in his stomach. Forensic analysis has shown that he was relatively short, about 1 metre 57 cm (5 ft 1 in) tall (although he may have shrunk a little after death), and about 45 years old – a very good age for the period. His long life had taken its toll on his body: his right hip joint showed signs of arthritis and he had healed breaks to his nose and a number of ribs. On his skin there were also patches of discrete tattooing on areas used today as acupuncture points, possibly made in an attempt to relieve the pain in his joints. His fingernails showed he had been stressed during the last months of his life, perhaps because of illness, and his teeth were worn from a lifetime of eating coarsely ground cereals. His lungs were also blackened with soot from living around open fires.

Ötzi's last meals

The contents of Ötzi's stomach showed that he ate a meal of ibex with some grains (possibly in the form of bread) not long before he died. The presence of very well-preserved pollen in this meal also tells us that he ate it somewhere in the alpine foothills, in a coniferous forest in late spring or early summer. Later, at a higher altitude, he had another meal, this time of red-deer meat and more grain. How much he enjoyed either is a matter of some speculation, since eggs of the whipworm parasite were also found in his colon, an infestation that would have caused him great discomfort, not to mention diarrhoea.

The world's oldest mummy. Ötzi's body was in an excellent state of preservation, first dried by the summer winds on the glacier and then covered in a thick layer of ice.

The value of Ötzi comes from the near perfect preservation of one man and the possessions he used in life. Not only has the glacier preserved the organic material that is otherwise almost entirely absent from the archaeological record of this time but, thanks to his isolated and lonely death, we have a snapshot of his life. His body was never prepared for burial, his everyday objects were not handed on to other people or thrown away. The objects in his tomb are not special funerary goods, just the ordinary necessities of life and as such he stands as a prehistoric 'everyman', an alpine traveller from a spring day 5300 years ago.

DEATH OF AN ICE MAN

The recovery of a 5300-year-old body from a Tyrolean glacier is one of the most surprising finds in archaeological history, but what is even more puzzling is how it got there in the first place.

Initial investigations of the body and the find location suggested that the Ice Man had climbed into this high alpine pass sometime in the autumn. Perhaps exhausted from his climb, he lay down to rest and froze to death only to be engulfed in ice and preserved in the exact position in which he died. But the truth about the circumstances of his death would emerge only after his body had made one final journey over the mountains.

In 1998 Ötzi the Ice Man was transferred by special convoy from Innsbruck University to the South Tyrol Museum of Archaeology in Bolzano in northern Italy following a geographical survey which proved that the body had been found on the Italian side of the border. As part of their preparations for the new display the museum authorities called on a forensic pathologist in the hope of commissioning a facial reconstruction of Ötzi to show the public what he would have looked like when he was alive.

Peter Vanezis, then professor of forensic medicine and science at the University of Glasgow, was the man for the job. Vanezis was used to examining modern human bodies, often in very poor states of preservation or even terribly mutilated, and he had a good reputation for being able to reconstruct facial details. He agreed to try to reconstruct the Ice Man's face. The problem for Vanezis, however, was that in this unusual case he did not have a skull to work with. Usually the skull of the victim can be used as a scaffold on which to reconstruct the facial features, but the idea of removing the skull from the oldest perfectly preserved human body on earth was of course ridiculous.

Vanezis therefore turned to an x-ray technique – CAT (Computerized Axial Tomography) scanning – in which a series of x-ray 'slices' through a body can be digitally combined to produce a 3D image of the interior. By scanning the inside of Ötzi's head, a virtual model of his skull was produced, which could then be reconstructed in resin and fleshed out.

The reconstruction was hailed as a great success, but Vanezis did not want to leave matters there. Ötzi's body had been examined by archaeologists who were used to analyzing artefacts, but they did not have a forensic pathologist's skills for teasing the truth out of a crime scene. From his perspective, Vanezis was unhappy with a number of the conclusions reached by the archaeologists. Firstly, there was the time of death. Pollen from surrounding ice suggested that the Ice Man had died in the autumn, but it was impossible to prove that this ice had formed immediately after his death. Analysis of fresh pollen in his stomach showed that it came from the hop hornbeam which only flowers between March and June, making the idea that Ötzi simply froze to death in the autumn far less likely. A new analysis of the positions of the body and the objects as they were found also suggested that the idea that everything had been found *in situ* and not moved at a later date by the glacier was wrong; therefore the Ice Man could not be shown to have simply sat down and died.

It was time to turn to the one clue that Vanezis was most used to dealing with – the body. As it was not possible to perform a full autopsy, a new CAT scan was ordered on the rest of the body. In one image from the scan, the head of radiology at Bolzano hospital noticed a strange shadow that had previously been overlooked. Lodged deep in the left shoulder was a dense object, which looked like an arrowhead. Returning to the body, Vanezis found an entry wound that showed signs of blood loss and no healing. Shortly before Ötzi had died, he had been shot.

The exact course of events leading to Ötzi's death is still not fully understood but it is clear that his resting place by the Similaun glacier was a crime scene. Recent DNA tests on his arrow, knife and clothing have identified the blood of four people, suggesting that several people were involved in the fatal fight. At some point in this skirmish Ötzi was shot in the back, probably while fleeing. The arrow entered his shoulder, severing an artery and stopping him in his tracks. He fell to the ground and died within moments. The following autumn his desiccated body, dried by the warm summer winds, was encased in the encroaching ice which would become his tomb for more than 5000 years.

SONG OF THE ICE MAIDEN

The Frozen Tombs of the Altay Mountains, 1993

In 1993 Russian archaeologist Natalia Polosmak was surveying a site high in the Altay mountains of Siberia near the borders with China, Kazakhstan and Mongolia when she came across a low permafrost-encased mound which looked suspiciously like a *kurgan* – an ancient burial site.

Archaeology this far north is hampered by the fact that the ground is often permanently frozen but this has one surprising benefit. When the first *kurgans* were explored between 1929 and 1949 in the nearby Pazyryk valley, some incredible finds had been made. Sometime after each burial, water had seeped into the tomb and then quickly refrozen, remaining that way for the next 2400 years. Normally any organic material in a burial, such as wood, leather, fabrics and the body itself quickly decays, but in their frozen vaults the bodies and possessions of these people had escaped the ravages of time.

A unique collection of frozen artefacts

Those early excavations had uncovered the remains of a group of nomadic horsemen and women who lived in the region around the middle of the first millennium BC. They had been buried in shafts dug into man-made mounds which had then been filled with logs and stones to seal them. All of the tombs found had to some degree been robbed, but it was what had been left behind that interested archaeologists. The robbers had concentrated on imperishable valuables such as gold and silver, but they left behind a unique record – a collection of frozen organic artefacts. Inside were felt wall hangings showing moustached men on horseback, leather cut-out silhouettes of deer, clothes and wooden furniture. There was even a pile carpet, the oldest known. The bodies of the occupants of the tombs had also been preserved. One, buried in a hollowed-out larch trunk, bore extensive tattoos of griffins, horses, deer, donkeys, mountain rams and fish.

For all the wonders of these early discoveries, no complete tomb had ever been found – robbers had removed much of their contents, and the disturbance had defrosted parts of the tombs, allowing their precious organic contents to rot. The archaeologists of the 1930s and 1940s had seen a glimpse of this strange culture, but what Natalia Polosmak was looking for in 1993 was an intact burial. Her chosen site was on the Ukok plateau, just metres from the no-man's-land between Russia and China, and the stones on the

mound had already been scattered, a worrying sign that the tomb had been robbed. Clearing out the logs and stones blocking the shaft, however, Polosmak rapidly changed her opinion. The whole of the burial area was encased in ice that had clearly been too hard and time-consuming to remove, even for the most dedicated grave robber.

As Polosmak's team excavated down, the first objects they came upon were perhaps the most valuable things the tomb's owner could take to the afterlife: six horses, each killed by an axe blow to the head. Shrouded in their icy tomb, they retained their chestnut colouring and even their felt saddles. Melting the permafrost as they went, the team arrived at the wooden burial chamber itself, and at the bottom lay what they had all been hoping for – a larch coffin, sealed with copper nails and covered with leather cut-outs of deer and snow leopards. Opening the coffin initially proved a disappointment, however. Inside it was filled with opaque ice completely obscuring whatever lay behind. They had to resort to heating water from the local lake with a blowtorch then pouring it over the ice, little by little, to melt it. But the result was worth the painfully slow work.

Dressed for the afterlife

Lying in the coffin was the beautifully preserved body of a young woman, not a concubine or slave sacrificed with her master but an important woman in her own right. She was young, perhaps 25, and lay on her side, her body arranged as though she was asleep. She seemed unusually tall for the period – 1.67 metres (5 ft 6 in) – an effect heightened by the extraordinary 1-metre- (3.3 ft-) high black felt headdress she wore, decorated with gold and wooden birds, and beneath which her blonde hair could still be

The elaborate animal tattoos on the arm and shoulder of the 2400-year-old Ice Maiden are remarkably well preserved and still a brilliant shade of blue.

seen. At her throat was a necklace of wooden camels, and she wore a dress woven from sheep wool and camel hair tied at the waist with a colourful tasselled cord. Beneath the dress was something rarer still – a blouse made of wild silk, possibly imported all the way from India. On her legs the leather of her thigh-high riding boots was still supple.

Her body had been mummified, the internal organs removed and the cavity filled with peat and bark whose tannins helped preserve her remains; her eyes had been removed to prevent the soft tissue collapsing into the orbits, and the space stuffed with fur. Beneath the clothing on her arms, the archaeologists saw that, like earlier discoveries, her skin was tattooed. Mythical animals twined up her arms, their horns ending in flowers. There were deer with huge antlers, goats and predators, variously identified as large cats or wolves.

Buried with her was a small wooden table on which a cut of mutton still lay frozen and a drinking vessel made of yak horn, perhaps a meal to help her on her way to the next life. There were personal possessions as well. Between her knees rested a red pouch containing an intricately worked mirror while at her feet a stone dish held coriander seeds. These aromatic seeds may have been burnt to cover the smell of the body. Tomb shafts could only be dug in the frozen ground during the short summer so her body may have had to wait some time for burial.

Was she a Scythian?

But for all the secrets the Ice Maiden's tomb revealed, her identity is still a mystery. Clearly she was an important and wealthy individual, and her elaborate headdress and tattoos suggest she may have held a special position in society, perhaps as a religious shaman or a storyteller. As for the culture she belonged to, there are strange resonances with descriptions of a people recorded by the Greek historian Herodotus (*c.*484–425 BC), who calls them Scythians. These nomadic horse people ranged from the Black Sea over the European and Asian steppes, something which might explain the exotic items found in the *kurgans*. Herodotus also tells us that they embalmed their dead in much the same way as the Ice Maiden had been prepared for burial and would carry their bodies huge distances back to their homeland. The High Altay is certainly distant from Herodotus's world and contains evidence of thousands of *kurgans*. Furthermore, he mentions that rulers are buried under mounds and often accompanied by sacrificed horses. Intriguingly he suggests they used cannabis – both for clothing (hemp) and for cleansing themselves in its smoke – and cannabis seeds have been found in other Altay tombs.

Herodotus is not, however, an entirely trustworthy source and he freely combines second-hand tales, myths and his own observations to paint a picture of a bloodthirsty, barbarian nation. The answer to who the people in the ice tombs of the Altay really are and whether they are the ferocious Scythians he describes may lie not in his books but in the mummified bodies. So perfectly preserved are some of the human remains in the *kurgans* that attempts are now underway to remove DNA from them. The results might finally reveal who the Ice Maiden was and how she came to her last frozen resting place.

THE ARCHAEOLOGY OF BODIES

Human remains found at archaeological sites give an important insight into the past, but it is a field filled with controversy. At what point does a body become an archaeological artefact suitable for study or display rather than a human who should be left in peace in their final resting place?

In many societies strict rules govern the excavation of human remains, and an exhumation licence is usually required. It can specify how long the remains can be held by excavators and what should happen to them after that. In the case of Christian burials, for instance, it may be a requirement that the body should be re-interred in a Christian manner. Obviously, where relatives can still be traced their wishes are taken into account, but the legal situation concerning older and non-native bodies is less certain.

The Pazyryk nomads were renowned horsemen, and their horses, as depicted in this felt wall hanging from c.300 BC, were often fitted with ornate costumes.

When archaeologists and anthropologists began exploring societies beyond their own in the 19th century, however, their attitude was much more cavalier. When Yagan, a warrior of the Noongar people of western Australia, was shot dead in 1833, his head was removed and sent to England to be displayed in a museum. Of course the idea of displaying an English head in a museum at that time would have been abhorrent. After years on display and then in storage it was finally buried in 1964 in Liverpool, but was exhumed at the request of the Noongar people in 1997 and returned to them.

Even in the case of ancient remains, local people often considered themselves to be descendants of the buried person. When the Egyptian mummies from the Deir el-Bahri cache were discovered in 1881, local people lined the river and wept as their 'relatives' were transported down the Nile to Cairo.

In the United States, the case of Kennewick Man (see pages 240–3) became a cause célèbre in 1996 when several Native American groups tried to use the Native American Graves Protection and Repatriation Act of 1990 to reclaim the remains of a 9000-year-old skeleton found in the banks of the Columbia river. The case went to court, which ruled that the modern Native American groups could not provide evidence of kinship and therefore could not claim custody.

All too often such events pit local people against archaeologists, the former wishing to respect their ancestors and traditions, the latter keen to use the information that can be gleaned from human remains to further our knowledge of the past. In the case of the Ice Maiden, the removal of one of the most spectacular finds in Russian history from the poor and underdeveloped High Altay region to Moscow caused particular friction, as permission was not sought from any local groups. Archaeological data regarding her ethnicity, particularly a facial reconstruction, were used insensitively to suggest she was not related to any of the modern inhabitants of the region and to claim that they therefore had no say over her fate.

The debate still rages over whether the Ice Maiden will return to a purpose-built museum in the High Altay, stay in Novosibirsk for study or be reburied as an honoured ancestor, as many local people wish. Whether or not it is ever possible to prove that the Ice Maiden is a Scythian or is related to the modern people of the High Altay, the passions aroused on the subject should warn any archaeologist stumbling on human remains of any date that they have found much more than just another artefact.

AMERICAN PIONEERS
Kennewick Man, 1996

The town of Kennewick in Washington State is home to an annual hydroplane event on the Columbia river which flows through the local park. By this point on its course the Columbia is a wide, slow-moving waterway with flat banks which on 28 July, 1996 were lined with spectators watching the races. Among them were two men, Will Thomas and Dave Deacy. To avoid paying the entrance fee they had reached the race site by wading down the shallows of the river, and Thomas was still standing knee deep in the water when he noticed a round boulder beneath the surface.

Turning back to look at his friend on the bank, he decided to play a trick and pretend he had discovered a skull. He reached into the water, took a grip on the rock and pulled. As the lump came away from the mud he held it aloft in triumph. But something was wrong. The rock was unusually light and, as the mud washed away from it, he noticed something else – teeth. It was indeed a skull, and a human one at that.

After the races Thomas reported the find to an off-duty police officer and soon the river bank was cordoned off as forensic teams searched for more remains. In the end, an almost complete human skeleton was recovered and the police opened an enquiry. But this was no modern murder victim. The bones were stained a dark brown, indicating they had been in the mud for a very long time. The forensic laboratory suggested using carbon-14 to date the remains and when the results came back it was clear that the police would not be needed. The bones were 9000 years old, making Kennewick Man, as the skeleton was named, one of the oldest American ancestors ever discovered.

The closing of the police case did not mean an end to legal disputes over the skeleton, however. Kennewick Man is perhaps best known today not for the important part his bones play in retelling the history of North America, but for the legal fight over who owns his bones and what should be done with them.

Native Americans claim custody

Shortly after the discovery, several local native American tribes applied for custody of the remains under the Native American Graves Protection and Repatriation Act (1990), which allows tribes to reclaim the graves of their ancestors if they are found on federal land. They wished to bury the skeleton in their tribal tradition without further

The facial features of Kennewick Man have been reconstructed in this model by the sculptor Tom McClelland, under the guidance of anthropologist Dr James Chatters.

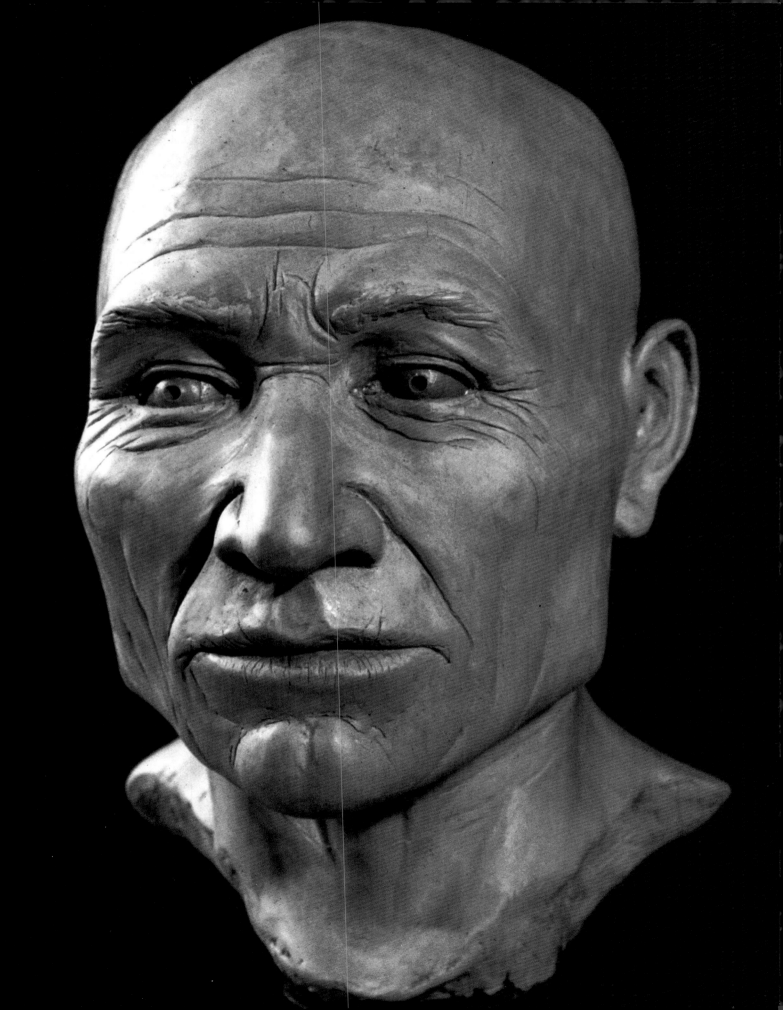

TIMELINE

24,000 BC Possible early migrations of humans across the Bering Strait into North America

c.7000 BC Kennewick Man lives and dies

AD 1996 During an annual hydroplane event at Kennewick in Washington State, a spectator discovers a human skull in the Columbia river bed. Subsequent searches uncover a near complete male skeleton, and police open a murder enquiry. Carbon dating later establishes that 'Kennewick Man' is 9000 years old, and the murder case is closed. Native American groups claim custody and try to prevent scientists from studying the remains; a long legal battle begins, to establish ownership

1998 A federal judge orders the remains be moved to the Burke Museum at the University of Washington, Seattle

1999 A team of federal scientists begin the study of Kennewick Man

2004 The Ninth US Circuit of Appeals finally rules against native Americans and rejects their custody claim

examination. Archaeologists, however, were insistent that the remains should be kept and intensively studied as they potentially held a vital key to understanding how North America first came to be colonized by humans.

What followed was perhaps an unlikely court case, pitting native Americans against archaeologists, but it highlights an important area of archaeology in which wider moral issues impinge on the simple desire for knowledge. Human remains are often found on archaeological sites but should they be treated as artefacts or as people? In Western museums we display the bodies of ancient Egyptians in glass cases, but we would be horrified to find modern Western humans displayed in this way. And yet human remains are among the most eloquent archaeological finds. A skeleton can reveal important information about a person's age, sex, the diseases they suffered from, what they ate and even, through DNA, who they were related to.

For the native Americans involved in the Kennewick case, however, studying and displaying this body was unthinkable – another example of Western colonial powers treating native peoples as lesser creatures suitable for study and classification. In the end, the legal case was not fully resolved until 2004 when the Ninth US Circuit of Appeals ruled that the tribes were unable to show any evidence of kinship and their bid for custody was rejected. Kennewick Man is now kept at the Burke Museum in the University of Washington but is technically owned by the US Army Corps of Engineers on whose land the body was found.

Tracing the origins of Kennewick Man

If Kennewick Man was not an ancestor of these modern native Americans, however, who was he? Analysis of the skeleton has shown he was a man aged between 38 and 55 who had lived a relatively violent life. He had a fracture to one arm and a broken rib, both of which had healed, a compression fracture to the skull and a 5.5-centimetre- (2.2-in-) long stone spear point lodged in his hip – all of which he had survived.

Reconstruction of his facial features had proved almost as contentious as the discovery itself, with early work suggesting in one case that he displayed Caucasoid European traits and in another that he resembled the peoples of Papua New Guinea. More recently it has been suggested that he may be related to the native Ainu people of Japan or to Polynesians. DNA analysis may prove this one way or another, if enough genetic material can be recovered from the skeleton. However, all other early human remains from the United States that have been DNA-sequenced to date have proved to be of the same genetic group as modern native Americans.

If Kennewick Man is genetically distinct from modern native Americans he will gain an even more important place in American history. Traditionally archaeologists have believed that the first Americans came to the continent only via a land bridge that stretched across the Bering Strait between Russia and Alaska during the most recent ice age. Kennewick Man may prove that the Americas were populated at various times by peoples from more than one homeland and that even 9000 years ago America was a cultural melting pot.

REACHING THE NEW WORLD

When the first Europeans arrived in continental America they discovered a world that was 'new' only to them. The entirety of two continents was already occupied but the question then, and ever since, has been: how did those native Americans get there and where did they come from? Many ideas have been put forward to explain the peopling of America, and the most influential of these fall into two groups: the 'short chronology' theories, which state that humans arrived in the Americas some 12,000 years ago, and the 'long chronology' theories, which claim that the continents were already settled when they arrived and had been for perhaps 40,000 years.

The most well-known short chronology is the land-bridge hypothesis. Around 70,000 years ago the northern hemisphere underwent an ice age which reached its maximum extent about 17,000 years ago and lasted until 10,000 years ago. With so much water caught up in icecaps, sea levels were up to 60 metres (200 ft) lower than they are today, leaving a wide land bridge from Siberia to Alaska across what is now the Bering Strait. This theory suggests that hunters in Siberia who tracked herds of large game followed the animals across the land bridge and into the new continent. These people arrived in North America around 12,000 years ago and rapidly spread south, reaching the tip of South America just 1000 years later.

These early hunters can be identified on North American sites by their distinctive flint tool technology, in particular a notched and fluted spear point known as a Clovis point, named after the site of Clovis in New Mexico. The 'Clovis culture' can be found all over North America, providing support for the land-bridge theory.

The problem with Clovis cultures, however, is that they are nowhere near as easy to spot in South America, where there seem to have been many more cultural types. This would suggest that a single human invasion from the north was not the only means by which the Americas were settled. There are also

dating problems, with some recent carbon-14 dates from South American sites apparently predating Clovis culture by up to 1000 years. A yet more extraordinary North American site (the so-called Topper site in South Carolina), has produced 14C dates of 50,000 years ago. Such finds imply that, whilst there was an invasion of Clovis culture big-game hunters beginning around 12,000 years ago, they might not have been entering an uninhabited land.

Examples of Clovis spear heads. Sharply honed flint points like these would have been used to hunt large game.

Long chronology theorists claim that the Americas were first colonized by peoples who used seagoing craft to hop from island to island and travel along coasts. This is not impossible, since the remains at Lake Mungo (see pages 184–7) tell us that Australia was inhabited at least 40,000 years ago, and those people can only have reached Australia by sea – at no point in human history has Australia been anything less than 30 miles (50 km) away from other continents.

These theories variously suggest migrations from north to south and south to north on Pacific and Atlantic coasts, originating in Australia, Japan, Southeast Asia and even Europe (for the Atlantic model). But like the land-bridge theory, this idea has its problems. The dated evidence from before 12,000 years ago is fragmentary and not wholly reliable. Finding more evidence, even if the model is correct, could also prove difficult since the coasts such people moved along were from an era of much lower sea levels. Today any of their coastal sites would be under 60 metres (200 ft) of water.

That is why remains like those of Kennewick Man are so important. If he is one of a group of 'pre-Clovis' inhabitants of the Americas, he is a rare find indeed. Clovis culture quickly came to dominate in North America and what happened to any previous inhabitants is unclear. If it proves possible to extract DNA from his bones that links him to native groups in Japan or Australia, then the human history of the Americas may have to be rewritten.

NEW ARRIVALS
The Grave of the Amesbury Archer, 2002

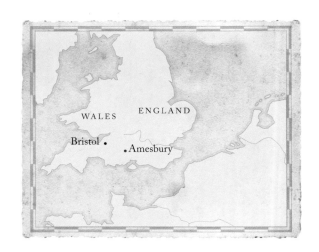

On Friday 3 May 2002 a professional archaeology unit was excavating on Boscombe Down by Amesbury, Wiltshire, in southwest England, ahead of a new housing development. Although the site is only 3 miles (5 km) southeast of the famous prehistoric monument of Stonehenge, all that was expected from the dig was further evidence of a small Roman cemetery which was already known there from earlier work. But that morning one of the team working in an area designated for the site of a new school found a grave. What was inside was one of the most remarkable finds in British archaeology, and the application of the latest scientific techniques has demonstrated how much archaeologists can now learn from apparently silent artefacts.

The grave contained the skeleton of a single individual surrounded by some of the objects he had known in life, which had lain there since around 2300 BC. There were three small copper knives, a bone pin that once helped to hold his clothes in place, five beaker pots, a spatula used to work flints, four boar's tusks, two wrist guards (to protect the owner's wrists from the recoil of a bow string), two gold hair tresses, 16 flint arrowheads, numerous flint tools and a small polished stone. It hardly sounds like a find on the scale of Tutankhamun's tomb, but these few artefacts tell the story of a man who stood on the brink of a revolution.

A traveller from continental Europe

With the site fully drawn, mapped and photographed, the objects were removed and sent to various archaeological laboratories and it was here that the story of the man dubbed 'The Amesbury Archer' unfolded. The bones themselves told the first part of his tale. The skeleton belonged to a man aged between 35 and 45. He had been carefully buried on his left side with his legs bent and his face pointing to the north. Oxygen isotope analysis of the enamel from his teeth shows that he was a foreigner, a traveller from Europe, probably from the vicinity of the Alps in either Switzerland, Germany or Austria. Another body found in a grave next to his, which has a similar peculiarity in the formation of some foot bones, must be a relative, perhaps even his son. Tests show that the latter was brought up in the Bristol region, so perhaps the Amesbury Archer came across to Britain and then had a family. The Archer's bones also tell a more

The ancient sacred site of Stonehenge, one of the greatest monuments of prehistoric Europe, was built in several stages over hundreds of years. The stone circle itself was completed in c.2000 BC. It would have taken a very powerful and important man to organize its construction, since the massive stone blocks would have to have been dragged to the site over long distances by hundreds of labourers.

sinister story: in life this stocky man would have been noticeable both because of the distinctive limp in his withered left leg, which through some traumatic injury had lost its kneecap, and because of the terrible smell emanating from the infection which still festered within.

But this man was no outcast. He was a collector and a magician. Although he is referred to now as an 'archer' because of the two hunting kits buried with him, it is unlikely that this partly crippled man made his living from hunting alone. Clues to his real value in society lie elsewhere in his grave. The decorated pottery vessels were of a distinctive type known as 'beakers', some of which may have come from as far away as Scotland, implying he had access to rare and valuable commodities. More important still, and almost unique in Britain at this time, is the unimposing smooth stone buried with him. It is a 'cushion stone', the tool of a goldsmith, and perhaps the stone on which he made the curls of decorated gold sheets – the tresses – that he and his relative wore in their hair.

Britain's earliest gold objects

What makes this stone and the gold tresses found near it so important is that they are the earliest known gold objects ever found in Britain and are made from imported metal. This man lived in a world of change. After thousands of years of stone technology, metalworking was being introduced to Britain from the continent at this time, probably by men like the Amesbury Archer.

The Amesbury Archer was surrounded by burial goods, including beaker pots and flints. The black object at his back is a cushion stone for goldworking.

His gold tresses and copper knives were radical departures from the everyday stone tools that were usual for the time, and his ability to make them marked him out as someone special. The mere fact that he was buried alone with these objects demonstrates that he was someone of note. In the earlier New Stone Age (Neolithic) most burials that we know of were communal and usually involved the simple cremation of the human remains. The Amesbury Archer, however, was not buried in a communal site nor was he cremated; he was placed in an individual grave, with over 100 objects for company. If there was any form of social differentiation in the Neolithic, if differences

THE FUTURE OF ARCHAEOLOGY

Archaeology is still a relatively young subject but its journey has already been a long one. Since Antonio da Magdalena first stumbled into Angkor Wat in 1586 we have gone from simply staring dumbstruck at the monuments of an apparently unknowable past to beginning to piece together the story of humankind across the world. It is a story whose canvas covers not just the few millennia that, even 150 years ago, people thought was the entirety of human history. We now know it covers millions of years and is told not in a single thread but in the form of innumerable complementary narratives taking place across many continents and centuries.

The inspiration for the birth of archaeology was undoubtedly treasure, in the form of Greek statues or gold coins, but as time has moved on archaeologists have come to realize that their subject can uncover treasures more valuable than any piece of art or cache of bullion. Archaeologists today are engaged in searching for clues to the whole human story. They are interested not simply in the famous or the powerful but in everyone – all of the people who came before us, most of whom left no mark in written history (if it even existed in their day) but many of whom left an imprint of their lives in the archaeological record.

How we go about that task in the future will undoubtedly be different from the methods we use today. New techniques, new sciences and new philosophies will change both what we can find and how we interpret it. Archaeologists may study the past but they live in the present and that will always influence their work.

For this reason, what all archaeologists must do is to record what they unearth as clearly as possible. The best gift today's excavators can give to those in the future is an easily understandable account of what they have done, since each dig is a one-off experiment that can never be repeated. We must also try to preserve those sites we have excavated and protect those we know of but have not touched so that future Howard Carters can find their own 'sealed doors'.

No doubt we are making mistakes today which we cannot yet see, just as only now do we notice the mistakes of those archaeologists who went before us. But hopefully those to come will look charitably on our efforts and perhaps even thank us for the sites we have left for them, a legacy that will enable them to write the next chapter in the history of archaeology and of the world.

in wealth and status existed, archaeologists have been unable to discover them. The Amesbury Archer, standing as he does at the beginning of the Bronze Age, is different. He was buried in a key position in the most elaborate ritual landscape in Britain of the time, in a bend in the River Avon in line with a processional avenue that ended just out of sight, over the hill at a place that was then just nearing completion: Stonehenge. As someone with 'wealth' he may have been involved in the construction of the monument, perhaps even its originator – certainly the newspapers have been keen to christen him 'the King of Stonehenge'. Such a title may be a little misplaced this deep in prehistory, but the people gathered around the pit on Boscombe Down on the day of his last rites were certainly mourning the passing of a notable figure, one of the first 'important' people in the British archaeological record, and the herald of a new age.

One of two gold hair tresses found in the grave of the Amesbury Archer, dated to c.2300 BC. The Archer's evident skills in metalworking would have given him great status among the essentially Stone Age local people.

GLOSSARY

Words in SMALL CAPITALS refer to other entries in the Glossary. Cross references to extended box feature articles are given in brackets.

adobe A sun-dried unfired brick of clay and straw; also a structure built using this type of brick.

aerial photography Photographic survey of the ground from the air; used to identify and record sites. (*See also* page 160.)

animal (faunal) archaeology The study of animal remains in the archaeological record. Faunal remains can aid in identifying hunting and farming strategies and help to characterize a past environment. *(See also* page 187.)

anthropologist Someone who studies past and present variations in human culture, biology and society. The field is generally split into biological (or 'physical') anthropology, which is concerned with the biological development of humankind, and social (or 'cultural') anthropology, which is the study of human culture.

artefact Anything made or fashioned by humans as distinct from objects that occur naturally.

astrolabe An instrument for measuring the altitude of the sun in the sky and hence calculating latitude. Historically used in astronomy and navigation.

bas relief Carving in low relief in which objects project from the background to a distance of less than half their true depth.

birch-bark writing Writing on thin slivers of boiled birch bark, commonly in use in parts of Medieval Russia before the advent of paper. (*See also* page 149.)

Bronze Age The period in the development of human civilization when the most advanced common metal technology was bronze. As a technological development it has no set dates, occurring in different parts of the world at different times. Where it is present, it occurs between the STONE AGE and the IRON AGE. (*See also* page 72.)

Byzantine Belonging to Byzantium (former Constantinople, modern Istanbul). Usually refers to the Medieval Byzantine empire which flourished around Byzantium from the sixth to the 15th century AD.

carbon-14 dating The scientific measurement of the amount of decay of the long-lived radioactive isotope carbon-14 that is found in all organic materials, which can be used to date the material. (*See also* page 121.)

cartouche The oval or oblong figure in Egyptian HIEROGLYPHIC texts signifying that the enclosed name is a royal or divine title.

cave art The depiction of animals, figures and abstract designs on the walls of caves by mainly STONE AGE cultures. (*See also* page 77.)

classical The art, language and culture of a civilization considered to be at its height. In archaeology the term is often used to refer to the ancient Greek and Roman worlds. In the New World, it is applied to the height of Mayan civilization.

classicist One who studies a CLASSICAL civilization.

concubine In the ancient world, a woman kept by a king or potentate as a wife but without formally being married; or in some cases the most senior wife.

conservation The study and practice of the prevention of physical deterioration of archaeological ARTEFACTS and deposits. (*See also* page 179.)

Copper Age A term used to define a period in some parts of the world between the New Stone Age (NEOLITHIC) and BRONZE AGE, when copper tools were prevalent.

cuneiform script The script of a number of ancient Middle Eastern languages including Sumerian, Babylonian and Akkadian; written in wedge-shaped characters often impressed into wet clay.

demotic script In Egyptology the everyday, fluid script used to write the ancient Egyptian language, as opposed to formal HIEROGLYPHICS.

dig An archaeological excavation.

experimental archaeology The reconstruction of past objects, technologies and behaviours, used to obtain practical information on how ancient societies produced and employed them. (*See also* page 25.)

fl. (flourished) Where the birth or death dates of an individual are unknown but other information exists on the period in which they lived, the abbreviation fl. is used to indicate the period in which they were living and working.

forensic archaeology The application of archaeological techniques to modern crime scenes. (*See also* page 223.)

geology The study of the earth's physical composition and the processes acting upon it.

geomorphologist Someone who studies the branch of geology dealing with the formation, evolution and configuration of the earth's surface.

geophysical survey A general term covering a group of scientific methods for locating buried features that are not readily visible on the surface. They include ground-penetrating radar, magnetometry and resistivity. (*See also* page 230.)

gilded Covered with a (usually thin) layer of gold plate or gold leaf.

glyph A symbol representing a unit of an ancient script. Often used to mean a single hieroglyphic symbol.

gridded site An archaeological site that has been overlaid with a measured grid to allow the accurate location of objects and features found during the excavation.

hieroglyphics The script of the ancient Egyptians.

ice age One of a number of periodic reductions in the temperature of the earth's climate, characterized by an expansion of continental ice sheets.

Iron Age The period in the development of human civilization when the most advanced common metal technology was iron. As a technological development it has no set dates, occurring in different parts of the world at different times. Where it is present, it follows the BRONZE AGE or in some cases the STONE AGE. (*See also* page 72.)

lapis lazuli A gemstone highly prized in the ancient world for both its colour (a deep blue) and its rarity (the best sources being in Afghanistan).

liminal Pertaining to an edge or threshold. Can be applied to a physical place, such as the shores of a sea or lake, or abstractly to the edges of human experience or consciousness.

lost-wax process A method of casting metal by making a wax model, enclosing it in clay and then firing this to melt the wax out; the process leaves behind a ceramic mould into which the molten metal can be poured.

magnetometry The measurement and mapping of minute variations in the direction and strength of the earth's magnetic field, which can indicate the presence of buried structures and objects, notably magnetic metals such as iron.

marine archaeology The archaeological study of human interaction with seas, lakes and rivers, including the recording and excavation of sunken structures and vessels. (*See also* page 117.)

Medieval Relating to a period of time characterized as being between ancient and modern. In Europe, specifically that which related to the Middle Ages, the period between the collapse of the CLASSICAL world and the advent of the early modern world in the 15th century.

Mesopotamia Literally 'the land between the rivers'. An ancient region between the Tigris and Euphrates rivers covering parts of present-day Iraq, Syria, Iran and Turkey.

Neanderthal A species of the *Homo* genus to which modern humans belong, originating at least 130,000 years ago. Until recently Neanderthals were thought to be a sub-species of modern *Homo sapiens,* but increasingly they are now thought to have been a separate species that became extinct in Europe around 24,000 years ago.

Neoclassical A style of art, music and literature, etc. based on classical models; used especially to refer to a style of 18th-century art and architecture influenced by the rediscovery of Roman sites such as Pompeii.

Neolithic The last of the three periods within the STONE AGE, which begins with the PALAEOLITHIC (Old Stone Age), is followed by the MESOLITHIC (Middle Stone Age) and ends with the NEOLITHIC (New Stone Age). The Neolithic is characterized by the advent of farming and ceramics and the development of finely flaked stone tools. It is followed in Europe by the development of metal technology leading into the BRONZE AGE. (*See also* page 72.)

Palaeontology The branch of science dealing with the (often extinct) fossil remains of humans, animals and plants.

Palaeolithic The Old Stone Age, the first of the three periods within the STONE AGE; followed by the MESOLITHIC (Middle Stone Age) and the NEOLITHIC (New Stone Age). It is characterized by the development of stone tools and begins around 2.5 million years ago, ending in Europe around 10,000 years ago; often sub-divided into three periods, characterized as the Lower (earliest) Middle and Upper Palaeolithic. (*See also* page 72.)

papyrus A tall aquatic plant native to the Nile Valley; its stalks were used in ancient Egypt to make a paper-like material. Also the name given to that writing material and individual texts written on it.

phonetic character A written character that represents a specific sound rather than an abstract idea or object.

pollen analysis The study of pollens preserved in archaeological deposits to deduce information about the local environment in the past. (*See also* page 211.)

portico The formal entrance to a building consisting of columns at regular intervals supporting a roof, either of or in the style of CLASSICAL temples.

Prehistory The period before written records or recorded history are available.

radiocarbon dating *See* CARBON-14 DATING. (*See also* page 121.)

Renaissance The revival in the arts and sciences following CLASSICAL models, begun in Italy in the 14th century and continuing through the 15th and 16th centuries in Europe.

sarcophagus A stone coffin, often inscribed or decorated.

soil archaeology The study of the contents and structure of ancient soils. Soil science can reveal the presence of seeds, pollens, shells and small animal parts in samples that are indicative of the environment from which they came. The make-up and structure of a soil itself can also be studied to identify its origins (i.e., in wet or dry lands, as plough soil or domestic floor, etc). (*See also* page 211.)

Stone Age The first period in the development of human civilization when the most advanced common technology was stone tool-making. As a technological development it has no set dates, occurring in different parts of the world at different times. It usually occurs before the metal ages (copper, bronze or iron) and is often divided into three sections. (*See also* PALAEOLITHIC, MESOLITHIC and NEOLITHIC.) It is first attested in Africa around 2.5 million years ago, and is first superseded by the Bronze Age in the Near East around 3500 BC. (*See also* page 72.)

stratigraphy/stratigraphic levels The study of the order and relative positions of layers (strata) of rock, in the case of geology, or soils and sediments in the case of archaeology, to deduce a sequence of events. (*See also* page 82.)

stucco A fine plaster used for creating mouldings and decorations on walls.

tablets (clay) Clay rectangles onto which the CUNEIFORM SCRIPT was often impressed before firing the tablet to make the inscription permanent.

terracotta A fine-quality unglazed pottery used in the manufacture of tiles, bricks, vases and statuary.

theoretical archaeology The study of the practice of archaeology and the interpretation of its results within philosophical frameworks. (*See also* page 175.)

torc A collar or neck ring consisting of a twisted band or bands of metal, often a precious metal such as gold or silver, and usually open-ended.

tree-ring dating (dendrochronology) The counting of the annual growth rings in the trunk of a tree to calculate its age. As the width of each ring varies depending on the climate in a particular year in a specific region, a unique pattern forms. This can be matched to similar patterns in the remains of older trees found in the archaeological record; hence tree-ring lines can be extended back longer than any individual tree has lived. (*See also* page 121.)

Upper Palaeolithic The last phase of the Old Stone Age. The period is characterized by the development of more sophisticated stone, bone and antler tools and the earliest evidence we have for organized settlements. In Europe it lasts from around 40,000 years ago until approximately 10,000 years ago. (*See also* STONE AGE.)

votive Something dedicated or given in consequence or fulfilment of a vow. Often applied in archaeology to objects deposited in a ritual context.

x-ray tomography The process of taking x-ray images of 'slices' through an object or body. These can then be combined by a computer to render a three-dimensional image of the inside of the object.

ziggurat A stepped tower or pyramid in which each successive stage is smaller than the one below. The term is most often applied to the distinctive stepped temple mounds found in Sumerian, Babylonian and Assyrian cities.

INDEX

AUTHOR ACKNOWLEDGEMENTS

The acknowledgements for this book would sadly be too long to list in the proper manner for they include everyone who has inspired and developed my love of archaeology and history from childhood onwards. They include family, friends, teachers and the many wonderful field and academic archaeologists I have met and worked with along the way. I hope you all know who you are.

For their support and help with this book I would like to thank Richard Milbank and everyone at Quercus, Graham Bateman and the team at BCS, Julian Alexander at Lucas Alexander Whitley, Richard Foreman at Chalke and, as always, Steph and Connie for their patience and support.

PICTURE ACKNOWLEDGEMENTS

2-3 Shutterstock: 4 Shutterstock/Lagui (top), Shutterstock (bottom): 5 Shutterstock/DMK 13 Shutterstock/Vova Pomortzeff; 14 Shutterstock/Vova Pomortzeff, 17 Corbis/ © Bettmann; 18 Corbis/ © Mimmo Jodice; 19 Corbis/ © Bettmann/Corbis; 20 Corbis/ © Bettmann/Corbis; 21 Shutterstock/ John Lumb; 23 Corbis/ © Wolfgang Kaehler; 24 Corbis/ © O. Alamany & E. Vicens; 27 Shutterstock/Florin Cirstoc; 28 Corbis/ © Christel Gerstenberg; 29 Corbis/ © Archivo Iconografico, S.A.; 31 Corbis/ © The Art Archive; 35 Shutterstock/Yazid Masa; 37 Corbis/ © Historical Picture Archive; 39 Corbis/ © Corbis; 41 Corbis/ © Michael Jenner/Corbis; 42 Corbis/ © Bettmann/Corbis; 43 Corbis/ © Archivo Iconografico, S.A.; 45 Corbis/ © Christie's Images; 46 Shutterstock/ Vladimir Korostyshevskiy; 48–49 Corbis/ © David Lees; 50 Corbis/ © Bettman/Corbis; 51 Corbis/ © Gianni Dagli Orti; 52 Corbis/ © Stapleton Collection; 53 Corbis/ © Reuters; 55 Shutterstock/Suzanne Long; 56 Corbis/ © Vianni Archive; 57 Shutterstock/Lagui; 60 Corbis/ © K. M. Westermann; 61 The Ancient Art & Architecture Collection Ltd. © Ronald Sheridan; 62–63 Corbis/ © Wolfgang Kaehler; 65 Corbis/ © Gianni Dagli Orti/; 67 Corbis © Roger Wood; 69 Corbis/ © Adam Woolfitt; 71 Corbis/ © Kevin Schafer; 73 Corbis/ © Adam Woolfitt; 75 Corbis/ © Archive Iconografico S.A.; 77 Corbis/ © Hubert Stadler; 79 Corbis/ © Archive Iconografico S.A.; 81 Corbis/ © Hulton-Deutsch Collection; 82 Corbis/ © Bettmann/Corbis; 83 Corbis/ © Archive Iconografico S.A.; 85 Corbis/ © David Reed; 87 Shutterstock/Lakis Fourouklas; 89 Shutterstock/Duncan Gilbert; 92 Corbis/ © Richard A. Cooke; 93 Corbis/ © David Muench; 95 Corbis/ © Roger Wood; 97 Corbis/ © Gianni Dagli Orti; 98 Shutterstock/ Vova Pomortzeff; 101 Corbis/ © Bettmann/Corbis; 102 Corbis/ © Bettmann/Corbis; 105 Corbis/ © Archivo Iconografico, S.A.; 109 Shutterstock/ Paul Cowan; 110 Corbis/ © Gustavo Tomsich; 112 Corbis/ © Archivo Iconografico, S.A.; 115 The Ancient Art & Architecture Collection Ltd. © Ronald Sheridan; 116 Corbis/ © Jonathan Blair; 119 Corbis/ © Paul Almasy; 120 Corbis/ © Adam Woolfitt; 123 Shutterstock/Galyna Andrushko; 125 Corbis/ © J.C. Kanny/Lorpresse/Corbis Sygma; 127 Corbis/ © Archivo Iconografico, S.A.; 129 Corbis/ © David Lees; 130–131 Corbis/ © Bettmann/ Corbis; 133 Corbis/ © Werner Forman; 135 Shutterstock/ Paul Vorwerk; 137 Corbis/ © Stapleton Collection; 139 Corbis/ © Hulton-Deutsch Collection; 140 Corbis/ © Sandro Vannini; 143 Corbis/ © Charles & Josette Lenars; 144–145 Corbis/ © Paul Almasy; 147 Shutterstock/DMK; 148 Corbis/ © Hulton-Deutsch Collection; 151 Corbis/ © Araldo de Luca; 155 TopFoto © Picturepoint; 157 Ronald Sheridan/Ancient Art & Architecture; 159 Shutterstock/ Dan Bannister;161 Corbis/ © Gianni Dagli Orti; 163 Corbis/ © West Semitic Research/Dead Sea Scrolls Foundation; 164–165 Corbis/ © Richard T. Nowitz; 167 Shutterstock/ Styve Reineck; 169 Shutterstock/Vova Pomortzeff; 170 Shutterstock; 173 Corbis © Yann Arthus-Bertrand; 177 Corbis/ © Archivo Iconografico, S.A.; 178 Corbis/ © Corbis; 181 TopFoto © Topham Picturepoint; 182 Corbis/ © Adam Woolfitt; 185 Corbis/ © Dave G. Houser; 186 Corbis/ © Alan Thorne/epa/Corbis; 188–189 Shutterstock/Ian MacLellan 191; The Ancient Art & Architecture Collection Ltd. © C.M. Dixon; 193 Corbis/ © Jacques Langevin/ Corbis Sygma; 194 Corbis/ © Sophie Bassouls/Corbis Sygma; 195 Corbis/ © Bettmann/Corbis; 197 Corbis/ © Bettmann/ Corbis; 199 Shutterstock/Timur Kulgarin; 200–201 Shutterstock/ Pozzo di Borgo, Thomas; 203 Corbis/ © Charles & Josette Lenars; 205 Corbis/ © Gianni Dagli Orti; 206 Shutterstock/Grigory Kubatyan; 207 Shutterstock/Grigory Kubatyan; 209 © Flag Fen Bronze Age Centre; 210 © Flag Fen Bronze Age Centre; 213 TopFoto © The British Museum/HIP; 214 TopFoto © AAAC/ TopFoto; 216–217 Corbis/ © Christophe Boisvieux; 219 © Corbis; 220 Shutterstock/ Gordon Galbraith; 221 Corbis/ © Stapleton Collection; 223 Corbis/ © Horacio Villalobos; 225 Corbis/ © Bettmann/ Corbis; 226 Shutterstock/SueC; 229 Shutterstock/ Alexei Novikov; 231 Shutterstock/Ivan Cholakov (top) US National Archives (bottom); 233 © South Tyrol Museum of Archaeology, Bolzano; 234 Corbis/ © Reuters/Corbis; 237 Corbis/ © Charles O'Rear; 239 Corbis/ © Charles & Josette Lenars; 241 © James C. Chatters; 243 Corbis/ © Warren Morgan/Corbis; 245 Shutterstock/Markus Gann; 246 © Wiltshire Archaeological Trust 247 © Wiltshire Archaeological Trust

Quercus Publishing has made every effort to trace copyright holders of the pictures used in this book. Anyone having claims to ownership not identified above is invited to contact Quercus Publishing.

For Sally Sharpe
(1968–1990)

Horas non numero nisi serenas

First published in Great Britain in 2007 by

Quercus
21 Bloomsbury Square
London
WC1A 2NS

A CIP catalogue record for this book is available from the British Library.

Cloth case edition: ISBN-10 1 84724 183 2
ISBN-13 978 1 84724 183 2

Printed case edition: ISBN-10 1 84724 011 9
ISBN-13 978 1 84724 011 8

Printed and bound in China

10 9 8 7 6 5 4 3 2 1